The German Colonies
in
South Russia

1804 to 1904

by

Rev. Conrad Keller

Translated from the German edition

by Anthony Becker

Second Edition

with some revisions by Adam Giesinger

American Historical Society of Germans from Russia
Lincoln, Nebraska

Printed by
Augstums Printing Service, Inc.
Lincoln, Nebraska

Die deutschen Kolonien

in

Südrussland

Ein Ueberblick der Culturentwickelung derselben im
Verlaufe von 100 Jahren, nebst den Chroniken der
katholischen Kolonien: Kleinliebenthal, Josephstal,
Marienthal und Franzfeld, als Jubiläumsgabe zum
100 jährigen Bestehen derselben.

(Mit 20 Porträts)

von

P Conrad Keller,

freiresigniertem Pfarrer.

———— ❈◦❈ ————

I. Bändchen.

Preis 1 Rbl. 20 Kop.

Verlag von Stadelmeier in Odessa.

Deribasstraße № 18.

ОДЕССА.
Типографiя. Л. Шульце, Ганжероновская ул., № 30.
1905

*This is a reproduction of the original title page of Die Deutschen
Kolonien by P. Conrad Keller, published in Odessa, Russia in 1905.*

CONTENTS

Foreword to the Second Edition

Dr. Becker's translation of the first volume of Keller has now been out of print for some time, but inquiries for it are still frequent. In view of this, but mainly because of the basic importance of this work, the American Historical Society of Germans from Russia, with Dr. Becker's permission, decided to re-print this translation. We offer it herewith to the many members of our Society who are interested in this pioneer work on the Black Sea Germans.

Although it was written primarily for the people of the Liebental district, near Odessa, who were celebrating their centennial in 1904, Father Keller's first volume has information of interest to all Black Sea Germans. It provides a description of the geographical features of the region; quotes a lengthy extract from Tsar Alexander's decree of 1804 regarding foreign immigration to the region; gives a list of *all* the German mother colonies, Lutheran, Catholic, Mennonite and Separatist, founded there from 1787 to 1852; describes the administrative arrangements made for their government; gives biographies of some of the leading personalities among the early administrators appointed by the Tsar; and outlines the regulations issued by the central government for the guidance of both administrators and colonists. It describes as well the progress in education, agriculture, industry and trade, and the part played by the Black Sea colonists (in a non-combatant capacity) in the Russo-Turkish War of 1828 and the Crimean War of 1853-56. Of special interest to descendants of Catholic colonists is a section on the spiritual administration of Black Sea Catholics before the formation of the Diocese of Tiraspol in 1856.

For the Liebental district specifically there is a section on all the colonies of the district, Lutheran and Catholic, with interesting statistics for the year 1858. Finally, for the four Catholic colonies of this district, Kleinliebental, Josephstal, Mariental and Franzfeld, there is an account of their hundred-year history, including for each village a list of the founding families, biographies of the parish priests who served them, and a year-by-year chronicle of events through the century.

The many descendants of Black Sea Germans in the United States and Canada owe a debt of gratitude to Dr. Becker for making this translation available to us. He translated and published this work as a labor of love, at a time (in 1968) when it was still far from clear that our people were really interested in the history of their forefathers in Russia. As the growth of our Society clearly demonstrates, interest in this history is growing at an accelerating rate. There is therefore no doubt that Dr. Becker's pioneer work will receive increasing attention and appreciation in the years to come.

We have taken advantage of this reprinting of the translation to correct typographical and other errors that have been found in the first edition. We have also revised the wording of a number of passages that readers have found somewhat obscure.

Adam Giesinger
President, American Historical
Society of Germans from Russia

Foreword to the First Edition

In translating and publishing German Colonies In South Russia, Anthony Becker has performed a valuable service not only to descendants of German migrants to Western Canada but to the history of this country as a whole. The original book was written by Rev. Conrad Keller, and published in Odessa, Russia in 1904. It outlines the culture of those early migrants during the period 1804 to 1904 as well as detailed chronicles of the colonies of Kleinliebenthal, Josephstal, Marienthal and Franzfeld, along with names of the original settlers. Many German migrants to Western Canada, particularly Saskatchewan, came from these colonies.

The book is extremely rare. Indeed, one academic microfilm company searched the University of Michigan catalogues, the United States Library of Congress catalogues, the Cumulative Book Index, the British Museum and the Keyser Bücher Lexikon, for a copy or even a trace of 'German Colonies in South Russia,' with no success. It was by chance that Dr. Becker, while carrying out literary and historic research for an article on his own colony, St. Josephs, located 18 miles east of Regina, came upon Mr. John Bichel of Macklin, Sask. who had an old copy of the book. Mr. Bichel was good enough to lend the copy to Dr. Becker who, with the help of his friends, spent over 2 years of spare time translating it into English. This extremely rare book has now been made available through Dr. Becker's industry and generosity to the children and grandchildren and to generations to come who trace their origins back to the Russian colonies.

The place names, weights and measures have been left in the original spelling. The reader can find the approximate equivalents indexed at the end of the book. The wording of the translation, has been left as close to the original as possible.

It is indeed a valuable contribution to the story of a fine and sturdy race whose contribution to the advancement of Canada has been quite significant.

R. H. Macdonald,
Executive Editor,
The Western Producer,
Saskatoon, Sask.

ACKNOWLEDGEMENTS

This translation would not have been possible without the help received from my many friends. I wish to thank Dr. E. Fieguth, Mr. R. P. Penner, and particularly Professor C. P. Brockett for his unstinting assistance. I also wish to thank Mrs. H. Reimer for her help with the many Germanised-Russian words. A special thanks is due the typists, Delores Hedlund and Monica Mollan for their patience and endurance, and to my wife for her help in proof reading.

The two maps in this book have been reproduced, with the kind permission of Dr. Karl Stumpp. The map showing the migration routes is from Dr. Stumpp's book "Die Russland Deutschen" ["The Russian Germans"]. This book is now available in English. The map showing the location of the colonies in South Russia is from Dr. Stumpp's personal file. Professor J. S. Height has kindly provided the plans for the colonies of Josephstal and Franzfeld.

A.B.

AUTHOR'S PREFACE

The purpose of this little book is to inform succeeding generations in a general way about the circumstances and the events of the founding of the first German settlements in South Russia and their gradual development since. Although no world-shaking events are recounted, there is, I believe, much of interest to all colonists in South Russia. The book gives them a historical-geographical survey of their new homeland, now grown so dear to them, from misty antiquity to the time of their forefathers' settlement in this region. It gives them information regarding the sad conditions under which their forefathers settled here, about the first accommodations provided for the settlers, about their relations with officialdom in the early years, and about persons who took an active and sympathetic interest in their weal and woe. In a word, the book gives a brief survey of the development of the German colonists in South Russia in the last 100 years. Detailed reports about the various aspects of the development I have reserved for future volumes.

To the Catholics of the Liebental district the appended chronicles bring more exact information about the life of their ancestors, especially in the first years of the settlements. If not everything described here is praiseworthy and exemplary, it is not my fault, for the sources in the archives force me to tell it as it was.

I have not included in this book the German colonies on the Volga and in other provinces of the Russian Empire, because it is my intention, when circumstances are more favorable and God restores me to health, to write separately about these. Nor have I included here the new colonies founded on bought land, because I do not have adequate information about them.

The circumstances under which this book was written, I must state openly, could not have been more unfavorable. Persons from whom I could have expected, according to accepted standards of behavior, obliging kindness, provided the greatest obstacles for me. As a result I was obliged to make many abridgements in the book and let it go out into the world with many defects. The most distressing features of the book are the many disfiguring typographical errors, which my kind readers can ascribe to the unfavorable conditions of this time. The frequent workers' strikes while the printing was in progress in Odessa and the shortage of experienced German typesetters exonerate the printer to some degree.

I must not fail on this occasion to express my warm thanks to all persons who helped to make this work possible. I am grateful above all to Actual State Councillor Somow, who most graciously placed at my disposal for my work the Archive of the former Colonist Welfare Committee, and the Ministerial Councillor Müller, who gave me access to the Archive of the former South Russian General-Gouvernement. I also thank Professor von Stern and University Librarian Brun, the first of whom permitted me to use the library of the Society for History and Antiquities, and the latter the library of the New Russian University. Nor must I forget to give recognition to the services rendered to me by the community of Kleinliebental.

That this little book has many deficiences and errors is well known to me. I therefore beg friends of the truth to point out to me without reservations and without diffidence any errors that they find and to give me their individual opinions of this work. It is only by united striving for truth and clarity that we shall succeed in presenting the history of the German colonists in Russia in its proper light. So, out you go, little book! out into the wide world. Tell the people that you are indeed a deficient creation, which saw the light of day in a difficult period, but that you can tell them many things about the old days and that you can announce to all Germans in the great and mighty (?) Russian Empire the memorable news: that they have now become a free people, enjoying equal rights with the natives, that they now have the right to develop their abilities, as bearers of civilization, in all directions, and as such to struggle and to strive in the new era for the first prize in the cultural development of the new Russia.

God grant that this may come about!

Odessa, November 23, 1905, on the feast of St. Clement.

The Author

The German Colonies
in
South Russia

1804 to 1904

The German Colonies in South Russia

The Land of the Scythians

When an inquiring person lives in a house, he is usually curious to find out who previously occupied the home. As in the case of the house, the same curiosity extends to the land. I believe, therefore, that for the reader, it may prove to be interesting to review the early inhabitants of South Russia.

Even before man possessed any historical knowledge of western Europe, the area now called South Russia was well documented and its geography accurately known. For this information we are indebted to the "Father of History," the venerable Herodotus of Halikarnassus. He lived in the fifth century B.C., and himself visited the land of the Scythians, as South Russia was known at that time. However, before the Scythians came to this land, the old Kimmerians or Teutons, our forefathers, lived there, as the renowned jurist Ivering reports. But history does not provide any information about this period. Only archaeology and paleontology occasionally provide information of the vanished people of that day, who in unknown times lived in the vicinity of the Black Sea.

Now I will allow Herodotus himself to tell the story about the Scythian land and its people. He writes as follows: The Pontus Euxinus, (now known as the Black Sea,) has on its shores the most barbarous people of any country, the most civilized inhabitants in that region being the Scythians.

The Scythian race had made one discovery that no other group had made, so far as we know. They discovered that they could not be conquered so long as they killed all who attacked them and so long as they could not be found by their foes.

The people did not live in towns or fortresses. On the contrary, they all lived a nomadic life, shot bows and arrows from horseback, lived by ranching, not by agriculture, and dwelt in wagons. It is difficult to conquer such a people, since they cannot be brought to bay; this they had discovered. Their land was suitable for this type of living, and their rivers were in their favor. The land was a large plain, very rich in grass and well watered, and the rivers flowing through these plains were no less numerous than irrigation ditches in Egypt.

I wish to mention only the main rivers, especially those that are navigable from the Black Sea. First, there is the Istros (now known as the Danube) with its five estuaries; there is the Tyres (now called the Dniester); the Hypanis (now called the Bug); the Borysthenes (now called the Dnieper); the Pantikapes (now called the Ingul); the Hypakris (now called the Inguletz); the Gerrhos (now called the Besuluk); and the Tanais (now called the Don).

The Danube is by far the largest of all known rivers, and is always deep, both in summer and in winter. It is the first river in the western part of the Scythian land, and it is the largest because so many other rivers empty into it. The reason the Danube is deep in both the summer and winter, I believe, is that in the winter it rains very little in this country, but the snowfall is very heavy. In the summer, this enormous amount of snow that fell during the winter, melts, and runs from all sides into the Danube. This snow also attracts frequent heavy rains, which fall in the summer.

The second river in the Scythian land is the Dniester. This river comes from the north and arises in a large lake which forms a border between the Scythian plains and the land of the Nauris. On its estuary live the Hellens, or Greeks, called the Tyrians.

The third river, the Bug, originates in Scythia itself, from a large lake around which wild white horses graze. This lake is truly called the Father of the Bug. It is a short river, and for a drive of five days, its water is sweet; but at a distance of only four days' journey from the sea, it is extremely bitter. Here it is joined by a bitter spring, which, even though it is insignificant in size, affects the whole Bug.

This spring is on the border of the land of the agricultural Scythians and Alazones, and the name of the spring, according to local legend, is Exampaos, which means the Holy Way. The Dniester and the Bug come close together near the Alazones but then the one wends its way in one direction and the other in the opposite, leaving a wide stretch between them.

The fourth river is the Dnieper. This is the largest river after the Danube, and in my estimation, flows through the most fertile land. It has the most beautiful grazing country, attracting wild animals, and without question, the best and the most fish. Its water tastes fresh and sweet, and it is very clear. Beautiful corn grows on its shores, and where there is no corn planted, there is very high grass. An endless quantity of salt flows from its mouth, and it affords pickling of large boneless sharks named Antakäer, and many other wondrous things. Its course from the north is known as far as the land of the Gerrhos, a distance of fourteen days' travel; but what the people are like in the land it flows through no one knows. It is, however, most likely that it flows through a wilderness until it reaches the land of the agricultural Scythians. These Scythians live on its banks, and where they live is a ten-day drive away. It runs as the Dnieper until it is near the sea, where it is joined by the Bug, and runs on with it into the same swamp. The point of land between these two rivers is called the Hypolaoshorn, and on this point there is a temple to the goddess Demeter. On either side of the temple, but on the Bug (where the ruins of the Parutino lie) live the Borysthenes people.

The fifth river is the Ingul. This also arises in the north from another lake, and between it and the Dnieper live the agricultural Scythians. It flows into the Hyläa land, and when it has crossed there, it joins the Dnieper.

The sixth river is the Inguletz. This also arises from a lake and flows through the middle of the nomadic Scythian region, passing the city of Karkynitis. In doing so it surrounds Hylaa and the district on the right, which is called the Achilles heel.

The seventh river, the Besuluk, divorces itself from the Dnieper in this region. It carries this same name in every district through which it passes, and flows toward the sea. It forms the boundary between the nomadic Scythians and the land of the Royal Scythians, and then flows into the Inguletz.

The eighth and last river is the Don. It comes from the far north and arises from a large lake. It empties into a larger lake named Mäetis, where it forms the boundary between the Royal Scythians

3

and the Sauromates. Into the Don flows another river named the Hyrgis. So the land of the Scythians extends from the Danube in the west to the Don in the east, and from the Crimean Peninsula in the south to the provinces of Volhynia and Poltava in the north. It was approximately these boundaries that formed the region of the present South Russia, which was soon to become the home of our German colonists.

The People of Scythia

As Herodotus tells us, the Scythians considered themselves the progeny of Zeus and the daughter of the river Borysthenes, and called themselves Skolotans; but by the Greeks they were named Scythians.

The Scythians were divided into three communities: the agricultural Scythians; the nomadic Scythians; and the Royal Scythians. The agricultural Scythians lived in the west, approximately in the region of the present city of Odessa and Ananiev, and in the western region of the district of Cherson. The nomadic Scythians lived in the easterly district of the present-day Cherson, Elizabethgrad, Alexandria, and a portion of the province of Jekaterinoslav. The Royal Scythians lived in the region of the Dnieper, as far as the Don river. The remaining region of the Scythian land was occupied by other people, who were kinsmen of the Scythians or their allies.

According to Herodotus, the customs of the Scythians were as follows: They prayed only to the following gods. The Histia was above all, then Zeus and the Earth. They believed that the Earth was the wife of Zeus. After these came the gods of Apollo and Aphrodite, followed by Hercules and Ares. The Royal Scythians also worshipped Poseidon (Neptune). They had no necessity for images, altars, or churches, except to worship the god Ares.

The Scythians also made animal sacrifices. The animal to be sacrificed stood with its front feet tied together with a rope. The sacrificer stood behind the animal and pulled back sharply on the rope, throwing the animal to the ground. As the sacrificial animal fell, the celebrant called on the god to whom he was making the offering. Then he threw a rope around the animal's neck, placed a stick through the rope, and twisted it, thus strangling the animal, without saying any words of consecration or lighting a fire. When the animal was strangled and skinned, it was cooked. In the Scythian land there is a tremendous scarcity of wood, so they frequently resorted to the following procedure. When the skin had

4

been removed from the sacrificial animal, the flesh was removed from the bones and placed into a pot. The fire under the kettle was then lit from the bones of the animal. If there was no kettle available, they threw the flesh into the skin, added water to it, and made a fire under the hide with the bones of the animal. So the sacrificial animal cooked entirely by itself.

It was also customary among the Scythians to make human sacrifices. From those of the enemy captured, countless numbers were sacrificed to the gods.

When in war a Scythian slew his first man, he would drink his blood. As many of the enemy as he killed in battle, that number of heads he had to bring home to the king. Only those who brought heads had a share of the booty that they had captured in the war. Once a year, every chief of each district blended a jug of wine, from which every Scythian who had killed an enemy could drink. Those who had not yet done so were not allowed to taste the wine, but had to sit quietly by. This to them was a great disgrace.

An alliance was made by the Scythians as follows. Those who wished to make the alliance stuck themselves with a knife or dagger, scratching the skin slightly. They poured wine into a large earthen jug and blended it with a small quantity of their blood. Then they dipped a sword, an arrow, a battle axe, and a spear into the jug of wine. After they had done this, they said a long prayer, and those who wished to make the bargain with one another drank from the jug, as did also the most distinguished ones from their midst. The remaining customs and manners of the Scythians were also quite barbaric and not to be recommended. Should anyone, however, wish to know more about the customs of the old Scythians, he should read the fourth book of Herodotus.

In the year 513 B.C., the Persian king Darius started a war against the Scythians. But the Scythians, through their strategy, compelled the proud king to retreat, devoid of any success. They were determined never to relinquish their homeland.

King Phillip of Macedonia had better luck, as in the year 399 B.C., he conquered the Scythians in battle and carried away 20,000 women and children. From this time on, the power of the Scythians was broken. They lost most of their homes near the Black Sea and intermingled with other peoples. Once in a while they appeared under another name on the scene of history, until they completely disappeared in the chaos of the vast migration of nations.

While the Scythians lived in the area of the present South Russia, the Greeks also had several trade colonies in this region. The most important city was Olvia, the ruins of which can still be seen near the colony Parutino, on the Bug River. Other colonies

5

were Ordessos on the Beresan estuary; Tyras, today called Akkermann; Cherson near Sevastopol; Pantikopea, today called Kertsch; Feodosia, today called Kaffa, and many others.

Different People who Lived in the Region of South Russia after the Scythians

After the Scythians, the Goths and the Dakis lived in this region; they were called the Sarmatian Roskolans until 61 B.C., when the Romans through their victory over the Bosporus Empire gained the area of the Black Sea, thus obtaining a firm foothold. After a number of successful wars, they gained the whole region, so that the entire Scythian land came under their rule. Under Domitian, Trajan, and subsequent Roman emperors, there were many Christians and other persons considered dangerous to the state, banished to this region. In the year 93 A.D., the venerable Pope Clemens Romanus, along with many Christians, was banished to the Tauric (Crimean) Peninsula, where, through his apostolic diligence, he christianized the whole region. He died a martyr's death in the waves of the Black Sea.

About the year 200 A.D., the Goths came to this region. Through many evil wars, the government of the Romans was severely weakened, and piece by piece annihilated, until Constantine the Great stopped the victorious Gothic march and again drove them back beyond the Danube. After the Goths came the Huns, and displaced the former. The Huns in turn were driven from their homes by the Alani.

Around the year 555 A.D., a wild Tartaric people, the Avares, overran the region of the Black Sea and crowded out all those who had lived there. They spread out from here over the Danubian region as far as Germany, where Charles the Great in 796 A.D. vanquished them, and drove them back to their former homes. The might of the Avares was completely broken by the brave Bulgarian named Chan Kuwrat, who, after the defeat of the various provinces on the Danube, founded a large Bulgarian kingdom. At this time there appeared in this region the Chasars, who are kindred to the Bulgarians. Later, the Petscheneges, Rossians, Romanians, and Magyars resided here.

From the year 1214 on, the Mongolians, Tartars, Venetians, Pisans, and Genoese lived here. In 1475, the Turks conquered the strong fortress Kaffa, and drove out all the above-named people of the region. From 1475 until the conquest by the brave Prince Potjomkin in 1788, this region was alternately occupied by

Lithuanians, Poles, Tartars, Cossacks, and Nagaians. The last two peoples named lived in this region immediately before the German colonists arrived. I find it relevant to introduce two short chapters about these people.

The Zaporozhian Cossacks

According to the Russian historian, Skalkowsky, the word Cossack is derived from Chasar. Others assert that Cossack is synonymous with Caisak, as the Kirghiz call themselves. The Ukrainian Cossacks are said to have originated from the Poles and Lithuanians. Later refugees also came from Russia, Moldavia, and other regions, and asked for asylum in the Setch, as their headquarters was called. In this way they collected a large number of daring rascals who were always ready to rent out their strong arms for money and privileges to any warring party. They set up a military organization, elected a ringleader named Ataman (Cossack for headman), and from the beginning were nominally under the Polish crown.

On the fifteenth of January, 1655, through a decree issued by the chief, Bogdan Chmelnizky, the new headquarters was moved to the far side of the waterfall on the Dnieper, near the island of Chortitz. They made a military treaty with the polish King Stephan Bathory, which was ratified and confirmed. From this time on, those Cossacks who lived here were called the Zaporozhians.

The Zaporozhians had from the beginning conquered almost all of South Russia, except for the western portion of the province of Cherson. In times of peace they had the task of defending the boundaries of Poland and Russia against the Crimean Tartars, the Nagaians, and other plundering neighbors. In war time, a certain number usually had to serve in the cavalry, at first for Poland, and as they later placed themselves under Russian jurisdiction, for Russia. But their tremendous desire for freedom frequently brought them into grave conflict with, and sometimes into rebellion against, the prevailing sovereignty. The famous chief Masepa rebelled, and with some of his subjects, went over to Charles XII, King of Sweden. Consequently, in the year 1750, as the country of New Serbia in South Russia was being settled, they took a large piece of land from the Zaporozhians and gave it to the foreign immigrants, leaving the Cossacks a limited quantity of land. The Cossacks protested this reprimand to Petersburg, stating that it offended them to the highest degree, and they prayed for a return of their old regions, but it remained unchanged.

When Catherine II ascended the Russian throne, they stood by their demands, and after long negotiation, so the story goes, their community was put to an end, since they no longer lived in conformity with their calling, and they were counted among the farmers of the Crown. Many refused to accept this outrage, and preferred to settle in Turkey. Others obtained permission to settle in the Kuban River area, where they later received some of their old privileges. But this was a poor substitute for the indignant Zaporozhians. Thus, the big, brave warriors who had often made courageous and brave decisions over people and lands from Poland to Russia, found themselves scorned, annihilated, and driven away from their dear old homes on the steppes. This was where they had defeated many enemies, and where they had won many victories of which there are no records, except those that live on in words and songs, proclaiming the fame and deeds of the famous Zaporozhians.

The present Cossacks with various designations of Kuban, Don, Terek, in Siberia and other areas are entirely different, and are a weak and degenerate generation. The name of Cossack had in the early 1800's commanded such tremendous respect among the French and Turks, that the mere mention of the name itself put many hundreds and thousands to flight. But things have changed. In the last war, and particularly the war with Japan, the Cossacks did not make a very good showing. The present Cossacks are more interested in agriculture, gardening, fishing or loafing, than they are in waging war.

The Nagaians

According to the writings of the research historian, Skalkowsky, the Nagaians descended from the remnants of the Golden Horde, who for two hundred years previously, had held the whole of Russia in disgraceful bondage.

A portion of the same Nagaians still live in Melitopol region, province of Tauria; formerly they lived all over South Russia. They divided themselves into three tribes. The first tribe called themselves the Budschack, and lived in Southern Bessarabia, where they had approximately three hundred colonies with 9,000 families. They had a singular leader, named Seraskian, who was a subject of the Chan (ruler) in the Crimea. His home was located in the present-day Gankishla near Akkermann.

The second tribe was named Eedisan, and occupied the present region of Odessa and Tiraspol, between the rivers Kutschurgan, Kujalnik, Tiligul, and Beresan. This tribe had 10,000 families; their chief lived in the upper Tiligul region near the present-day city of Ananiev.

The third tribe was the one from Chambuluz. They lived as nomads in the northern part of the province of Tauria in the so-called Nagaian steppes, and were mixed with the Kirghiz. Their total number was 2,000 families. They had alternately Seraskian and Kaimakans as leaders, whose homes were in Perekop.

The Nagaians were the immediate neighbors of the Zaporozhians and their sworn enemies. Kleeman, who visited this region at the end of the 1700's described the way of life of these Nagaians in the following manner.

"The houses of the Nagaians are quite durable and well built. The construction is round and approximately eight feet in diameter. The walls are approximately four feet high, and are interlocked crosswise with one another, made of thick sticks approximately one inch square, which occasionally are painted with blood. Between these sticks, all sorts of things are packed. On these walls rests a cupola, which is also fastened with such wood. The outside, from the top to the bottom, is covered with reed mats, and these in turn are covered with a brown felt blanket, through which neither wind nor rain can penetrate. In the middle of the cupola there is a round hole about two feet across. On the outside of the cupola there is a thick white or blue flag, which is an ancestral religious flag. The fire is made on the bare ground in the middle of the tent house, and the smoke draws out very well through the hole in the dome when the door is closed.

"The doors of the house are narrow and low, so that one can hardly crawl through. Always, the door is covered with a blanket. Furniture in these living quarters consists of a reed mat; two hair-filled cushions on which the Nagaian is accustomed to sleep; and a small wooden box containing a sword, a flint, and a pistol. If the Nagaian does not have these, he has a bow and slender arrows.

"A few steps from this tent, one finds a similar building in which the wife and children of the Nagaian live. One also finds the cooking utensils, consisting of a tripod and two or three wooden bowls. Such a house as it stands can be loaded on a wagon and moved to another place if necessary. Attached to these tents are cattle pens and barns. The walls of these are built of small stones, some of reeds and pointed sticks, and the outside covered with manure. A barnyard is enclosed with a reed fence and separated from neighbors by fifty to sixty steps.

"In the center of the colony, there is usually a large, round place where the young Nagaians play. In another place is the prayer hall or mosque. It is very small, and has no tower; it is built on a square with field stones, and covered with hollow tile.

"Instead of wood to burn, they use peat, reeds, or hay. Bread is a rare food. They eat mostly raw millet or barley; horseflesh is their favorite food. The Nagaians' chief occupation is cattle-raising, and also agriculture and bee-keeping."

These two peoples, the Cossacks and the Nagaians, lived side by side for centuries, and were very hostile to one another. This hostility resulted from their past origin. As the Cossacks had the mission of protecting the two Christian kingdoms, namely Poland and Russia, from the invasion of Tartar bands of robbers, so also did the Nagaians have the mission of checking the Christian powers bordering them on the north, from advancing into Crimea and Turkey.

Both sides were cunning and cautious when it came to setting a trap for the enemy. They were an equal match in bravery and speed, and likewise of equal agility and skill in pursuing the enemy, or escaping him by flight. Two advantages were on the side of the Cossacks. They had better guns, swords and pick axes, whereas the Nagaians were armed mostly with bow and arrow. Also, the Cossacks had a ruthless leader, and were dexterous in the use of their weapons. The Nagaians, however, were poorly equipped for war, and were mostly led by chance on their predatory excursions.

The Conquest of South Russia by the Russians

Since the victory of the brave Polish king, John Sobiesky, outside Vienna, over the Turks in the year 1683, the whole world had known that the Turks were no longer invincible. The Christian world no longer shook with fear and trembling at the mention of the Turkish name, and the Christian people could once more breathe more easily. Turkey was weakened, and started to decline very rapidly. No one knew this better than the clever Czarina, Catherine II of Russia. Immediately after she had ascended the throne in 1763, she devised a plan to weaken both Turkey and Poland, or if possible, to divide them. Both were suffering from decay. Her first aim, of course, was to have a navy on the Black Sea as soon as possible. As the boa constrictor surrounds and crushes the tiger, so Catherine wished to do to Turkey.

She therefore left not only her entire army in South Russia in readiness, but also immediately sent a fleet under Alexis Orlov into the Mediterranean Sea, to attack Turkey from the South, and to frighten her through insurrections in Greece, Egypt, Syria, and Trans-Caucasia. The weapons of the Russian army won a brilliant success. By the seventeenth of September, 1769, the fortress Chotin was surrendered to Prince Galizin. On the twenty-first of July, 1770, Rumjanzow beat the main Turkish army at Kaghul. Then on the twenty-seventh of September, 1770, Count Panin stormed the fortress Bender. Soon, thereafter, the fortresses Akkermann, Ismail, Kilia, and Braila fell into the hands of the Russians.

In 1771, the brave Dolgoruky conquered the Crimean Peninsula and installed a new Chan (Ruler), who had sworn an oath of allegiance to the Czarina Catherine.

In the year 1774, the Treaty of Kutschuk-Kainard was signed between Russia and Turkey. Through this treaty, Russia got permission for free shipping on the Black Sea. The Russian conquests were returned to Turkey, but the main gain, namely, the privilege of free navigation on the Black Sea was retained. But the conquest in the south was not yet concluded. In 1788, the second Turkish war started. This time we find that the Russian army was led by the two greatest field marshals in Russia, Suvorov and Potjomkin.

On the sixth of December, 1788, after a six-month siege, Potjomkin stormed the strong frontier fortress Otschakov, as a result of which the power of Turkey on the Black Sea was completely broken. After this, all of the fortresses on the Black Sea and the Sea of Azov, one after another, fell into the hands of the Russians. On the twenty-second of December, 1790, Suvorov stormed the fortress Ismail, and forced the Turks to sign the Peace Treaty of Jassy, on the ninth of January, 1792. By this treaty, all of the area which extended from Otschakov to the Dniester, fell to the Russians.

In 1812, by the Treaty of Bucharest, the region known as Bessarabia, as far as the Prut River, fell to the Russians. Since that time, Turkey has been "a sick man," whose poor existence was saved from collapse by time alone, since it was deprived of any European power on the diplomatic table. And still this "sick man" has the most holy spot in Christendom in his hands, namely Jerusalem with its holy places; and no one in the Christian world troubles himself to put an end to this horrible outrage. Because man does not treat the holy place with proper respect, there is misfortune, discord, rebellion, and ungodliness.

Potjomkin was the main Russian hero in these successful wars. But Potjomkin was not only a hero in war, but was also one of the first culture bearers of the eighteenth century. The founding of many cities in South Russia is his work. Thus in 1779 Cherson was founded, in 1778 Mariupol, in 1783 Sevastopol, in 1787 Jekaterinoslav, in 1789 Nikolaev, in 1793 Tiraspol, and in 1794 Odessa, the capital of South Russia.

Potjomkin was also a zealous promoter of science. Through his urging, a proclamation was issued on the fourth of September, 1784, starting a university in Jekaterinoslav; four professors had already been posted there. But when another Turkish war broke out later on, the building of the new university was discontinued. Even so, Potjomkin founded an agricultural school in 1790 in Vitovka near the present-day city of Nikolaev on the Bug River. It appears that this project also collapsed, at his death in 1791.

In an order dated the fourteenth of June, 1790, Potjomkin directed the governor of Jekaterinoslav as follows: "Vineyards are to be established in all crown settlements and in all good privately-owned land along the sea coast and from Chortitz to the Bug estuary, under the direction of the professors and assistants of the University of Jekaterinoslav. The seedlings should be obtained from the Don, but if insufficient, from the Crimea and Moldavia."

The Political Administration of South Russia
Following the Conquest by the Russians

Until 1774, the conquered provinces in South Russia were under military rule. The same year, the New Russian Gouvernement of South Russia was founded. It included for the most part the present provinces of Jekaterinoslav and the region of Elizabethgrad of the Cherson province.

In 1783, Jekaterinoslav was made a governorship. This included the present-day regions of Cherson, Elizabethgrad, Olviopol, and Alexandria in the province of Cherson. In 1795 the governorship of Vosnesensk was founded. To this new governorship belonged the district capitals Vosnesensk, Cherson, Elizabethgrad, Novomirgorod, Bogopol, Tiraspol, Jelensk, Olgapol, Uman, Tschigerin, Jekaterinopol, and Tscherkass. Other towns were Otschakov, Nikolaev, Berislav, Odessa, Ovidiopol, Dubossary, and Grigoriopol.

In 1796, all of the previously named provinces that had been annexed in 1783, along with the Crimea, were placed under the New Russian General Gouvernement. Those that were annexed in 1802 were included in the Gouvernements of Nikolaev, Jekaterinoslav, and Tauria. In 1803 the Nikolaev Gouvernement was renamed the Cherson Gouvernement.

The first Governor-General lived in Jekaterinoslav until 1805, in which year Duke Richelieu took over the important position and moved his residence to Odessa. When Bessarabia was included as part of Russia in 1812, all of these provinces were grouped together under the name of South Russia. At present the gouvernements in South Russia are as follows: The Gouvernment of Cherson with six counties and two governorships; the Gouvernement of Jekaterinoslav with eight counties; the Gouvernement of Tauria with eight counties and one governorship; and the Gouvernement of Bessarabia with eight counties.

Hydrography, or the Description
of the Seas and Rivers in South Russia

The Black Sea and the Sea of Azov form the southern boundary of South Russia, and in their wide expanse extend from the Danube on the west to the Don on the east. The Black Sea is joined to the Sea of Azov by the Strait of Kertsch.

The Sea of Azov is joined to the Lazy or Siwash Sea by the Narrows of Genitschi, and together they may be regarded as a small bay of the Black Sea. Both of the two previously named seas have many bays and inlets, more or less suitable for ships and steamboats. The Black Sea is almost completely land-locked, stretching between South Russia, the Caucasus, Asia Minor, European Turkey, Bulgaria, and Rumania. The expanse of the Black Sea from the east to the west is approximately 1160 kilometers; from the north to the south it is approximately 600 kilometers. The whole surface area amounts to approximately 432,800 square kilometers.

As in the Crimea, the east and south coasts are steep, but shallow elsewhere. Because of the heavy flow of fresh water rivers into the Black Sea, it contains very little salt, Ebb and flood tides do not occur. The depth is favorable for navigation, being 70 to 110 meters along the northwestern coast and as much as 1870 meters along the northeastern coast. The Black Sea has few reefs or sunken rocks, but very heavy storms occur on it in the fall and winter. The fishing industry is significant, especially around Otschakov. The most important ports and trade areas on the Black Sea in South Russia are: Odessa, Nikolaev on the Bug River estuary, Eupatoria, Sevastopol, Yalta, Feodosia, Novorosiisk, and Kertsch.

The Rivers of the Black Sea

The Donau or Danube River

The Danube forms the southern boundary between the Bessarabian portion of south Russia and Turkey, while its tributary, the Prut, forms the western border between Bessarabia and Rumania. After the Volga, the Danube is the longest river, and also the only one running diagonally from the west to the east; in olden times it was called the Istros or Ister. Now it is called the Donau, or Danube. It originates in the Grand Duchy of Baden, near Martin's Chapel, on the eastern slopes of the Black Forest, where it is named the Brege. Before it reaches Donaueschingen it is joined by the Brigach and other spring-fed rivulets and is then called the Danube.

From Tuttlingen on the border of Baden, it runs toward Würtemberg, makes several sharp turns, and then runs on to Ulm, on the Bavarian border, where it becomes navigable. It was from the city of Ulm that many of our forefathers, one hundred years ago, left their beautiful Fatherland and embarked on their distant excursions into the wild, unfriendly Russia. The Danube makes many turns as it flows from the north to the south; its total length is approximately 2,850 kilometers, and it drains an area of 817,000 square kilometers. It flows into the Black Sea from the west.

The beauties of the landscape through which the Danube flows are charming and wildly romantic, and in its diversity it emulates the Rhine. There are, however, large stretches that are monotonous, wild and bleak. It contains many hazards such as swift currents in its upper portion, sudden changes in its headwaters, and countless turns. But in spite of these drawbacks, navigation extends far inland, and there is considerable traffic on the river, forming the lifeblood of all those who live on the Danube.

The Austrian Danube Steamship Company alone owns 189 steamboats on the Danube. In Rumania and other states there are Steamship Companies which move trade and commerce, using the Danube. The Danube is joined by the Prut at Reni, and then flows for 200 versts (1 verst = 0.6629 miles) in the Russian territory, where it forms a delta above Tulcea. This is a large, triangular, marshy island overgrown with reeds; through this marshy bottom the main current divides into three branches: the Kilia, the Sulina, and St. Georges, and so empties into the Black Sea.

The Danube Commission converted the Sulina into a canal in 1858, as a result of which traffic was much improved.

The fishing industry on the Danube is not insignificant. In particular, one finds many Russian fishermen on the Danube islands of Tschetal, Leti, and Georgievsk. The main Russian cities on the Danube are Reni, Ismail, Kilia and Sulina.

The Dniester River

The Dniester, first called Tyras, then Danaster, by the ancients, springs from the Carpathian mountains, not far from Turka in Austrian Galicia, from where it is navigable. It flows past Chotin toward Russia, forming the boundary between the provinces of Bessarabia, Podolia, and Cherson; then it flows between Akkermann and Ovidiopol and empties into the Black Sea. At its mouth it has formed a shallow sand bar 27 versts long and 8 versts wide. The river is 1,000 versts long, of which approximately 350 versts are very crooked. The river drains an area of approximately 76,800 square versts.

Because of the many curves, and the swift current at Yambol, navigation on the Dniester is not without danger. Previously, much wheat and other produce from Galicia and the surrounding provinces was shipped south on this river. But since the railway was built, only wooden rafts and barges are used for shipping on the Dniester.

The Dniester is very rich with fish. The river bank everywhere is high, steep and stony. Because of the sudden onset of warm weather and heavy rains, the Dniester frequently overflows its banks and causes heavy damage by these floods.

The tributaries of the Dniester from the right, i.e., Bessarabia, are: Ramenez, Anuta, Tschernaya, Reut, Ikil, Byk, Botnya, Volschanez, and Yashtubei. From the left: Yagorlik, Shibka, Kamarova, Kutschurgan, Turuntschuk, Maly-Karagatsh, Bolshoi-Karagatsh, and Tomaschlik.

The following small rivers between the Dniester and the Bug empty directly into the Black Sea. They are: Baraboi, Dalnik, Maly-Kuyalnik, Bolshoi-Kuyalnik, Bolshoi-Adshelik, Maly Adshelik, Tiligul, Safik, and Beresan.

The Bug River

The Bug, previously called the Hypanis, originates in Podolia, in the district of Proskurov near the village Bubnoyka; it flows through Podolia and past the city of Olviopol into the Province of Cherson. It divides the latter into two unequal parts; and after a distance of 600 versts it forms a large sand bar near Otchakov and empties into the Black Sea. From Vosnesensk onward the Bug is navigable. All of the banks are high, stony, and covered with small trees and shrubs. At Olviopol the Bug is 100 Faden (1 Faden = 6 feet) wide; at Nikolaev where a strong bridge is built across the

15

river, it is only 2½ versts wide. Above Vosnesensk, the Bug has many rapids, due to granite rocks. These rocks are hauled to Odessa for paving stones.

The tributaries of the Bug on the right are: Sinyucha, Kagarlik, Tschorny-Taschlik, Suchoi-Taschlik, Vis, Bockschalu Tshertalu, Tshishaklei, Solenaya, and Korenicha. From the left side they are: Miklya, Bolshaya, Karabelnaya, Vordvavod, Gniloi-Yelanez, Kuzoï-Yelanez, Belousovka, and the Ingul with its fifteen tributaries.

The Dnieper River

The Dnieper, previously called the Borysthenes, originates in the Volkonski forest, near Dnieprovo in the province of Smolensk, and becomes navigable at Dorogobusch. It flows through the provinces of Smolensk, Mohilev, Minsk, Kiev, Tschernigov, Poltava, and Jekaterinoslav. It flows below the city of Cherson through its own sandbar, and becomes intermingled with the Black Sea at Otschakov. The Dnieper is approximately 1,700 versts long, of which over 700 versts are very crooked. The watershed covers an area of approximately 526,900 square versts. The width of the river varies from 90 to 360 meters; its depth is also very variable. From its origin to Kiev, it flows through beautiful, picturesque meadows, in a fairly large valley. Below Alexandrov, the rapids begin, thirteen in number. Near Kiev, there is a strong bridge across the river, and in many other places one finds pontoon bridges or ferry boats. By way of the King's Canal, the Dnieper is joined to the Vistula, the Niemen, and the Dvina.

The Dnieper is very rich in fish, particularly in its sandbar, which is overgrown with reeds and rushes, and is composed of forty small islands. The important tributaries from the right are: Drut, Beresina, Pripet, Tererev, Ross, and Ingulez. On the left are: Sosha, Desna, Sula, Psiul, Worskla, Orel, Samara, and Konskaya.

Besides these, the following rivers of the Crimean (Taurian) Peninsula flow into the Black Sea, and a few into the Lazy Sea: Kalantshak, Tshemerlik, Samartshik, Tobe-Tshokrak, Bulganak, Alma, Katsha, Kokos, Baidar, Alushta, Temirdsha, Kuru-Ufen, Andusudern, Suuksudern, Uskut, Usen, Schelen-Usen, Woran, Taraktasch, Kazkali, Salgir-Bulganak, Andal, Subasch, and Tshuruksu. The last five empty into the Lazy Sea.

The River System of the Sea of Azov

The Don River, previously called Tanais, originates in the Ivanovskoye Osero province of Tula. It flows through the provinces of Tula, Ryasan, Tambov, Orel, Voronesh, and the vicinity of the Don Cossacks, as far as Voronesh, where it becomes navigable. It flows in a southerly direction, breaks through the flat steppes of South Russia, flows within a distance of 50 versts of the Volga River, then turns southwesterly. It then forms a broad, shallow sand bar, and flows past Azov into the Sea of Azov. The river is approximately 1500 versts long, of which 1300 versts are navigable. The Don has no waterfalls or swift currents, but there are many shallow areas, sand bars, and small islands. In many places it is 360 meters wide and very rich in fish. In the spring, when the snow melts, the river often overflows its banks for many miles around, flooding large areas of land.

The tributaries of the Don from the right are: Sosna and Donets. From the left: Voronesh, Bityug, Chozer, Vorona, Medvediza, and Manytsch. Besides these, there are small rivers that run into the Sea of Azov: Torez, Bachmut, Lugan, Luganshik, Kalmius, Mius, Tshaltyr, Sambeck, Bugas, Karesa, Samartshik, Berda, Berdyanka, Tshenalgish, Tshetatil, Solonaya, Yantshokrak, Molotshnaya, Maly-Utlek, and Bolshoi-Utlek.

The Composition of the Soil in South Russia

The large land area from the Dniester to the Don River is for the most part flat, crossed only by the above-named rivers, and is usually called the South Russian Steppe. Various geographers divide it into the Otchakov, the Dnieprov, and the Don Steppe. Real mountains are found only on the south, separating it from the Crimean Peninsula. In the northwest arise the foothills of the Carpathian Mountains. They extend in a southerly direction across the Dnieper, where they form the rapids, and on both sides of this river, they spread out into wavelike hillocks. Another chain of the Carpathian hills extends over northwest Bessarabia, and at Bender gives way to flat prairie. This steppe, which extends farther than the eye can see, at first glance appears to be a poor, treeless waste, unproductive, and arid. This, however, is only deception, for this steppe contains a rich, productive, fertile soil for almost every cereal, the so called "Black Earth." Much has been written, and there has been considerable discussion about the formation of this black earth called humus. Here are opinions of some specialists about the genesis of this soil.

The Englishman, Murchison, contends that the black soil is composed of sea mud. The learned Ermann argues that this black soil has the same composition as the soil on the Rhine, between Basel and Andernach. Others believe the soil originated from peat bog, which is supposed to have existed here in prehistoric times. Whether one or the other of these opinions is correct or even close ot it, is impossible to decide. The constituents of the upper part of the black soil, according to the chemist Schlippe, are as follows:

Hydroscopic Moisture	5.68%
Organic Material	11.72
Pebbles (Silica)	60.80
Aluminum and Iron Oxide	18.01
Calcareous Material	1.67
Magnesium	0.41
Potash and Soda	1.70
	99.99%

The layer of black earth is usually two to five feet thick, and sometimes fifteen feet thick, in the valleys. It is assumed that this black earth covers a third of European Russia, extending over approximately 87,000,000 dessatine (1 dessatin = 2¾ acres), stretching across twenty-two provinces. The northern boundary of this black soil begins in the west, below 51 degrees north latitude, turns in various directions from Podolia to Shitomir, Kiev, and Tshernigov, then easterly to the provinces of Kursk and Orel, then extends to the rivers Oka, Sura, Volga, as far as the Ural River. The southern border starts in Bessarabia below 47 degrees north latitude, and extends across Odessa, Cherson, and along the Sea of Azov and the Don River, to Zarizin, then to the Volga, and without reaching its banks, upward to Saratov, then easterly toward the river Irgis as far as Orenburg.

One also finds a great deal of black soil in Siberia, but about the extent of this, geologists have not yet any accurate knowledge. The extraordinary fertility of the black soil is due to:

1. The top layers contain the humus which is very rich in nitrogen, a necessary ingredient of plant glutamines.

2. The looseness of the layer of black soil permits the moisture and air to penetrate to the plant roots and allows the roots to spread and become firmly attached.

3. Because of the sand it contains, and because of its black color, this soil warms rapidly.

Because of these characteristics it is able to soak up a significant quantity of moisture and yet permit it to evaporate slowly. Therefore this black soil is best suited to grow wheat but less satisfactory for potatoes, since they will rot if left in this damp soil very long.

The Black Earth is doubtless the best type of soil, as it has been very fruitful since time immemorial, without addition of any fertilizers. If only rains come at the right time, it always produces a rich harvest. The best witnesses for this statement are the German colonists in South Russia, with their one hundred years of experience. However, I do not wish to imply that the productiveness of the black soil cannot be increased with proper treatment and additional fertilizers. Especially now, after the last one hundred years have passed, is a good time to think of improving the agricultural methods of the German colonists, and to institute the necessary remedy to prevent imminent bankruptcy.

The Climate of South Russia

Since South Russia consists of a boundless plain, and is not protected by any high mountain ranges, it is exposed to winds and storms from all quarters. So the climate in winter is very raw, and in summer very sultry. Due to the nearness of the Black Sea, the climate is temperate, and in the winter the thermometer seldom drops to 20 degrees below zero (i.e., -4° F.) Spring usually starts in the beginning of March.

The frost and very cold spring winds interfere with growth, until at last the warm April sun stirs stubborn nature out of its winter sleep, and at its command nature rapidly weaves and puts on its glorious spring raiments. Spring is very short, and often it is already very hot by the 2nd of May. The critical time for the farmers is the end of May; if it then rains enough, they can count on an abundant harvest.

The summers often are so hot that all vegetation dies, and the heat does extensive damage to the farms. In July the heat often reaches 30 degrees R (100° F.), and in Odessa 40 degrees R (122° F.). The hot south wind and hail often spoil the beautiful grainfields.

The fall in South Russia is usually the most pleasant season. Even if there are cold days, heavy rainstorms and foggy weather in the second half of September, October is usually warm, friendly, and comfortable, to make up for it.

The winter usually starts at the beginning of November. It is, however, very capricious, for it is not unusual for the temperature to vary from ten below to ten above in a single night.

During the years 1806-1807, the cattle were able to graze in the pastures all winter. Then again, in the years 1812 to 1814, a lot of cattle died due to the extreme cold.

The wind in South Russia is a frequent guest all year long. There is a steady cool north wind all summer, but in winter it is accompanied by very heavy frost. The most fearful wind, however, is the northeaster. The west wind in winter is fairly general, and in summer is more damp than the other winds. But at times it is also accompanied by violent storms which exceed even the northeaster in severity. The south wind is noted for its agreeable warmth in the spring, and at harvest time for its fog banks. The east wind is not very strong; in spring and summer it often brings rain, and in winter slippery ice.

With the exception of winter in South Russia, the winds usually start before sunrise, gradually getting worse during the day until about two o'clock in the afternoon, when they calm down gradually until sundown, seeming to come quietly to rest.

Fog and hoarfrost are of frequent occurrence in South Russia and often have a damaging effect on the vegetation. It should rain more often in this region, as generally the cause of a crop failure here is the scarcity of rain. It snows more often in the northern part of South Russia than in the Crimea. But seldom does the snow last longer than two weeks, as the abundant warm weather melts the snow, turning the area into a sea of mud, so that all roads and byways are impassable.

The origin of the German Colonists in South Russia and Their Old Home

There is hardly a German district which does not have some representative in South Russia. However, it is historically verified that most of the German colonists in South Russia emigrated from the provinces of Alsace-Lorraine, Rhineland, Baden, Würtemberg, Bavaria, Switzerland, and Prussia. Therefore one must look for the ancestors of these colonists in these same provinces. The Roman historian, Tacitus, writes that before Christ, these provinces were occupied by the Gauls, Triboks, and Suevi. In the fifth century A.D., this region was overrun by the Allemanns, a mixed race composed of various Germanic stock. In the year 496 they were forced by Chlodwig to recognize Frankish sovereignty; they mixed with the inhabitants living there, accepted the Christian religion, and remained in this region. They are the present-day inhabitants of the middle Rhine area.

The territories of the Rhine endured a harsh destiny during the centuries of the Christian era. They were often the bone of contention between major and minor princes and tyrants. During the Peasant Revolt, the inhabitants of the Rhine suffered considerably through the hordes of aroused mobs. During the Thirty Years' War, Sweden overran the lovely Rhine district; under the pretext of protecting their Protestant brothers, they committed dreadful acts of cruelty. But all of this was put in the shade by the French Revolution.

A commissioner, named Von Dietrich, immediately started work in the spirit of the Revolution and later became mayor of Strassburg. A former professor, E. Schneider, started the whole Reign of Terror, aping the bloody methods in Paris. He held revolutionary talks, erected a guillotine and watered the "freedom tree" with a lot of human blood; and through the mayor had the famous Strassburg Cathedral converted to the "Temple of Reason." And soon the revolution sent its rapacious armies to the Rhine.

The old order was uprooted and the principles of the revolution instituted. Freedom, equality, brotherhood, were the passwords. The aristocracy everywhere was driven out, and the churches plundered. The French nationalists, who were officially installed as functionaries, stole in colossal ways. They sold state and public property, and forests, and shamelessly filled their purses. Every claim of those who were robbed was treated with scorn. Only bribery sometimes helped to save some worthwhile object. As accomplices of the French thieves, Jews made themselves notorious everywhere on the Rhine, acting as sleuth hounds for worthwhile goods and rare church treasures. Acting as brokers, they sold these treasures and shared the proceeds with the revolutionaries.

But not only the godless revolutionaries were such robbers; the German princes also robbed everybody and transformed the beautiful Rhine region into a waste. One notorious celebrity belongs in this group, namely, the Elector and later King of Bavaria, Max Joseph. He started the assault on the convents like a raging wind, leading a wild army, and swept over all of Bavaria. They trampled everything asunder that our devout forefathers had built and maintained since the year 1000. In a short time all of these worthwhile foundations and institutions were swept aside, so that today nothing remains but the memory.

More than seventy religious institutions and abbeys, and over four hundred monasteries, were robbed and dismantled in Bavaria alone. The contents of these institutions usually remained in the hands of the malefactor Jews. The magnificent buildings were made into barracks, homes for invalids, castles, or theatres. Many were torn down or still stand today as empty and desolate ruins, a witness as to how men in Catholic Bavaria desecrated the most sacred. Many churches were made into stables, breweries, custom houses, and powder magazines. Jewelry, sacred vessels, horses, wagons, furniture, buildings, farms, fields, meadows, and forests, were immediately made public property, and with zealous haste, often divided solely for the benefit of a single individual. At the frequent public auctions, Jews disguised themselves as wandering bishops and made a mockery of the Holy vessels. And this disgraceful procedure came to pass by the order and knowledge of a Christian prince, who was appointed by God to administer justice and righteousness to all his subjects, and to protect the defenseless people, including the monks.

All these things, crying out to heaven, were seen by our forefathers with their own eyes. It is therefore no wonder that they have a peculiar sense of values and possess few virtues but many vices. For under such confused and sad conditions as then existed, neither domestic nor civic virtues could take deep root in our forefathers. And that they still have some taint from that terrible period is evident today. To this can be ascribed their lack of respect for the sacred, their disobedience against their superiors and the disastrous management of their affairs.

The Invitation of
the German Colonists to South Russia
under Alexander I

When the present South Russia as described above was incorporated with Russia, through the gallantry of the Russian Field Generals, the Russian government endeavoured to populate this newly acquired province as soon as possible with new settlers. They searched everywhere in the Balkans to fill these requirements; e.g., the Serbians, Bulgarians, Montenegrins, and Greeks. But among all these there were no cultured or only poorly cultured people. The brave Potjomkin had already come to this conclusion, because he had already assigned German tradesmen and their families to Cherson. But his early death interrupted all of his grandiose plans which he had hoped to bring about for his dear South Russia. However, these plans were not cancelled on this account, but only postponed.

When Alexander I assumed the Russian throne in 1801, a new plan was made immediately to colonize southern Russia. As a result of the ill success of the Volga colonies and of the few German colonies in the south, Alt-Schwedendorf, Danzig, Jamburg,

Josephstal and others, the Russian government had become convinced that one had to be careful in the choice of immigrants and not accept all the rabble that applied for entry. They issued a decree informing all of their commissars and agents in foreign countries about this decision.

Privileges to those Colonists
Who Settle in the Southern Provinces
of the Imperial Russian Empire

1. Complete religious freedom.
2. Freedom from taxes and other obligations for ten years.
3. After the ten free years have passed, the colonists become equal to other Imperial Russian subjects, with the exception that they will not be required to billet troops except on a march through.
4. The colonist will not be required to render military or civil service. He may volunteer to enter the service of the crown, but this will not free him from the payment of crown debts.
5. Each settler will receive on arrival a money advance to get himself established, which he will be expected to repay in the ten years following the tax-free years.
6. Every family can bring with them their furniture, duty free, and over and above this can bring articles to sell, the value of these articles not to exceed 300 rubles.
7. The craftsmen can enter the guilds and corporations. Also, each can carry on his trade unhindered, anywhere in the entire Imperial Russian realm.
8. Through the magnanimity of His Imperial Russian Majesty, all serfdom has been discontinued in the Imperial Russian State.
9. Every family will receive 30 to 80 dessatine of useful land from the Crown, depending on their ability to utilize same. The taxes which the family will pay after the ten free years have passed, in addition to any police fines, will be a land tax of 15 to 20 kopeck yearly for one dessatin.*
10. He who wishes to leave the Imperial Russian State and return home, must first pay his debts to the Crown and also the taxes on the land for three years.

Signed at Lauingen, 20 March 1804
Russian Imperial Colony Transport
Signature illegible

---

*A dessatin is in German equivalent to approximately one Tuch (Toch) or Morgen (2¾ acres). A Kopeck is slightly less than a Kreutzer (Farthing).

This document was published in foreign countries. The original of these privileges can be seen in Kleinliebental at the home of Widow Walz.

For a better insight I include this additional edict:

EDICT CONCERNING THE SETTLEMENT
AND RIGHTS OF THE COLONISTS
20 FEBRUARY 1804

(The original is endorsed:
　　　So be it!　　　　　　Alexander I)

"The foreigner Ziegler, who, in the last year (1803), has led a certain number of colonists from Germany to Russia, wishes to offer his services for a similar summoning of colonists this year.

"After examining his proposals and thinking over the whole state of affairs, I venture in all humility to make the following proposal to his Imperial Majesty.

"The invitation to the colonists was extended, and still is, on the basis of the Manifesto of 1763. This contained no limit on the type of people who were to be accepted; on the contrary, one sought generally some from every trade and profession. Consequently at the start, many worthless and for the most part very poor farmers migrated, who until now have benefited the state very little. The Saratov colonies and also some of the New Russian ones confirm the truth of this statement. As far as one can judge, the present invitations through Ziegler and Escher are also without selection. From the letters of the first colonists, it is evident that there were many superfluous artisans among them and frail, weak single persons, some with old ailments, the greater part of them very poor.

"The Empress Catherine II decided to invite foreigners, since she wished to populate the uninhabited steppes. Due to the population increase in the inner provinces, and the need to overcome the crowding of our own subjects, there is no longer an abundance of useful land available for colonization. One should therefore strive less for indiscriminate settlement by foreigners than for a restricted number of immigrants who can serve as models in agricultural pursuits and in trades. If accepting of people from foreign lands is to be continued, it is necessary to restrict it to those most needed and to able, well-to-do farmers.

"At the present time the immigration is directed mainly into the New Russian region. Since it is known that there is very little suitable crown land left there, and land is difficult to find, one has to determine, before accepting the immigrants, where they are to be settled, by searching out suitable crown land or buying land from private owners. If this is not done and settlement after arrival is delayed, the immigrants have to live for two years or so at crown expense at considerable total cost.

"Once land has been found and protected from diversion to other uses, its settlement has to be restricted to such foreigners as are most useful in this region: good grain farmers, people experienced in wine-growing, in the cultivation of mulberry trees and other useful plants, in cattle raising and especially in the breeding and raising of the best sheep, who possess all the necessary knowledge to pursue a rational agricultural operation. Such people as these shall be accepted in preference to all others. Rural tradesmen, such as tailors, shoemakers, carpenters, blacksmiths, potters, weavers and masons may also be accepted. All other artisans and tradesmen, not useful in a rural community, are not to be accepted as colonists, except in cases where it may be considered indispensable to invite a modest number of tradesmen to the new cities of the South.

"According to these principles it appears undesirable to entice people to come here by persuasion or other means or to set up special commissions for the recruiting of colonists or to appoint special agents. Instead, one can prescribe that those who wish to emigrate to Russia shall apply to our Ministers or other agents, who can provide them with passports for the journey to the Russian border. Before doing so these will check the credentials, certificates or testimonials from a magistrate or a community official certifying that the bearer is a person of good character. It will be expected also that the emigrant shall have fulfilled all the obligations toward his present government prescribed by the laws of his state and empire.

"Since the journey to the border might prove difficult for one or two families travelling by themselves, we can authorize our Ambassador in Regensburg to form those wishing to go to Russia into groups of 20 to 30 families to travel together by water or by land, whichever appears better. He could rent ships or wagons at Russian government expense and choose from among the emigrants leaders whom all are to obey on the journey. To assist the ambassador we could appoint the foreigner Ziegler, a man of much skill and adroitness, who could assemble the required number of families, could hire the sailors or wagon drivers for the expedition, and could examine carefully the testimonials presented by the colonists and their economic circumstances. When he hands in his report we could pay him a suitable salary for his efforts. A group of families who have agreed to emigrate could be permitted to choose one or more persons to send ahead to examine the pieces of land under consideration for them and determine their qualities. Finally, the annual emigration of colonists from Germany should not be allowed to exceed 200 families, for more than that can not be settled in a suitable way. The ambassador should therefore be instructed to accept and expedite only 100 to 150 families a year, on the assumption that some others will emigrate on their own from places close to the border.

"Our Ministers at foreign Courts, who might have to deal with this matter, should be instructed:

1) That they are not to make any advance payments, except for the rent of the ships and wagons for those who have been accepted as described above.

2) That those who report to them wishing to emigrate must show documents or provide a responsible guarantor to prove that they possess an estate of 300 guilders in cash or goods to take with them; and that those who can not provide such evidence are not to be accepted, for experience has taught us that settling people without means proceeds very slowly and succeeds poorly.

3) It is understood that the emigrants are to be people with families; single persons are not to be accepted, unless someone adopts them into his family.

4) Families that consist only of a husband and wife should not usually be accepted, for experience shows that it is difficult for them to manage a farm successfully, since they would have to hire some workers.

The Immigration of German Colonists
to South Russia

We see from the foregoing chapter that the colonization of South Russia with German culture bearers was undertaken by the Russian government according to a definite plan. One wished not only to bring under cultivation the barren stretches of land in the newly-won territory, but to settle colonists who could serve as models to the natives of the region in the practice of agriculture and related trades. The first purpose has been achieved, the second only partially.

The oldest colonies in South Russia are the Swedish colonies of Alt Danzig and Schwedendorf, founded in 1787. The next three oldest colonies, Jamburg, Josephstal, and Rübalsk date from 1789. Then in 1789, the Mennonites came to the Chortitz region. The settling of the Mennonites on the Molotschna began in 1803.

Besides the Mennonites, settlements began near Odessa in 1803. In this year, the agent Ziegler led 2,990 colonists, mostly Swabians, to Odessa, the port of entry for the southerly colonization. From the city of Ulm, the rallying point of the emigrants, various groups set out each year upon the arduous journey to distant Russia. In the years 1804-1805, the rush of the colonists to Odessa was already so great that no place in the entire area could be found as winter quarters for the newcomers.

Under these circumstances it was no wonder that the poor colonists were afflicted with problems of all kinds and a variety of miseries and illnesses, compounded by the heartlessness and unscrupulousness of Russian officials. Let us listen to the horrifying complaints which they directed to the authorities in a petition from Ovidiopol, where they were packed together like herring in a miserable building. I offer the document word for word:

"We colonists of Ovidiopol, your willing and obedient servants, can no longer avoid begging for help in our distress, from the most honored military and civil authorities of the Russian land, particularly from the fortress commander and his superiors, because we can no longer accept our fate. We had been hoping that the situation would improve in time, but instead it has got worse. Relying on the promises of Imperial Russian Commissar Ziegler we spent all our means and risked life and limb on such a long journey, believing that the promises made to us would be kept, that we would be paid the daily allowance of 40 kopeks from the day of departure, as well as the cost of the fare by water and land. This had been promised to us at every station since we left Ulm, but we have received nothing. Finally at the border at Radziwilow we received for the first time an allowance; persons over fifteen years received 10 Kopeks, and the younger ones received 6 Kopeks. Because of the exchange rate we lost 25 per cent. Those who still had a little money had to help the others, so that we were able to get here together, in the hope that it would all be repaid. But of this we have received nothing, only our daily stipend, and that with difficulty, as our leaders have had to be in Odessa eight days of each month in order to get it. All of this puts us to great expense.

"We have received very little wood and no light at all in the barracks, all winter long. In addition, we have had to lie so close to one another that we could not possibly maintain our health, because of the stale air and other annoyances. We all arrived here healthy, thank God, but in this prison many parents have lost their children, and many children their parents, God help us. And if we do not get help, all of us here will die.

"Whenever we complain to our Court Councillor, Böhm, he gives us nothing but abusive words in reply, reprimanding us as slovenly people and riffraff. And if we wish to show him our certificates of respectable citizens, he simply replies in the same way. If an upright man exchanges words with him, he threatens to cut off his hair and chase him out of the country. When we receive an order from Court Councillor Briganez in Odessa, and we wish to obey it, he berates him in the extreme. So, for our own protection, we must not contradict him. One dares not reply to him in any way, as he will listen to no one. Lately he hit our mayor, Götz, on the heart and on the head with his cane, without any provocation.

"And so we request from the most honorable Authority, not only alleviation of our troubled conditions, but also payment of monies; otherwise none of us can procure any clothing for ourselves.

"We hope also not to be treated harshly, like those who came before us. That this is the pure truth is witnessed by the following signatures: Jacob Götz, mayor, Jacob Modinger, Johannes Kalberer, Matthäus Maile, Andreas Haar, Wilhelm Mohr, Jacob Krass, Johann Georg Wolf, Matthäus Hagstolz, Jacob Bauer, Jacob Ildinger, Andreas Klinger, and Daniel Ekinger."

(Ovidiopol, December, 1804 or January, 1805)

To investigate this matter, a medical man, Dr. Korolenkov, was sent to Ovidiopol from Cherson. He found the state of the colonists shocking, and informed Commander-in-Chief Koble at Odessa. Accordingly, on the 8th of March, 1805, he wrote to Governor-General Rosenberg:

"The barracks in Ovidiopol are too small for the many colonists, poorly ventilated, damp and unclean. The people are all lying together in a disorderly manner, the well, the sick and the dying, all wailing, screaming, and begging for help. A horrible, heart-rending picture. One the 21st of February, 1805, there were 150 cases of fever; all died in a single day."

Dr. Pisenko was sent at once from Grossliebenthal to Ovidiopol to bring some help to the sick, until Duke Richelieu, who was expected as the new Governor-General from Petersburg, could provide other arrangements. This frightful calamity was most promptly abolished by the new Governor-General, who from that time on was like a father to the colonists.

Things improved for the subsequent immigrants who arrived in 1805 to 1812; winter quarters were established for them, mostly in the Liebenthal colonies. Without going into further detail about the German settlements, some of it already reported in a book,* I shall

---

*"Die Deutschen Colonien in Sudrussland" — P. J. Stach—Published by Schaab in Prischib.

give a statistical survey of all the German colonies in South Russia founded from 1787 to 1855.

Statistical Table* of the Colonies of South Russia and Bessarabia

I. Cherson Province Odessa Region	Year Founded	Amount of Land**	Number of people 1859	Number of people 1905	School children 1859	School children 1905	Houses 1859
1. Liebenthal District							
1. Grossliebental	1804	8828	2635	2997	429	510	256
2. Kleinliebental	1804	4204	1434	2227	197	260	148
3. Alexanderhilf	1805	3043	964	901	157	161	99
4. Neuburg	1805	2945	888	825	180	157	105
5. Marienthal	1805	2945	629	1156	83	133	91
6. Peterstal	1805	2994	869	187	193	163	116
7. Josephstal	1804	3458	741	1116	89	153	103
8. Freudental	1806	3829	1392	1326	270	205	162
9. Franzfeld	1805	2110	789	803	114	90	89
10. Lustdorf	1804	1109	503	461	80	78	45
11. Güldendorf	1829	5335	1058	1310	182	192	107
2. Kutschurgan District							
1. Strassburg	1808	3561	1023	1884	175	240	148
2. Selz	1808	5933	1523	2745	194	259	192
3. Kandel	1808	5966	1583	2824	213	203	193
4. Baden	1808	3561	1034	1649	206	155	149
5. Mannheim	1809	3561	1035	1727	162	209	117
6. Elsass	1809	3561	1175	1725	144	161	151
Community Pasture	....	1570	....	....	....	....	....
3. Bujalik District (Bulg.)							
1. Gross-Bujalik	1802	17107	....	....	....	....	....
2. Klein-Bujalik	1801	9570	....	....	....	....	....
3. Kubanka	1804	7590	....	....	....	....	....
4. Beresan District							
1. Landau	1809	8896	1958	2048	220	248	202
2. Speier	1809	7898	1514	2056	203	319	190
3. Katherinental	1817	5564	773	1726	118	206	104
4. Karlsruhe	1809	5390	1085	1410	137	107	129
5. Sulz	1809	4428	815	2569	67	116	92
6. Rohrbach	1809	8333	1581	2521	285	118	205
7. Worms	1809	4946	1533	1776	304	140	136
8. Johannesthal	1817	4149	625	1420	130	178	90

*The Jewish colonies are included because German model farmers lived there, the Bulgarian colonies for the sake of completeness.
**This figure is given according to the 1859 survey.

9. Waterloo	1833	2675	562	634	121	100	80
10. Neu Freudental	1828	2655	517	870	114	110	63
11. Helenental	1838	1704	247	485	68	80	29
Community pasture	....	1316	....	....	....	....	....

Ananyev Region

12. Rastatt	1809	5428	1303	3691	123	305	138
13. München	1809	2974	713	1928	95	150	80

Tiraspol Region

1. Glückstal District

1. Glückstal	1805	7035	1875	2143	364	324	259
2. Neudorf	1807	5810	1703	1956	327	262	222
3. Bergdorf	1809	3925	1360	1387	274	150	168
4. Cassel	1809	6948	1637	1388	332	266	214
Community Pasture		500	....	....	....	....	....
5. Klein-Neudorf	1855	1867	....	270	34	54	32

On own land — 1200 dess.
which was bought by 29 farmers from this district.

2. Separate Colonies

1. Hoffnungstal	1817	4457	1154	2375	242	260	120
2. Katarschina (Bulg.)	1806	14001	2734	....	100	....	210
3. Parkan (Bulg.)	1804	8165	1155	....	42	....	163

Cherson Region

1. Swedish District

1. Alt-Schweden- dorf	1787	3102	322	710	56	110	40
2. Mühlhausendorf	1804	2596	335	639	45	75	35
3. Klosterdorf	1804	3003	375	817	70		35
4. Schlangendorf	1804	2597	293	534	82	75	35
Community Pasture	....	350	....	....	....	....	....

2. Separate Colonies

1. Neu Danzig	1843	3886	553	555	100	70	72
2. Ternoffka (Bulg.)	1802	10019	1687	?	40	....	232

Elisabethgrad Region

Alt Danzig	1787	1635	478	....	70	?	58

II. Jekaterinoslav Province

1. Separate Colony

Jamburg	1789	2228	926	2028	128	130	71

2. Chortitz District

1. Chortitz	1790	2994	767	2105	90	123	83
2. Rosental	1790	2567	619	984	90	129	77
3. Rosengart	1824	1793	259	213	64	31	48
4. Burwalde	1803	1947	518	456	67	74	65
5. Blumengart	1824	914	193	240	52	38	40
6. Nieder Chortitz	1803	2190	729	670	141	63	100
7. Insel Chortitz	1790	2781	381	204	55	24	27
8. Einlage	1790	3219	771	715	112	66	99
9. Kronsweide	1790	3027	785	?	157	49	91
10. Neuenburg	1790	1233	338	?	76	....	47
11. Neuendorf	1790	3149	1007	811	119	....	118

12. Neuhorst	1824	847	218	165	64	....	49
13. Schönhorst	1790	2478	833	552	122	....	89
14. Kronstal	1809	1249	415	286	66	....	44
15. Neu-Osterwieck	1812	1911	723	1215	153	....	113
16. Schöneberg	1816	1177	377	315	53	....	46
Community Pasture	....	2924	....	....	....	....	....

Alexandrov Region

17. Schönewiese	1797	1463	322	....	52	75	46

Novomoskov Region

18. Kronsgarten	1797	1556	153	....	40	?	23

Separate Colonies

1. Josefstal	1789	3250	969	1300	165	180	110
2. Rübalsk	1790	1590	463	627	95	80	51

Alexandrov Region
1. Mariupol Mennonite District

1. Bergtal	1837	2144	399	375	99	60	67
2. Schönfeld	1837	1643	329	231	69	76	51
3. Schöntal	1838	2039	401	271	79	?	53
4. Heubuden	1841	1837	270	275	79	?	42
5. Friedrichstal	1852	1973	96	148	44	?	28

2. Mariupol Colonists' District

1. Kirschwald	1823	1560	421	367	80	46	39
2. Tiegenhoff	1823	1740	398	447	75	55	41
3. Rosengart	1823	1680	424	416	78	56	38
4. Schönbaum	1823	1860	347	421	75	53	45
5. Kronsdorf	1823	1620	497	530	93	105	44
6. Grunau	1823	1620	461	369	85	?	55
7. Rosenberg	1823	1560	512	308	91	49	40
8. Wikkerau	1823	1560	414	312	73	54	40
9. Reichenberg	1823	1680	386	292	76	40	43
10. Kampenau	1823	1800	423	784	121	65	50
11. Mierau	1823	1680	391	750	64	100	34
12. Kaiserdorf	1823	1560	318	494	56	85	42
13. Göttland	1823	1680	387	487	62	60	42
14. Neuhoff	1823	1380	223	464	53	75	38
15. Eichwald	1823	1680	430	963	94	85	44
16. Tiegenort	1823	1680	439	504	75	85	42
17. Tiergart	1823	1200	278	313	46	45	28
18. Elisabethdorf	1825	2100	425	724	75	95	44
19. Ludwigstal	1828	2160	419	652	75	75	47
20. Belowesch	1831	1800	612	413	95	....	38
21. Kaltschinoffka	1831	1920	449	390	70	60	32
22. Rundewiese	1831	1920	445	343	82	52	34
23. Klein-Werder	1831	1260	411	226	60	55	27
24. Gross-Werder	1831	2230	589	429	74	78	39
25. Darmstadt	1843	1860	278	420	110	?	39
26. Marienfeld	1843	1380	208	442	46	?	45
27. Neu-Jamburg	1848	2280	277	481	46	?	28
Community Pasture	....	2140	....	....	....	....	....

III. Province of Tauria
Berdyansk Region
1. Berdyansk District

1. Neu-Hoffnung	1822	3473	763	....	137	....	82	
2. Rosenfeld	1822	1671	328	....	45	....	42	
3. Neuhoffnungstal	1822	1602	241	....	73	?	45	
4. Neu-Stuttgart	1831	1392	234	....	90	?	48	
Community Pasture	....	1000	....	....	....	....	....	

2. Molotschna Mennonite
District

1. Halbstadt	1804	1605	593	849	75	41	57
2. Muntau	1805	1621	412	573	58	44	64
3. Tiegenhagen	1804	1732	296	424	50	43	45
4. Schönau	1804	1630	297	390	55	46	52
5. Fischau	1804	1575	344	464	57	50	51
6. Lindenau	1804	1695	310	517	54	51	51
7. Lichtenau	1804	1525	306	506	70	44	46
8. Blumstein	1804	1555	501	510	106	65	70
9. Münsterberg	1804	1668	280	369	50	52	51
10. Altonau	1804	1646	416	647	72	61	51
11. Tiege	1805	1483	260	449	51	51	42
12. Orloff	1805	1544	288	486	45	45	43
13. Blumenort	1805	1451	277	474	56	43	43
14. Rosenort	1805	1445	287	349	54	46	47
15. Tiegerweide	1822	1698	337	485	53	36	56
16. Ruekkenau	1811	1400	358	395	82	43	54
17. Kleefeld	1854	2600	396	567	84	84	65
18. Lichfelde	1819	1500	336	365	55	56	46
19. Neukirch	1820	1490	425	385	58	54	58
20. Prangenau	1824	1414	347	462	72	47	52
21. Elisabethal	1823	1777	343	356	54	57	59
22. Alexandertal	1820	1435	341	378	56	38	54
23. Schardau	1820	1382	406	382	77	32	47
24. Pordenau	1820	1390	305	227	57	21	46
25. Marienthal	1820	1371	394	396	56	42	46
26. Rudnerweide	1820	2318	550	446	65	63	74
27. Franztal	1820	1663	356	407	54	51	40
28. Pastwa	1820	1260	274	235	44	30	39
29. Grossweide	1820	1683	326	400	70	43	50
30. Sparrau	1828	2685	555	797	95	82	60
31. Conteniusfeld	1831	2029	464	489	80	58	69
32. Gnadenfeld	1835	2729	621	842	106	74	84
33. Paulsheim	1852	1682	182	259	37	37	26
34. Nikolaidorf	1851	1438	198	211	43	28	31
35. Margenau	1819	1756	487	605	78	47	65
36. Fürstenwerder	1821	2230	435	595	64	57	52
37. Alexanderwohl	1821	2240	401	495	85	47	48
38. Gnadenheim	1821	1680	345	414	66	45	60
39. Friendensdorf	1824	2063	372	365	53	46	52
40. Landskrone	1839	2648	520	519	107	55	67
41. Hierschau	1838	1993	390	330	103	37	54
42. Waldheim	1846	2928	982	638	160	101	86
43. Wernersdorf	1824	2095	497	483	75	47	64

33

44. Liebenau	1823	1435	265	483	37	40	50
45. Schönsee	1805	1440	323	504	43	39	40
46. Fürstenau	1806	1561	343	396	49	30	56
47. Ladekopp	1805	1530	297	391	63	41	50
48. Petershagen	1805	1460	291	382	44	49	42
49. Alexanderkrone	1857	2600	220	488	40	66	40

Melitopol Region

50. Huttertal	1843	2112	288	347	55	58	36
51. Johannesruhe	1852	1104	197	370	56	59	30
Juhanle Farm		505					7
Steinbach Farm		370			14		11
Felsental Farm		56					5
Factory Meadow		3000				13	10
Craftsmen's Colony		827					26
Community Pasture		3190					6

Molotsch. Colonists'
District

1. Molotsch., Prischib	1804	3090	1185	1042	204	100	84
2. Hoffental	1804	1408	369	378	67	60	36
3. Alt-Nassau	1805	2614	628	576	123	79	63
4. Weinau	1805	2380	511	315	116	55	50
5. Durlach	1810	799	198	110	55	13	19
6. Neu Montal	1816	1809	368	326	75	59	35
7. Grüntal	1810	683	213	224	34	41	19
8. Tiefenbrunn	1820	1949	451	373	83	67	36
9. Alt Montal	1805	2050	424	175	80	33	39
10. Darmstadt	1838	3100	636	508	137	84	53
11. Hochstadt	1809	2548	591	491	143	85	56
12. Friedrichsfeld	1810	4026	999	845	210	133	80
13. Neu Nassau	1814	1845	387	479	66	49	39
14. Wasserau	1804	1700	374	325	76	40	32
15. Reichenfeld	1810	2794	708	420	160	88	55
16. Kronsfeld	1825	1904	460	373	100	77	44
17. Karlsruh	1815	2390	678	358	149	80	49
18. Rosental	1804	2049	559	344	108	72	45
19. Kaisertal	1838	3100	517	663	146	120	51
20. Eugenfeld	1846	2435	375	507	115	89	40
21. Heidelberg	1810	5132	1094	1002	136	101	92
22. Hochheim	1847	2577	571	291	89	35	40
23. Blumental	1822	3912	760	729	120	82	67
24. Waldorf	1809	1768	333	162	39	28	37
25. Kostheim	1810	2298	443	396	74	51	43
26. Leitershausen	1810	3250	622	507	132	62	57
Community Pasture	....	9335	....	....	....	....	....
Plantations	....	31	....	....	....	....	....

Simpferop. Region

1. Neusatz District

1. Neusatz	1805	968	613	468	123	100	61
2. Friedental	1805	729	536	262	84	63	42

3. Rosental	1805	1459	559	344	96	105	59
4. Kronental	1811	3910	591	1249	103	77	68

2. Separate Colony
   Baltotschakrak

(Bulg.)	1806	797	112	... ...	...	....	13

Feodosia Region

1. Zürichtal District

1. Zürichtal	1805	2131	751	590	140	102	85

In addition Okratsch (Freudental)
land belonged to them,

containing 1200 dessatin.			65	141	23	38	12
2. Heilbrunn	1805	1140	296	225	85	40	44

The land of Islam Terek

(Neudorf), 1446 dess.			70	172	33	?	15
Koyanle, 707 dess.			43	112	8	34	9
3. Sudak	1805	300	168	99	30	27	29
4. Herzenberg	1805	100	39	38	5	?	4

2. Separate Colonies

1. Kischlaw (Bulg.)	1803	1937	1563	... ...	...	....	143

2. Starj-Krim

(Bulg.)	1802	1000	627	....	28	....	89

IV. Bessarabia

Akkermann Region

1. Sarata District

1. Sarata	1822	6219	858	1880	177	318	117
2. Gnadental	1830	4970	704	1168	138	203	95
3. Lichtental	1834	4860	640	1317	188	270	88

2. Malojarosl. District

1. Malojaroslavetz 1.	1815	4137	1074	1451	244	270	123
2. Malojaroslavetz 2.	1823	5139	889	1300	146	303	105
3. Kulm	1815	6488	1398	1326	257	240	135
4. Tarutino	1814	8164	1644	5257	370	549	229
5. Krassna	1815	6996	1205	1992	133	253	158
6. Katzbach	1821	3914	734	970	205	195	62
7. Fere-Champenoise							
1.	1816	3867	818	1212	196	216	109
8. Fere-Champenoise							
2.	1823	3864	695	1057	169	185	86
9. Teplitz	1818	6904	1073	1850	212	424	127
10. Dennevitz	1834	3860	639	767	173	130	71
11. Plotzk	1839	2364	411	421	67	74	47

3. Klöstitz District

1. Klöstitz	1815	8132	1294	2692	280	276	155
2. Leipzig	1815	7601	1273	2122	180	300	133
3. Borodino	1814	6949	1503	2197	250	391	172
4. Beresina	1816	8251	1350	2060	127	337	175
5. Paris	1816	7314	1298	1518	141	285	134
6. Alt-Arcis	1816	4947	936	1781	180	287	105
7. Neu-Arcis	1824	2475	449	626	84	119	48

8. Brienne	1816	5046	1151	1537	211	242	137
9. Friedenstal	1833	5312	987	1410	188	252	135
10. Hoffnungstal	1842	4816	743	1381	139	355	89
Superfluous Land	....	327	....	....	....	....	....
4. Single Colony Chabag	1829	4013	301	462	80	92	65

Bessarabian Bulgarian Colonies

1. Ismail District
   5 Colonies .... 40622 8006 .... 99 905

Akkermann Region

2. Lower Budjak District
   19 Colonies .... 116010 17006.... 213 2415
3. Upper Budjak Districk
   19 Colonies .... 127670 24068.... 138 2823

Hebrew Colonies
1. Cherson Region

1. Gross-Seidemenucha	1809	9848	2097	....	124	 211
2. Klein Seidemenucha	1840	1588	418	....	31	 35
3. Bobrovoi-Kut	1807	9748	1902	....	100	 192
4. Gross-Nagartav	1809	4635	753	....	27	 101
5. Klein-Nagartav	1809	1830	217	....	20	 33
6. Effenger	1809	5232	850	....	60	 102
7. Inguletz	1809	5759	1359	....	90	 136
8. Kamianka	1809	3457	568	....	30	 68
9. Islutschistaja	1824	2895	543	....	30	 65
10. Novo-Berislav	1840	3664	677	....	28	 94
11. Lvova	to	4907	1055	....	68	 119
12. Romanoffka	1841	5158	1001	....	50	 115
13. Novo-Poltavka		5569	1533	....	90	 149
14. Novo-Vietbsk	1848	3428	572	....	15	 76
15. Novo-Podolsk	to	2766	619	....	5	 62
16. Novo-Rovno	1850	1755	371	....	16	 42
17. Novo-Schitomir		3044	434	....	10	 68

2. Bobrinetz Region

18. Israilevka	1807	3861	874	....	50	 100
19. Sagaidak	1807	2197	467	....	21	 46
20. Dobrinkaja	1807	....	1435	....	14	 156

II. Jekater. Province
   1. Alexandrov Region

1. Novo-Zlotopol	1846	4480	1235	....	14	 92
2. Vesselaja	1846	1950	424	....	7	 44
3. Krassnoselka	1846	2240	623	....	13	 30
4. Mejiretsch	1846	2240	540	....	12	 50
5. Trudoljubovka	1846	2000	521	....	8	 23
6. Netschaevka	1846	1520	386	....	9	 18
7. Priutnaja	1846	2320	616	....	10	 24
8. Roskoschnaja	....	....	616	....	7	 11

9. Bogodarevka	....	....	607	....	8	....	10
10. Gorkaja	....	....	488	....	7	....	10
11. Graffskoe	1846	1960	450	....	9	....	20
12. Selenoepole	....	6711	557	....	8	....	20
13. Nadejnaja	....	7519	532	....	6	....	12
14. Sladkowodnaja	....	2310	562	....	6	....	8
15. Satischa	....	....	487	....	7	....	28

The Highest Legal Authority of the Colonists in South Russia

When Catherine II of Russia proclaimed the familiar Manifesto of the 22nd of July, 1763, in order to invite German colonists into her empire, she founded at the same time the so-called Guardianship Council whose first president was Count Orlov. This administrative authority had the assignment of assembling the emigrants, through its domestic and foreign commissioners, and of escorting them to the location of the new settlement in Russia.

The Council lasted until 1782, when all of Russia was divided into provinces, and the colonists, along with the farmers on the crown lands, became subject to the administration of the earlier directors of the domestic economy. In Saratov, from 1766 to 1782, there was a department of the Guardianship Council, called the Guardianship Office for Foreigners, but it was closed in the last year (i.e., 1782). By 1797, however, the administration had begun to recognize the error of this ordinance. Almost everywhere a decline in morals had spread; agriculture was neglected; everywhere the colonists lamented the harassment by the officials and their corruptibility, which was confirmed by an investigation.

Consequently, steps were taken again, toward organizing a special legal authority for the German colonies. On the 30th of June, 1797, a Guardian office was set up in Saratov for the foreign settlers on the Volga, and on the 26th of July, 1800, another such office was set up in Jekaterinoslav. This office, in some respects, was under the control of the Governor-General of New Russia, and was the highest ranking colonial authority for foreign settlers in the south until the establishment of the "Welfare Committee." The personnel of this office consisted of a director with two assistants, a secretary, and a number of subordinate officials. The first director of the Jekaterinoslav office was State Councillor S. Kantenius, about whom I shall give a report later on. He was a man of high reputation, very devoted to the good of the colonists. The office had to organize itself, as did the Welfare Committee later, in accordance with the government-approved Instruction of 1801 for the domestic regulation and administration of the New Russian foreign colonies. I shall give an abstract of this instruction, by which it can be perceived how well and wisely the administration was concerned with the welfare of the colonists.

The Welfare Committee for Foreign Settlers in Southern Russia

As the settlements in the south increased each year, the official personnel in the office at Jekaterinoslav could no longer cope with the situation; therefore the government created a new authority, the Welfare Committee for the southern colonies.

By Supreme Decree of the 22nd of March, 1818, this authority was appointed in accordance with the following regulations:

"The Welfare Committee is to consist of a president and two associates, along with the necessary number of officials. The President, also called Chief Curator, must belong at least to the fourth service class, and is appointed by the Emperor himself. The two associates are appointed by the Minister of the Interior, and confirmed by the Ministerial Committee. The director of the chancery is proposed by the President to the Minister of the Interior for confirmation. The other officials are appointed by the committee itself. The Welfare Committee is the highest authority for settlements in South Russia within the provinces of Cherson, Jekaterinoslav, Tauria, and Bessarabia."

The subjects of the administration of these authorities were all colonies already settled or yet to be settled in this region, without regard to their origin or creed. The aim of this administration was the acceptance of the colonists as Russian citizens, to conduct their settlements according to the prescribed rules, and the protection of the rights granted to the colonists.

Finally, the administration was to keep vigil over the obligations to be fulfilled on the part of the colonists toward the Russian crown. The committee supervised only the settlers in the colonies, but not those in the cities, where the individuals had established themselves as artisans and merchants. The artisan colony in Odessa and later the colonists' community in Berdjansk were an exception.

Three offices were subordinate to the Welfare Committee, one in Jekaterinoslav, one in Odessa, which had its seat in the Bulgarian colony of Katarschina, and one in Kishinev with the seat in Kauschau.

At first the head office of the Welfare Committee was assigned to Cherson, but it seems to have been established at Jekaterinoslav right from the beginning.

From 1818 to 1822, the Welfare Committee had its office in Jekaterinoslav, and from 1822 to 1833 in Kischenev. On the first of July, 1833, the status of the Welfare Committee was reduced by Supreme Decree; the three offices were abolished, and its residence was assigned to Odessa. This authority remained in Odessa until 1871 when it was completely abolished, and all colonists were put under the general authority.

The personnel of the Welfare Committee, with salary estimates, were as follows:

	Number of Persons	Salary of each in Rubles	Total Salary in Rubles
President or Chief Curator	1	3,000	3,000
Expense allowance for president	—	3,000	3,000
Two Members	2	2,500	5,000
Director of Council	1	1,500	1,500
Secretary	2	1,000	2,000
Assistant Secretary	2	750	1,500
Journalist	1	500	500
Bookkeeper	1	1,500	1,500
Assistant Bookkeeper	2	500	1,000
Translator	2	1,000	2,000
Rent Master	2	1,000	2,000
Official Receiver and Land Divider	2	500	1,000
Land Surveyor	1	750	750
Assistant Surveyor	2	500	1,000
Clerical assistance	—	—	4,000
Maintenance of Council	—	—	1,500
Maintenance of Buildings	—	—	3,000
Travelling Expenses for Chief Curator	—	—	2,000
Caretaker and Other Help	—	—	2,000
Total	21		38,250

The personnel of an office with the salaries of the officials.

	Number of Persons	Salary of each in Rubles	Total Salary in Rubles
Senior Member	1	2,500	2,500
Junior Member	2	1,500	3,000
Secretary	1	1,000	1,000
Assistant Secretary	2	500	1,000
Bookkeeper	1	1,000	1,000
Translator	1	750	750
Rent Master	1	750	750

Colonial Physician	1	750	750
Veterinarian	1	500	500
Clerical assistance	—	—	2,000
Maintenance of Council	—	—	1,000
Maintenance of Buildings	—	—	2,000
Travelling Expenses for Senior Member	—	—	600
Total in one office	11		16,850
In three offices	33		50,550

Besides the three above-mentioned offices, the following were subordinate to the Welfare Committee.

A. *Three Welfare Committee Stations:*

1. One for the Bulgarian Colonies in Bessarabia with seat in Kamrat (43 colonies in all);

2. One for the Jewish Colonies in Cherson province with seat in Grossnagartav (20 colonies in all);

3. One for the Jewish Colonies in Jekaterinoslav province with seat in Grunau (16 colonies in all).

B. *Eight Inspectorate Districts*

1. In Cherson province *First* Precinct—with the office of the inspector in Odessa (previously located in Grossliebenthal), to which belonged the Liebenthal and Kutschurgan territory, along with the Chabag colony near Akkermann (eighteen colonies). *Second* Precinct—with the office of the inspector in Gross-Bujalik (Kaschkova) formerly located in Landau, and including the Bujalik and Beresan territory (sixteen colonies). *Third* Precinct—with the office of the inspector in Parkan, supervising the region of Glückstal and the individual colonies of Hoffnungstal, Katarschina, and Parkan (seven colonies). *Fourth* Precinct—with the office of the inspector in Cherson administering the Swedish region and the individual colonies of Alt-Danzig, Neu-Danzig, and Ternoffka (seven colonies).

2. In Jekaterinoslav province *First* Precinct—with the inspector's office in Josephstal, administering the Chortitz region and the individual colonies of Josephstal, Rübalsk and Jamburg (twenty-one colonies). *Second* Precinct—with the inspector's office in Grunau, administering the regions of the Mariupol colonists, the Mariupol Mennonites, and Berdyansk (thirty-six colonies).

3. In the province of Tauria *First* Precinct—with the inspector's office in Prischib, administering the Molotschna colonists and Mennonite region (seventy-seven colonies). *Second* Precinct—with the inspector's office in Neusatz, administering

Neusatz and Zürichtal regions, and the colonies of Baltotschakrak, Krishlav, and Starikrim (eleven colonies).

4. Bessarabia *One* Precinct, with the inspector's office in Tarutino, supervising Sarata, Malojaroslavetz, and Klöstitz region (twenty-four colonies).

I now follow up with a number of short sketches of the most prominent guardians and benefactors of the colonists in South Russia. My intention was to present such a biography of each of the presidents of the Guardian Committees, but the continued riots in Odessa, during which all archives were locked, obliged me to give up this idea for the present.

Short Sketches of the Lives of the Most Prominent Guardians of the German Colonists in South Russia

Samuel Kantenius
Councillor of State, Chief Justice of the Guardian-Office
for Foreign Setters in South Russia 1800-1818

Samuel Kantenius was born in 1750 in Westphalia, the son of a poor Protestant pastor. He studied industriously, finished university while still young, and was well educated, especially in languages. He came to Russia, where he took a position as a private tutor in a wealthy, noble family. So much he related about himself. But the energetic gossip told much more; it surrounded good Kantenius with an aura of mystery, and asserted that he was a French prince.

In 1785 Kantenius entered the service of the Russian State and was promoted to Staff Registrar. He was promoted through the various departments of the Russian service. On the 8th of August, 1800, he was appointed Staff Counsel* and Chief Justice of the newly founded Guardianship Office for Foreign Settlers in New Russia, with the head office in Jekaterinoslav. The Russian Government could hardly have found a more capable and knowledgeable man for this important post, than Kantenius. He worked tirelessly and with inexhaustible patience for the accommodation and general welfare of the new colonies. He strove toward the elimination of all possible obstacles, as far as he could. With the help of his friend, the Duke of Richelieu, he was for the most part successful in this task. He usually sought out the best land for the location of the colonies, in the vicinity of a seaside town. He drew up the plans, checking them from all angles, and

---

*Soon afterwards Councillor of State.

presented them for confirmation to higher authority. Since he was known even to Emperor Alexander I as praiseworthy for his insight and knowledge, his proposals were usually approved.

Even the plan of settling the Liebental region near Odessa was Kantenius' project. Often he was present in person at the founding and settling of the new colonies, in order to grant suitable regulations and guiding principles. Kantenius made himself particularly deserving among the colonists, because he provided for them seed grain, young trees, vegetable seeds, and the necessary draught animals. He often visited the new settlements in order to advise the people, to encourage them, to settle their disputes and to reprimand the disobedient and lazy ones.

He was strict but kind and just with all. He requested but little from the people only their good will. No important branch of agriculture that could be essential to the colonists either in the present or future, escaped his notice. He was farsighted in both agriculture and cattle raising. He was like an anxious father who is steadfastly dedicated to make the best and most precious things available to his children.

Besides the cereals which were raised in South Russia, Kantenius ordered rye and flax for the colonists. In this way he established a new branch of business for them. He sought to improve the cattle which the colonists had brought along from Germany, with a better breed. At his instigation the government ordered expensive Spanish ewes and rams, so as to introduce sheep breeding to the colonists. As a result of this, joint sheep farms were established in all colonial districts, contributing much to the general welfare of the colonists. But his keen eye saw further. He attributed, and rightly, the lack of rain in South Russia to the complete absence of forests, and consequently drew up ·the regulation that a specified amount of land in every colony was to be planted with trees. Likewise he decreed that fruit and mulberry plantations be laid out, thereby starting a silk industry as an additional occupation in the colonies. In Jekaterinoslav there was a sizeable garden where all possible species of trees were planted. From this garden, which was under the custody of Kantenius, the colonists received seedlings for the plantations and forests.

In case of necessity, Kantenius even intervened in community and domestic life, usually beneficially and often very strictly. Many colonists' sons aged fifteen to sixteen had married girls thirteen to fifteen on their way through Kovno, in order to receive a whole farm plot at the location of the settlement, as was allotted to families. But Kantenius saw through this trickery and banished them back to their families, without giving them a farm plot.

In May, 1818, Emperor Alexander I visited South Russia. When the Emperor was travelling through the Molotschna colonies Kantenius came to see him. He had just previously been pensioned, and he wished to present himself to his gracious majesty to thank him for the pension bestowed. The Emperor was very pleased with the set-up of the colonies and ascribed their success primarily to the work and care of Kantenius. He kissed him tenderly and requested him to enter the service anew as assistant to General Inzov, to which Kantenius agreed.

Before his departure, the Emperor handed Kantenius a medal, First-Class, which until that time was held in all Russia only by the historian Karamsin. This high distinction aroused the envy and the malice of the more lowly bureaucrats, who could not bear to see a German's honor, faithfulness and honesty in service, rewarded. But the greying benefactor of the colonists cared little about the barking of the little lap dogs of bureaucracy. On the contrary, he kept on working for the welfare of the colonists to the end of his days. Even in his will he did not forget the colonists, his dear children, bequeathing a bank fund of 15,000* rubles for the education of qualified sons of the colonists.

Kantenius died on the 30th of May, 1830, in Jekaterinoslav, after a long illness. He was a good, fine, honorable German, whose remembrance will live among the German colonists in the south for many generations. His remains are buried in Josephstal colony, near Jekaterinoslav. It would be interesting to know what condition his grave stone is in.

Emanuel Joseph Armand
Duke of Richelieu, Governor of Odessa (1803)
and Governor-General of New Russia 1805-1814

Emanuel, Duke of Richelieu, was born in Paris on the 25th of September, 1766, the son of the Duke of Fronsak. After completing his studies, he went to Russia on the outbreak of the French Revolution. He took part in the Turkish campaign under Suvorov in 1790 and because of his bravery he was promoted to Lieutenant-General by the Russians.

When Richelieu came to Odessa in 1803, it had only four thousand inhabitants and was more like a village than a city. The low houses with roofs of reeds and detached mud huts were built in a rather spacious area. Odessa was supposed to be a seaport, but had no harbor where ships could land safely. Odessa was supposed to be an industrial city, but had no business firms and no

*The capital is in the Werner school in Sarata.

warehouses. Odessa, as a city, was to have educational establishments, but no trace of such facilities was yet in existence. After an eleven-year rule by the Duke, things looked entirely different.

First he built churches for most of the faiths, set up a sanctuary for the poor and foreign people, founded schools, and planned a spacious harbor. He established hospitals; started shops and markets; and provided the city with wells, gardens, barracks, theatres, and other useful and essential accommodations.

For the erection of such buildings, however, there was a lack of the necessary workers. In order to remedy this difficulty, Richelieu wrote to Rumianzov, the Minister of Trade, and requested him to send some tradesmen from Petersburg.

On the 14th of May, 1803, Rumianzov answered: "Your report, in which you have described the extraordinary shortages of tradesmen in Odessa, was presented to the Emperor. With the consent of His Majesty, I will be sending along to Odessa in a few days, a carpenter who is bringing two or three helpers, a baker with one assistant, and a locksmith with a helper." From this can be seen how short were the numbers of tradesmen at that time in Odessa. When Richelieu first came to Odessa, he had to write to Cherson for a dozen ordinary chairs, since none were to be found in Odessa.

The labor shortage was soon eased. In 1804 a large number of German immigrants arrived, among whom there were a significant number of tradesmen. These came in handy for Richelieu, for he was sorely in need of them. The Duke induced them to settle entirely in Odessa. In this way the colony of German tradesmen got its start in Odessa, beginning with forty-two families.

When the plague broke out in Odessa in 1812, Richelieu was an inspiration of love and dedication to his fellow men, giving rise to universal admiration. He issued the most exacting decrees immediately, in an effort to prevent the further spread of the epidemic. At his orders all of the yard-gates in Odessa were locked, leaving only a small sliding shutter open for handing food and drink in to the occupants. All street traffic was prohibited. Only the Duke and a retinue of servants laden with provisions, and his friend Father Nicolle with the Eucharist, and a priest's assistant, marched through the streets. Walking from house to house, they dispensed first strength-giving food to the sick and destitute, then extreme unction to the Catholics, and to the others, comfort and blessing in their last hour.

But the plan of completing the building-up of the city of Odessa was not the only aim of the restless Duke. He directed his special attention to the German colonies in the South, whose planning he

44

conducted mostly in person in the early years. It was a picture worthy of admiration, how the great man deigned to visit with the colonists, like a father with his children. He listened patiently to all their woes, comforted them in their sorrows, dispensed his always-ready alms to the poor, and was a comforter and advisor to them in all their concerns.

Whenever they were wronged or dealt with unfairly by an official, they went at once to the Duke, whom they all loved and revered as their father. He heard their complaints and anxieties patiently, and at once gave an order to investigate the matter. On Sundays and holydays he always rode through the city streets, to see whether his orders had yet been completed. If he saw a German colonist on the street and recognized him by his clothes, he would approach him and inquire, "Are you a Catholic or a Lutheran? After receiving an answer, he then would say, "Well, my dear fellow, be advised that the service in the Catholic church starts at ten o'clock, and in the Lutheran Church at nine o'clock."

Just as Richelieu was kind and thoughtful toward the good and the infirm, he was correspondingly strict toward the malicious ones, especially the lazy and thieving. Accordingly he had the colonists, Franz Grimm and Johann Spannagel, who arrived in 1810, committed for life in the prison-gang, for breaking into the Grossliebental District Office and robbing the safe.

Richelieu usually travelled through the German colonies with his lieutenants in May, when everything was cleaned, polished and well-oiled. The Duke, beloved by all people, was a great friend of order and cleanliness, and had a keen eye for the slightest faults and carelessness. The women were never sure whether their kitchens would pass his inspection for cleanliness.

Besides the German colonies, he also founded most of the Bulgarian colonies; likewise, he directed the settlements of the Greeks at Mariupol, of the Armenians at Nachitshewan, the Jews in Cherson and Jekaterinoslav provinces, and of the Nagaians at Nagaisk. To the Nagaians he gave an excellent administrator and wise chief, in the person of Count De Meson. He brought these half-wild people along so well by his humane treatment and convincing conversation, that they forsook their nomadic life, burned their wagons (kibitken), and settled down to domestic life in separate villages around and about the town of Nagaisk.

From this active and blessed activity, he was called away by his dear fatherland, France, which had been freed from the claws of the tyrant Napoleon, by the great powers.

The new king of France, Louis XVIII, summoned Richelieu to Paris in 1814, and assigned him to the Ministry of the Interior.

Compelled by circumstances, he resigned in 1818 and returned to private life, after donating the nation's gift to him of 50,000 francs, to the Bordeaux Hospital. Elected Prime Minister in 1820, he soon had to tender his resignation for reasons of health. Following a long illness, he died on the 17th of May, 1822, in the arms of his faithful friend, Father Nicolle. The remembrance of this noble man is dear to all colonists in South Russia. By his love and protection of them, he has earned the honor of being named, along with his friend Kantenius, the greatest benefactor in the history of the colonies.

Infantry General Ivan Nikitish Inzov
President, Welfare Committee 1818-1845

Ivan Inzov was born in 1768, but where or who his parents were, is unknown. The person of Inzov is puzzling, as much for his ancestry as for his childhood and upbringing. It was in the early part of the second half of the eighteenth century when Prince George Trubezskoy lived with his family on his estate in the province of Pensa, quite alone and forgotten by the world. Suddently his old friend, Count Jacob Pruss, called quite unexpectedly and brought the prince a little boy, with the request that he raise him as his own, that he would be liberally reimbursed for the expenses of this upbringing. The child's name was Ivan, and he bore the family name of Inzov. To all further questions of Prince Trubezskoy, Pruss answered, "You will learn everything later."

In this way little Inzov remained in the prince's home and was raised with his children. The promised money for raising him came regularly from an unknown source until Count Pruss suddenly died, and took the secret of Inzov's origin with him to his grave.

Soon afterward Inzov was transferred to the boarding school of Moscow University to complete his education, where he finished his studies quite successfully. Following the completion of his studies at this secondary school Inzov was brought by Prince Trubezskoy to Petersburg, where the mysterious story about the youth's origin soon reached the ears of Empress Catherine II. The Empress immediately decreed that three thousand ducats be paid to Inzov to buy uniforms, and that he be enrolled as a cadet in the Sum Cavalry Regiment (1785).

It is not my intention to report on the various fortunes or military designations in the life of Inzov since that would lead too far afield. I will only say here that Inzov was a brave officer, a loyal patriot and an honorable man, who carried out his assignments at all times.

When in 1814 and in succeeding years, the emigration of Germans and Bulgarians into South Russia reached ever-increasing proportions, and the Guardian-Office was no longer in a position to direct and watch over it, the Russian government formed the previously-mentioned Welfare Committee, and appointed General Inzov as its president. Inzov certainly had the best intentions to be a good and upright chief, but as a soldier he lacked many a special branch of knowledge which he needed to be a leader of a small colonial republic.

From 1818 to 1822 Inzov lived in Jekaterinoslav, where he always had the experienced Kantenius by his side as advisor in all colonial contingencies, as a result of which all regulations of the Welfare Committee at that time were always primarily for the benefit of the prospering young colonies.

The colonies in Bessarabia at first did not come under the jurisdiction of the Guardian-Office for Foreign Settlers in New Russia, but were subordinate to the Regional Authority. When Emperor Alexander I traveled through South Russia in 1818, the Bessarabian colonies asked through Inzov that they too be placed under the newly-founded Welfare Committee, and be granted the same rights and privileges as the other colonies in New Russia. Through the Ukase of the 29th of December, 1819, the request of these colonists was granted, and their rights and privileges were established and submitted to the Welfare Committee.

At this time, Inzov often traveled through the colonies, giving new regulations about various arrangements within the colonies, and demanded especially that in all instances the "Instructions for Local Administration" be strictly adhered to. On these excursions Inzov became acquainted with the weaknesses and vices of the colonists.

Accordingly he released the following order on the 20th of January, 1819: "Since it has been brought to my attention that intemperance and card-playing in the colonies have increased to the extent that the colonists waste their time until late in the night in taverns and colony houses, and spend time drinking and gambling, which inevitably must have serious consequences, I therefore order the district and village elders to put a stop to it immediately in a way that people will heed, and to prevent similar disorders later by dealing with these obstinate ones in accordance with the "Instructions for Local Administration".

Also on Inzov's orders, the neglected plantations, woodlots, and vineyards in the colonies had to be revived. In 1822 Inzov was temporarily designated administrator of the province of Bessarabia and also provisionally entrusted with the difficult office of

Governor-General of New Russia, from which Count Langeron had retired. That was entirely too much for the good-natured General Inzov, but he submitted as usual.

Upon this occasion he moved from Jekaterinoslav to Kischinev and took with him the entire civil service of the Welfare Committee, of which he remained president. It was in Kischinev where the famous Russian poet Alexander Pushkin served as a minor official under Inzov.

In 1833 Inzov moved with the Welfare Committee from Kischinev to Odessa, where he lived, secluded and alone. He busied himself mainly with the natural sciences and industriously studied mysticism. Ekharthausen, J. Stilling, and Böhmer were his favorite authors. In the latter period he devoted most of his attention to the Bulgarian colonies in Bessarabia. In Bolgrad at his instigation a large church was built, in which his remains now repose.

During his last years Inzov was continuously ill; consequently the management of the colonies was badly handled. Everywhere there were loud complaints about fraud and bribery of the officials. Because of this, in 1841, Privy Councillor Von Hahn was appointed as assistant to the elderly Inzov.

Inzov died in Odessa on the 27th of May, 1845. In November, 1846, his remains were transported to Bolgrad in Bessarabia and laid to rest in the above-named church. At present there is a committee to erect a monument to Inzov. Already 25,000 rubles have been collected for this purpose from the Bulgarians. The German colonists should also contribute to this praiseworthy undertaking, for Inzov was always a great benefactor to them.

Privy Councillor Von Hahn, Deputy President of the Welfare Committee 1841-1845 President from 1845 to 1849

Eugen von Hahn was born in Petersburg on the 15th of October, 1808. He apparently pursued his studies in Petersburg. When the Minister of Imperial Domains was travelling through the southern colonies in 1841, he found that the administration of the ill and aging Inzov was very deficient and in great need of improvement. The Minister appointed Privy Councillor von Hahn as deputy to Inzov.

Hahn was the very man that our colonists needed, for he made such beneficial arrangements everywhere that many of them have extended into our time. An example is the founding of the central schools. He had the ability to get acquainted with and thoroughly assess the colonists in a short time. When, at the beginning of his appointment, he requested records about the garden and wood lots, many localities replied that they could not grow trees on their "poor land."

To these communities he issued the command: "Trees must grow where you are." He was right, for after that, trees grew at his "command" in all the colonies. On one occasion he was on an inspection trip in the Molotschna, when a ranking official reported to him on the condition of the colonies entrusted to him.

"But trees do not grow here, your Excellence," he concluded.

"I tell you, Mr. Official," replied Hahn, "that trees must grow here, and you will see to it during the year, after which I shall return, that trees grow on this very spot." The command was clear. And truly, in the following year the designated spot was planted with trees.

Privy Councillor Hahn directed his special attention to the neglected colonist schools, and sought all means to arouse the colonists intellectually, to uplift them and to draw them out of their careless ways. To this end he issued wise regulations concerning schools, inaugurated compulsory education, and ordered that only reasonable and respectable men might be appointed as school-masters. He had come to know from sad experience that the schoolmasters of the time, apart from their traditional defects, could read and write only poorly, and accordingly were not in a position to impart the fundamentals of knowledge to the children. He therefore resolved to found the central schools in the colonies as teacher-training institutes.

Whenever he made inspection tours in the colonies he provoked much excitement and lively industry; in particular, the womenfolk were all "on their toes", for Privy Councillor Hahn had the unusual habit of closely inspecting the women's domain. Kitchens, cellars, larders, warehouses, were all closely inspected, to verify if Dame Cleanliness ruled here, or whether dirty people worked here.

During the visits with the colonists, Hahn was very affable and friendly, but he was strict with and had no pity on unscrupulous officials.

In 1849 Hahn was transferred to the Ministry of Imperial Domains, and the colonists lost in him their great benefactor and promoter of their general welfare. In 1859 he was Privy Councillor and Associate Counsel of the Ministry of Imperial Domains. About his further career I regretfully can report nothing more.

Now I will furnish the names of the subsequent presidents of the Welfare Committee, up to the time of its discontinuance. I must put off until later the report about the personalities of these presidents, because the necessary material is not yet at my disposal.

Extracts from the "Instruction on the Local Administration of New-Russian Foreign Colonies" [1801]

Section 1
On the religious duties of the colonists

1

One of the most important duties of all colonists is this: that each and every one take seriously to heart the commandments and teachings of his faith and scrupulously follow them as the rule of conduct of his life. To this end each one is dutifully to attend church service every Sunday and holy day; to listen with devotion in the house of God to expounded dogmas; and if he is worthy of it, receive holy communion. If any one without weighty cause, or through laziness or carelessness, stays away from church service, he then is to be emphatically warned the first and second time, but subsequently deposit 10 kopeks fine for each of his non-appearances at church service. And if any one has deposited such a fine three times in the year, without mending his ways, he is to bear twice the said penalty and do a whole day's work for the community. Such money fines flow into the general treasury.

2

Those colonists acknowledging the Lutheran and Roman Catholic religions are obliged at the expiry of their voluntary year, when their pastors are no longer paid by the Crown, to support these pastors of theirs and schoolmasters at the expense of the whole community. The stipulated salary for them is to be borne by the number of the menfolk from 16 to 60 years belonging to each parish, in three yearly installments, i.e., the 1st of January, May and September. To this end, church elders must be selected every year from each community; it is their duty to collect the salary due to its pastor, as mentioned above, and to deliver the money for each term, receipted, to the administrator of the district, who in turn is duty bound to lend to the church warden every necessary assistance for its collection, so as to bring it about without the slightest arrears. Any particular colonist who fails to pay the share of money assigned to him for the appointed term is taxed with a fine of 10 kopeks the first time, 15 kopeks the second time, but the third time is arrested and compelled to perform work for the community for however long it takes him to pay up. Also, the administrator of the district has to give a report to the Welfare Office about a colonist who does not pay up properly, along with a declaration of the causes and description of his status.

5   (3)

The Evangelical-Lutheran pastor is required, when he discharges the duties of his office in the Swedish and Elizabethgrad colonies, to watch carefully and to insist that the schoolmasters strive to fulfil their duty with befitting ardor and diligence, for which purpose the clergymen have a special and complete directive to draw up for the schoolmasters rules of conduct and deportment. In the Josephstal colony, where his permanent residence is, the pastor has constant charge of the schoolmasters. The Catholic priest* and the religious leaders of the Mennonites are duty-bound to carry out the self-same duties.

Section II
Regarding Establishment of District Governments and Election of District and Village Officials

8

Special district governments are to be set up for the colonies. Each of them is to be headed by an elected district mayor, assisted by two councillors and a secretary. In the district in which the district mayor lives space is to be found annually for a district office, either a temporary room in a farm house or by the building of a house for the purpose with funds raised by all the villages belonging to the district. Here, in a locked box, closed with the seals of the mayor and his councillors, are to be kept the records of income and expenditure, the money collected in the district to pay district expenses, the official correspondence and the directives from the Welfare Committee office. In addition to this, there shall be elected to govern each village a village mayor, two councillors and a representative for every ten families.

*It was the one from Jamburg.

The district and village mayors, the councillors and other village officials shall be elected in every region and village by majority vote from among those householders who are of legal age, have their own household and sensible judgment, who lead an irreproachable life, who think and behave honestly, are good managers, and so distinguish themselves in agriculture, horticulture, and cattle raising that they can serve as an example to others. Every eligible householder gives his vote free from partisan influence of friendship or enmity to the man whom he considers good and capable for this or that office. The choice of the one receiving the majority of votes is certified by the signature(s) of the voters and then presented to the Welfare Office for confirmation.

16

Announcements which have to be made by the district mayor in his district and the village mayor in his village:

I All lawful ordinances regarding which the people have to be informed are to be made known by public announcement. These, as well as instructions issued by the Welfare Office, should be read out and explained at the end of the religious service in the church or prayer hall, or wherever else the people are gathered.

II. It must be explained and taught that it is everyone's duty to live morally and peaceably with other people and whatever else needs to be known by the average person; that the young must respect their parents and all old people and obey them and that these in turn through their example encourage young people to industriousness, uprightness, temperance and to peaceable living with members of their household, their neighbors and all people.

III. The church regulations must be made clear to them and instructions given that each person dutifully sanctify Sundays, holydays and feastdays and that each confess according to the beliefs and the commandments of his faith and make himself worthy to receive the Lord's Supper.

IV. The community must be incessantly instructed that each person exercise all care and caution to prevent infectious diseases, livestock epidemics and fire damage, that all give legal weights and measures, and that nowhere and under no circumstances is forbidden and harmful brandy sale to take place.

23

The regional and village officials are to see to it dutifully and carefully that the colonists do not indulge in idleness, drunkenness, and in extravagance or outrageous behavior; that on the contrary they comport themselves soberly and lead a respectable life, also carry out diligently the duties of their occupation, such as farming and horticulture, cattle-raising and all other activities pertaining to agriculture. So that colonists who excel in promoting their own and the general good through diligence and industriousness can be distinguished, the village mayors, under the special supervision of the district mayor, are to draw up special lists of the good and diligent farmers, and also of the lazy and negligent ones. These lists, signed by district and village officials, are to be delivered to the Welfare Office. Thus trust can be reposed in the industrious and upright and withheld from poor and lazy farmers, and the latter can be made to mend their ways by fines or imprisonment on bread and water. The latter must also through coercion be made to do the ploughing and seeding of their plots of land and all other house and farm labor with the help of assignments under orders which they are responsible to carry out daily. In order to accomplish this properly, they will work under the supervision of an official. But in the event that some should not desist from negligence and laziness after such repeated urgings and punishments, a report on them, accompanied by a description of their guilt, is to be sent to the Welfare Office.

30

The district and village mayors are charged with seeing to it that poor and infirm colonists do not loiter about or take to begging. The healthy among such impoverished ones are to be constrained to earn their own keep by working. But if they have neither relatives nor the strength to work, then the community must have a poorhouse of two compartments built near the church, one for men and the other for women, in which their poor people are provided with food, fuel and needed clothing. For their support there shall be set up nearby, under lock and seal of the churchwarden, an alms-box, and in the church, a collection bag with bell, into which on Sundays and holy days contributions for the alms-house are to be amassed, such money collected in the bag and box being applied every month to the support of the needy. If such is not adequate, the colony must provide extra allowance. In order to maintain the alms-houses in the best order, the clergy are to supervise them.

48

When enmity, hostility or quarrels break out among the colonists, or if one charges another with false accusation, then the mayor is to try to reconcile them, the first time by emphatic warnings, but the second time by imposing community punishment. However, in case quarrelsome colonists were to incur such misdemeanors frequently, then each time there will be imposed upon the aggressor 25 kopeks penalty, to pay into the general treasury.

49

It is up to the mayors to bring it about with might and main that sumptuousness and wastefulness be rooted out among the colonists. To this end, those who yield to such vices are to be charged with the heaviest community toil and have dictated to them how much work they must perform each day, so that no time will be left over for them to continue so infamous and corruptible a life. This punishment of them must be repeated just as long as may be needed to bring them around. But in case they do not mend their ways thereby, they are to be reported to the Welfare Office

NOTE: A sumptuous life means having extravagant display in one's home and frequently entertaining beyond one's means. Wastefulness means playing cards for money and goods, the sale of cattle and of other effects without the compulsion of necessity but only to use the money gotten from the sale for drunkenness or the satisfying of other inordinate desires.

50

The mayors must strictly see to it that every single householder maintain his dwelling, barn and stables and fences in best condition, cleanliness, and repair. In the event that any one mismanages here and in spite of all repeated orders allows his farm buildings to become dilapidated or tumble-down, he is to be fined 20 kopecks, and beyond this, be required to repair immediately everything considered in disrepair, which improvement is to be brought about under the supervision of an official.

51

The mayors in all villages are duty-bound to insist that the streets are kept clear of trash and are always properly cleaned. For protection against storm and fire, the houses, barns and yards must be planted with all sorts of fast-growing trees which are compatible with this climate, and especially with mulberry trees, which do well everywhere, and from which the colonists, in view of the possibility of silk culture, can derive considerable profit.

The district mayors are charged with seeing to it that the colonists' deportment is friendly and pleasant toward their neighbors in their own and bordering villages and courteous and hospitable to passers-through, and that they avoid border disputes with the former and unpleasant confrontations with the latter.

68

District and village mayors must strive to the utmost to promote all manner of useful handicrafts and manufacturing plants in the colonies, to which everyone is to contribute, if he understands the work, or will be forced to, if he fails to do it because of laziness. Because the main branch of farming in this area is livestock-raising, especially sheep-raising, first consideration should be given to the processing of wool, which constitutes the leading product of these parts, as well as to tanneries, soap-making, and the casting of tallow candles.

69

It is the duty of the district mayor and village mayor to observe closely the characteristics of the soil and climate and to discover, and propose to the Welfare Office, such suitable means as will advance the progress of the colonies, and to make the usefulness of these clear and comprehensible to the colonists.

70

The district mayors and village mayors are most strictly directed to apply all means and care to have trees planted in every colony, particularly those which grow and can thrive best in each respective colony, according to the nature of its soil. Special attention is to be given to planting such fast-growing species as alder, willow, and aspen. From these and other useful wood species, the seeds must be collected at the time of ripening and be sown in suitably plowed and prepared land. But primarily, all possible effort is to be applied to planting mulberry trees.

72

The district mayor has to see to it, and bring it about, that the arable land in all colonies is subdivided into three fields, and also to investigate whether the subdivision into six or seven fields would be practicable and useful. The village mayors are charged with seeing to it that the colonists individually make repairs to their plows, harrows, wagons and other farm equipment and get their draught-animals into good condition for the working season; and if anyone cannot accomplish this because of misfortune, rather than through negligence, the entire community must help such an unfortunate person by rendering all possible assistance.

73

Just as soon as the time for ploughing arrives, the mayor has to direct all the farmers to betake themselves to the field, all at the same time, the first thing in the morning, so as to arrive before, or at least at, the break of dawn, and to work there industriously and tirelessly. The mayor must require his assistants to see to it, by their inspection and their pressure, that orders are obeyed by everyone exactly as prescribed. In the springtime and autumn the mayors and assistants in every village must inspect the cultivated fields of each landowner to note whether they have been worked as required by the character of the soil, whether ploughed deeply enough or the earth made loose enough. When a field is not prepared properly, the owner must be compelled to do it over again right away. In a like manner the owners collectively are to be urged and forced to carry out each type of seeding at the suitable time. The harvesting of the crops is to begin by observation of ripening. Threshing must take place in good weather, and everyone must have a dry granary or a masanka erected for the storing of the grain.

78

It must be strictly seen to that nobody spends the wintertime in idleness, but that everyone applies himself to taking the best care of his cattle, to keep his horses well groomed, and his house suitably repaired, to improve the fencing about his yard and garden, to put his entire house and business life into fit condition, to provide himself with adequate seeds for summer sowing and garden vegetables, and to maintain such things in the best of condition.

Those who understand how to weave linen and tablecloths, or know other useful handicrafts, must be made to busy themselves with these; just as the women are to keep themselves busy with spinning wool and flax, hatching poultry, making butter, and so on. In a word, the village authorities must see to it that the winter time is entirely devoted to industriousness. (Consequently, no arm-chair life, as happens today.)

14 *From the Appendix to the Instruction*

Experience teaches that those proprietors who pursue a handicraft along with farming, are in a better position to improve their living standard, and are able to earn their living even if (Heaven forbid) crop failure, cattle disease, or other potential misfortunes cause shortages. In contrast, those who spend not only the winter, but also most of the remaining seasons in corrupting idleness, must go hungry in hard times.

Linen weaving is now a highly useful craft for the farmer, since during periods when farming can not be done, the menfolk can earn wages with weaving. Women and even children ten to twelve years old can work at spinning for pay; consequently, all colonists are emphatically enjoined to set this handicraft more and more in motion, as a perpetual means of livelihood, wherever it is already being done, and to introduce it without fail wherever it is not yet established. So that this goal may be attained with certainty, every regional office of a colony (or if there is none, every mayoral office), is obliged to induce the heads of the families with grown-up boys to give their sons over to a course of instruction with good linen weavers, and allow them to apprentice long enough to permit them to learn the handicraft thoroughly.

In case a trained weaver cannot afford a spinning wheel to perform his handicraft, then such a beginner shall be loaned the necessary support from the communal fund, with the stipulation that he pay back his debt correctly in regular installments.

The district office (and where there is none, the mayoral office), is obliged to see to it that at the beginning of fall each year, an adequate supply of flax is brought up from those localities that provide the very best; and that each head of a household be provided with such a portion of it as he may require for keeping industrious hands busy in his house. The proprietors have to gather the necessary funds together for purchasing the best flax, or in case of necessity, the money can be taken from the communal treasury, conditional upon its being repaid promptly.

-0-

Truly, dear reader, this was a different era, when our colonies regulated their lives by these rules. Yes, it was a different time, but also a much better and happier one than the present. Now, as soon as winter sets in, all vices are indulged in through idleness, by the big and the little, by young and old. Not without truth is the saying: "Idleness is the beginning of all vice."

Ordinance of the Minister
of Imperial Domains — Count Kisselev
in 1841 in Grossliebental

On the 6th of September, 1841, Count Kisselev, Minister of Imperial Domains, was in Grossliebental Colony, where he disclosed his intentions about the South Russian (German) colonists to the assembled regional and village mayors, in the presence of the Provost, Granbaum, and the local pastor, Johann Wilsdorf, indicating that the points he was making applied to all district and village mayors. His remarks were translated by Pastor Wilsdorf.

1. The regional and village mayors, like those in the Mennonite colonies, are to supervise the colonists entrusted to them, with real enthusiasm and conscientiousness, as a father would his children.

2. The Mennonite colonies are to be esteemed as models; they are to serve as examples to the remaining colonies and colonists, in farming and management; therefore, the colonies are to set up an economic committee modeled after the Mennonites, the membership to consist of every twentieth or thirtieth farmer to be chosen from their midst. This committee, along with the regional office, is to be alert to order, diligence, industriousness, conduct and decency of the colonists; to assess whether a farmer can manage his farm; to dismiss worthless farmers without more ado, putting good ones in their places and letting a no-account farmer serve at menial tasks; and to advise and bring into being economic changes and improvements which will be best for all.

3. Only real farmers and actual landowners are to receive cash advances, not artisan colonists. The Mennonites have 900 actual landowners, with 35 dessiatines of land each, and also have 1400 landless artisans among them. They could give land to all of these, as they still have land in reserve but they will not do it because they do not want poor farmers to gain access to their ranks. Only genuine farm families receive cash advances, artisans must make a living with their trade. To act otherwise would soon put the Mennonites into the same sad condition as the other colonists. All colonists are to take note of that, said the minister.

4. If the colonists comply with the wishes and expectations of the central government, their privileges will be continued, but if they are negligent they will lose their privileges and revert to the status of Russian peasants and become subject to military service.

5. In case the district and village mayors chosen by the colonists, do not comply with the above aim of their office, then the minister will himself choose district and village mayors from the Mennonite colonies, and have them installed in place of the above. The new

officials will govern entirely by the power conferred upon them, just as they would their own people.

6. The Minister will do all in his power to help them with their agricultural development and will give them unfailing support.

7. The central administration of the colonies is to retain its present basic character, but he, the Minister, will supervise carefully its better progress and effectiveness. The Minister will keep a special eye on the district and village authorities and make the changes that are needed.

8. Churches, schools and parsonages are to be built everywhere, from now on. The Minister has issued instructions to the local pastors three times, that they impress this upon the colonists and all the local elders whenever possible. They are frequently to remind them, advise them and urge them on so that they might most eagerly fulfill the wishes and expectations of the central government for their own welfare.

The Spiritual Administration of
the Catholic Colonies in South Russia

The State of the Catholic Church in South Russia
at the Time of the Arrival of the German Colonists

For centuries South Russia was no foreign soil to the Catholic missionaries. Ever since the establishment of the Roman Empire in the east (1203 A.D.), these missionaries wandered through the provinces on the Black Sea and in the Caucasus, preaching the gospel to the heathen and Mohammedans, uniting a good many renegade Christians with the Mother Church, and founding mission-houses and school in all areas. When soon thereafter the Genoese founded a commercial republic in the Crimea, a number of Catholic bishoprics were formed in the same place.

As a result of the conquest of Kaffa (Feodosia) in 1475 by the Turks, all Catholics were slain or sold as slaves, and the Catholic churches were converted into mosques. From this time on, Catholic missionaries came only infrequently, mostly from Poland, to bestow the comfort of their religion to Catholics living there. At the start of the eighteenth century the number of Catholics living there increased by reason of refugees from Poland and war prisoners from Germany, Hungary and other countries.

At that time there was staying at the court of the Crimean ruler, the French physician Ferran, who was deeply stirred by the sad plight of the Catholics there. He informed the Jesuits at Constantinople about how, two years earlier, a Polish Jesuit had come to the Crimea, carried on very zealously among the Catholics, but after only ten months died from a severe illness; and the Catholics remained thus far wholly without ministration.

Immediately after that, through the intervention of the French envoy, Marquis Ferioli in Constantinople, three Fathers of the Jesuit order were dispatched to the Crimea: Fathers Ban, Kurbilion and Stefani. That was in 1704.

When they had received permission from the chancellor, Hasi-Girei, to settle in his capital, Backshisarai, they erected there a small church and college. Soon thereafter they founded additional missionhouses in Karasubazar, Eskikrim, Kuslev (Eupatoria), and Perekop, and asked for more priests of their order.

The situation remained thus until the Russian General Münich conquered the Crimea in 1736, stormed the fortress of Backshisarai, put the Jesuit college with the rich library endowed with rare manuscripts to flames, and drove the Jesuits out of the Crimea. In 1787, Archbishop Sestrinzevitch was in the Crimea to look for source material for his work "Tauric Province," when the Catholics brought their problem to him and asked for help. Sestrinzevitch promised assistance and soon thereafter ordained a deanship to be founded in Karasubazar, and appointed the resident Armenian Catholic priest, Father Duchai, as dean of all Catholic churches of Roman and Armenian rites in South Russia.

Things remained thus until 1811, when a special inspectorship was established for South Russia, and Father Nicolle was appointed its first head.

The fathers of the Society of Jesus in the Catholic Colonies in South Russia

As the Catholic colonies in south Russia kept increasing each year, and already amounted to more than twenty by 1810, it was necessary to provide spiritual care and religious services for them. Duke Richelieu accepted this responsibility. In 1810 he wrote to Prince Galizin and urgently requested that a priest be appointed as soon as possible for the newly founded Catholic colonies. In Petersburg an attempt had been made to engage a Capuchin (Franciscan) monk from Germany, to look after the souls in the colonies. But when this plan miscarried, priests of the Society of Jesus had to be sent there again, as had happended six years earlier with Father Löffler and his companions.*

---

*Details below in Josephstal parish history.

In June, 1811, fifteen priests of the above-named Society came to Odessa and into the Catholic colonies located near this city. All of these priests were subordinate to the Inspector of all Catholic churches in New Russia, Father Charles Nicolle, who was, however, not a Jesuit but an Oratorian (Dominican). At first these priests were posted as follows: Father E. Vitry (a former Knight of Malta and Count) in Odessa, aided by Father Nicholas Brickmann and Father Joseph Liko; in Cherson, Father Oswald Rausch; in Josephstal, Father Theodor von Monfort; in Selz, Father Andreas Pierling; in Mannheim Father Franz Hoffmann; in Landau, Father Anton Jann; in Rastadt, Father Johannes Koervers. The rest of the fifteen were lay brothers.

The German Catholic colonists were from nearly every province in Germany; the majority of them had more vices than virtues. A good many were neglected, raw, ignorant in religious matters, and of loose morals; in a word, it was a rough, undisciplined mass. Consequently the work was not very attractive, but the fathers did not despair. They possessed all the personal qualities for sifting through this rough, ignorant mass and bringing it around to the form befitting a Christian life. The fathers were well trained, had abundant practice in redeeming souls, possessed inexhaustible patience, had a boundless love and devotion for their flock, and above all, an ardent apostolic devotion to the human spirit.

Just as a skillful general tries to probe the enemy's position before the battle so as to attack him where he is most vulnerable, the fathers surveyed their sphere of work and concluded that their greatest enemy was the ignorance of the colonists. They therefore drew up a plan of battle against this monster. Convinced that most people sin only through ignorance, they began to instruct these poor people about Christian doctrine in the school, in the pulpit, and in the confessional. The schools were very poorly organized in most colonies, but the priests took the utmost pains to improve them, so that the children would be well instructed in religion and acquire a knowledge of the essentials of life. As often as their other duties permitted, they visited the schools in order to explain to the children in person the fundamentals of their religion and to lay the foundation in their hearts for the coming of Christian life.

Another means of instruction was the Sunday School, which the older youths and adults often attended, and where they received information about their duties. The main features of the instruction were the impressive and soul-stirring sermons of the Fathers. Steadfastly the work of God resounded from the pulpit on Sundays and holy days, calling sinners to repent and promising the mercy of God and the remission of sins to the repentant. All were invited to use the means of grace of the holy Church assiduously and with the appropriate preparation. Deeply affected by these sermons, the colonists frequently came to the holy court of atonement, the confessional, in order to have their hearts cleansed and relieved of many distresses, and to reconcile themselves with their God and Father.

The Jesuits also accomplished a good deal through the inauguration of many Catholic practices, such as the Rosary Brotherhood, Sacred Heart devotion, and others, which had either fallen into oblivion among the colonists, or were entirely unknown. In this way the Jesuits carried on everywhere in accordance with the best principles of moral and pastoral theology, and on this account the success of their activity was everywhere equally fruitful and beneficial.

The colonists began to understand that their former way of life did not correspond with the teachings of the Catholic church. Convinced of this, they attempted to bring their way of life into line with the holy teachings under God's blessing, and to show fruitful results in atonement for their sinful ways until this time. They accomplished this mainly because they, acting as guardians of the soul, set the example of a model Christian life. The priests had the praiseworthy attribute of clarifying their sermons through their own holy lives, because the way of life of the preacher is the best illustration for his sermons. So our colonists had good patterns to follow, modelled according to the rules of Christianity.

When the priests first came into the colonies, there were no churches or chapels anywhere. Only in Josephstal was there a small church, built by Father Löffler in 1806. In this respect also it was necessary to take measures to remedy the situation. Soon churches and chapels were built everywhere in the colonies, as in Selz (1811), Rastadt (1811), Landau (1812), and likewise in other colonies, so that by 1820 a church or chapel was built in every colony.

But not for long were the priests permitted to remain as the educators and soul-guardians of the Catholic colonists. Already a furious storm was developing against them in the north; this put a quick end to their stirring activity. How this came about I will now relate briefly.

The Withdrawal of the Jesuits from the Catholic Colonies in South Russia in 1820

"Those must be real he-men (these Jesuits) since the whole world hates and chases them."
—Göthe

Through the seizure of Poland and Lithuania by Russia in 1772, all then-existing Jesuit institutions came under Russian domination. Catherine II recognized the value and usefulness of these institutions in a country where there were so few facilities for educating the young. She protected the Jesuits and wished to retain them, even when Pope Clement XIV, yielding to the pressure of various courts, had already released a papal brief for their suppression. At the request of the Russian empress, Rome agreed to the continuation of the Society of Jesus in Russia.

When Pius VII renewed the Order, the Jesuits thought they could live and work quietly in Russia, but it was not so. By their vigorous activity, particularly in educating young people, they had incurred jealousy and the grudge of evil individuals, who sought to ruin them.

The storm which broke over them had been foreseen for some time by some of the priests. They had fallen from favor with the Minister of Public Worship and Education, Galizin, who could not forgive them for having converted his nephew, who was raised in a Jesuit institution, to the Catholic religion. They were also reproached for having converted ladies of aristocratic families to Catholicism. Thus arose the decree of the 1st of January, 1816, by which the Jesuits were expelled from Petersburg and Moscow.

This first blow was but the prelude to other odious regulations and persecutions. The leader of the Jesuit order, who was called to Rome after the restoration of the order, was forbidden to make the trip, and was ordered not to leave Russia. The members of the Order living in their colleges and at their missions were disquieted. Their enemies seized every opportunity to assign ignoble intentions to their behaviour. The (Russian) bishops and priests looked with annoyance upon the Jesuits and begrudged their insight, talent and zeal in fulfilling their duties, and the fact that by their good conduct and thoroughness they had won the general respect of the laity in education of the youth.

The proximity of such vigorous, educated workers to the lazy members of the ignorant Russian clergy certainly offered no flattering subject for comparison. Hence the hatred and enmity toward the Jesuits. These miserable people themselves could not accomplish anything, and in their malice, consequently hindered others from accomplishing anything. In this way complaint piled on complaint, and reproach on reproach, until minister Galizin was won over and enacted the decree.

Galizin handed over to Emperor Alexander I a long-winded report about the reasons why the Jesuits must be driven out of Russia. The Emperor, with whom Galizin then stood in highest favor, signed the decree of the 13th of March, 1820, whereby the Jesuits were entirely banished from Russia.

Now follows the account of the departure of the Jesuits from the Catholic colonies near Odessa.

On the 21st of April, 1820, order number 1396 of the Odessa Councillor of State informed the Welfare Committee as follows: "The Cherson Military-Governor, Count Langeron, transmitted to me an order from Petersburg from the administrator of the Ministry of the Interior, which contains the exact instructions for the departure of the Jesuits from Odessa and the Catholic colonies.

"While instituting these instructions, with reference to the Odessa Jesuits, I find myself called upon to request your Excellence to issue the necessary orders covering the departure of the Jesuits from the Catholic colonies." (Signed) Acting Councillor of State Trajgubov.

The decree of the Minister of the Interior, referring to this, reads: "All Jesuits are to be banished from Russia, under the supervision of the police, and under no condition are they to be allowed to return to Russia in the future. Everything belonging to the Jesuits is to be taken over by the deans or spiritual inspectors, in the presence of representatives of the city authorities, and the inventory of the same is to be signed. The funds needed to send the Jesuits away and to provide priests to take over the parishes from them, may be taken from miscellaneous funds of the provincial administration, but the debt is to be repaid later from the Jesuit capital. The governors must see to it that the surrender of the property is carried out exactly according to regulation and that the removal of the men takes place without delay. A list of the names of the Jesuits and of the places to which they were dispatched across the border is to be sent to the Minister of the Interior.

"If there are some among the Jesuit order who want to leave the order and remain in Russia, they must express their wish in writing immediately to the government. In that event they may no longer call themselves 'Jesuits', and are deprived of all the rights and privileges of that order. It is further ordered that immediately after the arrival of the priests who are to succeed them, the Jesuits are to be expedited across the border, according to the following regulations:

1. Those Jesuits who have no movable or fixed property to manage, and do not wish to leave the order, must immediately be dispatched across the border, to whatever place they themselves wish to go.

2. The civil authorities with the deans, religious inspectors, and deputies, must draw up an inventory of the movable and fixed

property of the Jesuit Order. In the inventory, the value, weight and size of every article is to be estimated. Additionally, the inventory is to be forwarded to the Crown Depository, where the wealth will be stored away for the Catholic clergy and other worthwhile purposes(??).

3. The cash of the Jesuits is to be deposited in the fund for general charity, likewise, the other things are to be stored in a safe place."

The assignment of banishing the Jesuits from the Catholic colonies was given to the senior member of the Odessa Office, Von Lau, by General Inzov.

I give here the personnel involved in the transfer of the parishes, exactly according to authoritative sources*.

Census of the Catholic Parishes in the German Colonies Near Odessa in 1820. When the Jesuits Were Expelled

JOSEPHSTAL PARISH—Pastor Anton Jann, S.J.

	Men	Women
		Population
1. Josephstal Colony	168	153
2. Marienthal Colony	133	132
3. Kleinliebenthal Colony	236	231
4. Franzfeld Colony	137	132

The transfer occurred on the 4th of June, 1820, to Father Peter Stettmann. Signatures of those present: Father Antonius Jann, S.J.; Father Petrus Stettmann; officials of Josephstal: Mayor Grad, councillors Scherer and Neigel; officials of Kleinliebental: Mayor Stein, councillors Götz and Merklinger: officials of Marienthal: Mayor Schütt, councillors Beck and Stärk; officials of Franzfeld: Mayor Fix, councillors Frank and Nold; District Mayor Wolf, Councillor Strenger, District Secretary Max; colonial inspector Repey, Senior Member von Lau. Father Jann left via Grossliebental.

PARISH OF MANNHEIM—Father Oswald Rausch, S.J.

	Men	Women
		Population
1. Mannheim Colony	160	159
2. Elsass Colony	165	161

*Archive of Welfare Committee—1820—Number 34—Odessa.

The transfer occurred on the 3rd of June, 1820 to Father Anselm Siegmund, who was posted as pastor at Selz. Signatures of those present: Father Oswald Rausch, S.J.; Father Anselm Siegmund, secular priest; Mayor Scherer, church warden Estreicher; District Mayor Kieffel, Councillor Knoll; Inspector Wesmann, Senior Member von Lau. Father Rausch left via Grossliebental.

PARISH OF SELZ—Father Theodor von Monfort, S.J.

	Population	
	Men	Women
1. Selz Colony	263	252
2. Kandel Colony	267	255
3. Baden Colony	140	104
4. Strassburg Colony	177	140

The transfer occurred on the 4th of June, 1820, to Father A. Siegmund. Signatures of those present: Father Theodor von Montfort, S.J.; Father Anselm Siegmund; Mayor Werner, Mayor Schneider, Mayor Engelhart, church warden Eichenlaub; District Mayor Kieffel, Inspector Wesmann, Senior Member von Lau.

PARISH OF LANDAU—Father Franz Scherer, S.J.

	Population	
	Men	Women
1. Landau Colony	271	255
2. Speier Colony	219	255
3. Sulz Colony	119	122
4. Karlsruhe Colony	163	177

The transfer occurred on the 26th of June, 1820, but no priest had yet been appointed to replace Father Scherer; therefore he gave the church treasury, which contained 6 rubels, 10 kopeks, to the District Mayor. Signatures of those present: Father Franz Scherer, S.J., church warden Marsal, District Mayor Fischer, Councillors Zimmermann and Wanner, District Secretary Stelzer, Senior Member von Lau. Father Scherer left directly from Landau.

PARISH OF RASTADT—Father Johannes Koervers, S.J.

	Population	
	Men	Women
1. Rastadt Colony	245	214
2. München Colony	122	113

The church treasury, which had debts of 32 rubels, 92 kopeks, was given over to Church Warden Schmitt, since no priest had yet arrived. This was on the 28th of June, 1820.

Signatures of those present: Father Johannes Koervers, S.J., Church Warden Schmitt, Mayor Schmitt, Councillor Zimmermann, Senior Member von Lau. Father Koervers travelled via Koshkova to Landau, where he received his passport.

Father Charles Nicolle, Inspector of All Catholic Churches in New Russia, 1811-1820

Father Charles Nicolle is an interesting and famous personality in all of Russia, but particularly in South Russia, where, in his Pedagogic Institute and later in the Lycee Richelieu in Odessa, he gave to the sons of the aristocracy in the south, a superior and timely upbringing and education. Nicolle ranks as one of the greatest pedagogues of the 19th century, thus surely a great man.

He is important to the German Catholics in South Russia, for he was their first inspector who contributed not a little to their development and welfare.

Dominik Charles Nicolle was born on the 4th of April, 1758, in the village of Poville, near the city of Rouen, in France. Quite early the boy exhibited extraordinary abilities, and studied very industriously in the college of Rouen, where he won the attention of his teachers and the love of his schoolmates by his kindness and hard work. Soon an important event took place in his life. One of his teachers was promoted to Paris as Professor in the Jesuit College of St. Barbara. He took little Nicolle along with him and procured a stipend for him in the same College.

Here progress of young Charles was so brilliant and so successful that he was offered a teaching position at the conclusion of his studies in this institution. In 1782 he assumed the position of Conference Leader, and soon afterward, that of a Prefect (Dean) of Studies. As a young priest, Father Nicolle was already burning with the desire to raise true sons and valuable citizens for his native country and for Holy Mother Church. "Father Nicolle was a priest of exemplary morality and mode of life, a friend of the sciences and a true son of his Church; and of boundless devotion and reverence, for her precepts."* One of his chums said of him: "It is not possible to know Father Nicolle and not love him."

Thus lived Nicolle in the College of St. Barbara, busying himself with ecclesiastic knowledge and practicing Christian virtues, until the French Revolution raged over the entire country like a cyclone, and unhinged all of the decaying French political system then in

*words of a high prelate.

existence. Even St. Barbara College had to forfeit its existence, according to the principles of the revolutionaries, because its religious professors would not take the oath of the Constitution and were therefore removed. The professors, with sad hearts, left the scene of many years of activity and scattered to many lands.

Nicolle, by good fortune, found a place of refuge as tutor in the family of Count Choiseul. Count Choiseul was at that time French ambassador in Constantinople, and was a faithful adherent of luckless King Louis XVI. After the execution of the king, he fled with his family and Nicolle to Petersburg, in order to elude the traps of the revolutionaries. Here, in Russia's capital, Nicolle founded an educational institute for aristocratic youths, which soon won such renown that most Russian aristocrats transferred their sons to this Institute for their education. In this school the sons of Orlov, Galizin, Menshikov, Pletsheev, Benkendorf, Volkonsky, Poltorazsky, and Dimitriev, and many others, obtained their education.

But the envy and illwill of malicious persons soon found ways and means to make suspect and to slander the Institute. The rumour was spread about that Nicolle was educating the youth in the spirit of Catholicism and anti-Russian ideas. These reasons and his weakened health caused him to transfer his Institute to Father Makard in 1800 and to withdraw to Moscow, where he took the position of private tutor in the family of Prince Dolgorukov.

When, in 1805, Duke Richelieu, a friend and classmate of Nicolle, became governor of New Russia, he found public instruction there in a wretched condition. He then thought of his old-time friend, Nicolle, and induced him, by repeated entreaty, to consent to move to Odessa. Concurrently the Duke wrote to the Minister of Education of that time, Prince Galizin, and urgently requested permission from the highest authority to bring about the appointment of Nicolle as Inspector of all Catholic churches in New Russia, with extensive powers for the regulation of ecclesiastic affairs. The Duke's request was fulfilled. On the first of June, 1811, the appointment ensued, making Nicolle inspector of all Catholic churches in South Russia. Soon after his arrival (1814) Nicolle founded a teaching institute in Odessa for aristocratic young men, which in 1817 was made the Lycee Richelieu. Its first director was Nicolle. This lycee (secondary school) was one of the best centers for study in all of Russia, and continued until 1865, when it was converted to the New-Russian University. In addition, Nicolle drew up the course of instruction for the Young Ladies' Institute in Odessa, which exists to this day.

But Nicolle had also a lively concern for the Catholics in his district. Outstandingly, he founded a three-year parochial school near the Catholic church in Odessa, which still exists today. Likewise, he took the pains to improve the schools in the Catholic colonies and, where none were yet in existence, to establish them. He often toured around in the colonies, exhorting the new colonists to application and industry, comforting them in their poverty, and himself aiding where necessary. He always urged his priest subordinates to treat the people with love and friendliness, to enlighten them on their duties and rights, and to constrain them to upright and edifying conduct. But whenever it came to looking after the rights of the colonists, he was steadfastly ready to defend them before higher authority. One time the Welfare Committee had forbidden the colonies to make wax and incense offering at church service, as was the prevailing custom; and no colonist could get married without permission of the secular authorities. But Nicolle arranged things with the authorities so that this enactment was rescinded, and the rights of the colonists remained inviolate.

After Nicolle had worked beneficently nine years in Odessa, he was invited by Duke Richelieu—then the Prime Minister of France—to come to Paris and direct an educational institute there. In this way Nicolle returned to his homeland. Following many labors and sufferings, the high-minded man died the death of the just in Paris on the 2nd of September, 1835.

Father Ignaz Lindl, Inspector of All Catholic Churches in New Russia, 1820-1822.

Ignaz Lindl was born the 8th of May, 1774, in Baindlkirchen, in Old Bavaria. Ordained as a priest in 1799, he was appointed as parish priest in his native locality, where he produced theatrical plays with his parishioners.*

He soon became acquainted with Jung-Stilling, Gossner, Boos, and other lesser mystics. In 1812, converted by Gossner to the mystical way of life, he began with fanatical zeal to spread the mystic heterodoxy among his parishioners. In so doing he came into conflict with religious authority, had to abandon his fallacy under oath (1818), and was transferred from Baindlkirchen to Gundremingen. But in his new parish he carried on even further. Into what absurd vagaries he ventured we see in a letter from his friend Boos: "Lindl," it reads, "now believes (that) we, the living, will not die at all but will be transformed instantaneously according to I Thessalonians 4:16, and then at once right into the

*Hergenrother, "Kirchengeschichte," 1st Ed., Vol. II, P. 983.

1,000-year Kingdom."** As he kept on spreading his fallacies, heedless of the warnings of his superiors, he was locked up in the house of correction in Augsburg.

Baron Berkheim, who at that time was recruiting colonists in Germany for South Russia, delivered him from his imprisonment. Through Prince Galizin, Lindl received an invitation to Petersburg, as preacher in the Maltese Catholic church there. This invitation was much desired by Lindl. At the end of October, 1819, he set out on his journey to Petersburg. In his entourage was a certain Steinmann, Lindl's sister, and the sister of his earlier chaplain, Völk. After a trip of three weeks, Lindl arrived in Petersburg on the 15th of November, 1819.

The first impressions Lindl had of Petersburg were stimulating. "The gracious Prince Galizin," wrote a friend of Lindl, "received the unceremonious country parson not *simply* with rare friendliness, but his first request was, 'Bless me.' " Soon Lindl was received in audience by the emperor. Alexander I, who, since his association with Frau von Krüdener, had become initiated into the mystique of the "Awakened", was so impressed by the apocalyptic religious fanatic, that he received him in great humility and knelt down before him to receive his blessing.*

After such a reception Lindl could assume his ecclesiastical office in Petersburg with good hope of success. The fame of his impressive sermons soon spread throughout the city. All, Catholics and Protestants, jammed into the Maltese church, Sundays and holy days, in order to hear the preacher. At the very time when Lindl was revelling in the blissful feeling of his fame in Petersburg, an event intruded which gave a new ominous twist to the life of the famous preacher.

By the decree of the 13th of March, 1820, the fathers of the Society of Jesus who were active in the German Catholic colonies at Odessa as spiritual advisors, were completely banned from Russia. Just then, through the departure of Father Nicolle, the office of the Inspector in South Russia became vacant. The preacher in the Maltese church, Father I. Lindl, was now proposed for this post by Prince Galizin. The designation of Lindl as Inspector of New Russia and Provost of the Catholic Church of Odessa dates from the 13th of April, 1820. The salary of the new inspector was set at 3,000 rubles, then another 1,000 rubles quarterly allowance, 2,000 for his household establishment, 3,000 as travelling expenses for the trip from Petersburg to Odessa, and 2,000 rubles for the purchase of a stagecoach for the trip.

**Aichinger, J. W. Sailer, p. 303.
*Aichinger, J. W. Sailer, p. 311.

Before this departure from Petersburg, Lindl took another step which stamped him as a weak, sensual creature. On the eve of his departure he invited his friends to a farewell banquet. Then, when all were assembled in the brightly illuminated hall, a side door opened suddenly and in strode the new Provost of Odessa with a richly adorned bride on his arm—it was his housekeeper Elizabeth Völk—and bade his successor in office, Father Gossner, to consecrate his marriage "already concluded in Heaven." Gossner and all the guests were dumbfounded to the highest degree by the strange request of the marriage-bent provost. But, so as not to make the scandal even greater, Gossner pronounced his blessing and the apocalyptic provost was wedded. Next day the newly-married but long-intimate couple started out on their journey to the south. Lindl arrived in Odessa in May, 1820.

The arrival of the new Inspector, accompanied by women, did not make a favorable impression upon the local ecclesiastics and laymen. Yet, one bided his time. The new provost soon gave himself away by disavowing reverence for the Virgin Mary and the Saints in his sermons, and attacking other Catholic teachings and rites. These sermons made for bad blood among the Catholics in Odessa. Preaching and saying mass were forbidden him until further notice, and the case was reported to Petersburg and Rome. The apostolic prefect in Constantinople, Antonius, was dispatched by Rome to Odessa to investigate the Lindl affair. Soon, for the same purpose, came an ecclesiastical judge from Petersburg.

Lindl was summoned before the religious court which the Governor-General, Count Langeron, also attended. At the outset he denied charges obstinately, but the evidence of his guilt was so abundant and overwhelming that he was forced to silence. Lindl was relieved of his post of Inspector and Provost and was suspended. Lindl had brought along to Odessa grandiose plans. He wanted to bring all Catholic colonists to the rejection of their religion and to conversion to his sect. In Josephstal (on the Baraboi) he wanted to throw out of the church all religious pictures, which he called "false deities."

In Rastadt, he preached his sham mysticism for a few months, until the community locked him out of the church. In the colony of München he brought more than thirty families to apostasy, most of whom, however, returned to the Catholic church subsequently. Even in Landau in the Beresan, he was about to preach his new gospel; but the Landauer armed themselves with scythes and hay forks, congregated at the town's end toward Speier, and did not allow the new prophet into their village. Then Lindl thought up another grandiose project.

At Ovidiopol a tract of land was promised him, where he could set up a seminary for preachers and establish a colony of his former parishioners from Baindlkirchen and Gundremingen, with a church and school. Building up the seminary and the layout of the colony was estimated at 250,000 rubles. The money was to be taken from the confiscated wealth of the Jesuits.

But architect Charlemann anticipated 567,141 rubles for the expenses. Over and above this, Lindl required 300 dessatine of land for cultivation, meadows and a garden, and 100 dessatine for the setting out of a forest. In like manner, 151,174 dessatine were promised to Lindl for the settlement of his followers. In the Lindl seminary, clergymen for the Catholic colonies on the Volga were to be educated, thus a larger and broader project. The pastoral seminary was to have three teachers at the outset, who were to train the twelve pupils (count of the apostles).

On June 7, 1820 the Minister of Public Instruction, Galizin, proposed the Lindl seminary project to the Minister of the Interior, recommended it and asked that construction be started as soon as possible. For the support of the seminary 2000 dessiatines of land were set aside.* But the whole grandiose plan collapsed and Lindl received only a small parcel of land in Bessarabia, where the colony of Sarata is now located. He moved there from Odessa on March 13, 1822, accompanied by his followers — a caravan of 50 wagons — whom he had invited from Germany as early as the summer of 1820.

A good many members of the mystic persuasion in Gundremingen followed the invitation of their "spiritual father," sold their possessions, said farewell to their homeland, and migrated enthusiastically and with good cheer to the east, in order to await there the "thousand-year kingdom," united in the blissful covenant of love. But how scandalously they found themselves betrayed. Here, on his own property, Lindl was no longer their brother and father in Christ, honey-mouthed in love and tenderness, but a very strict overlord. Instead of divine revelation there was harsh work, and the kiss of freedom often had to give way to coarse abuses. Impoverished and in misery, many of these disillusioned colonists returned years afterward to their homeland and told their countrymen what they had undergone.

"Upon our arrival in the steppes," so they related, "we had at first to spend our time at breaking stone, and had to build a large and stately house for Lindl. The timbers came all the way from the sea, and we had to fetch them with our draught animals, ten to twelve hours distant; not until then were houses built for the individual families. Land, houses and everything belonged to Lindl.

*Archive of the General Government of New Russia, Annual Set of Publications No. 4, 1820.

He was simultaneously the worldly official and treated his underlings with inhuman harshness; his words following upon the slightest mistake were always, "I'll have you beaten until your blood flows down to your feet!" He intruded into the most trivial family affairs, and nothing could take place without his foreknowledge, nor could any one leave the place without his permission. He jeered at religion and demanded of the emigreés that they renounce completely the Catholic church directly for him, and adhere solely to his teaching."* While Lindl was now setting up and running his little republic in Bessarabia, a frightful tempest was rising in the far north over his head.

When Emperor Alexander I was travelling homeward from the conference of sovereigns in Verona (1822), he had a parley with the Austrian statesman von Metternich in Vienna. The latter informed the Emperor about the diabolical doings of the bogus mystics; how in their fanatical madness they had recently crucified two of their members in Austria, and that he, the Emperor, was harboring in his federation the two worst instigators of this sect, Lindl and Gossner. He reported also that Lindl had had himself secretly married to his maid. The Emperor was indignant over what he heard, and had the matter most strictly investigated upon his return home. The investigation confirmed von Metternich's report.

Suddenly, in December of 1823, an examining magistrate with General Inzov's adjutant, Güldenschanz, came to Sarata. When the gentlemen entered the yard, they found a child at play in the care of a maid. To the question of to whom the child belonged, the maid, having a presentiment of trouble, answered that it was hers.

When the pastor's house was then investigated and a woman was found under the same roof with Lindl, the gentlemen asked him who this woman was. Lindl, was "utterly stunned in guilt."** and answered: "That is my housekeeper." But upon further investigation, the case assumed a different aspect. Lindl was ordered to prepare himself at once for a trip. When all accounts were settled and affairs had been put in order, Lindl travelled with the gentlemen to Kishinev, and from there across the border.

Soon after Lindl's departure, his friend Johann Gossner wrote a message of consolation to the community of Sarata and exhorted them to submit to the inscrutable decree of God; he praised Lindl and elevated him far above himself. But it was of little help, for the community soon abandoned Lindl's tenets and turned to Protestantism, as Lindl himself had done shortly before then in Leipzig (1824). Since the structure erected by Lindl was based upon

*Aichinger, W. Sailer, p. 312.

**Dalton J. Gossner, p. 268.

sand and not upon rock, it quickly fell to pieces. After losing wife and children through death, he advocated and favored celibacy once more. When violent emotions subsided, he returned to reason. Lindl died on the 31st of October, 1845.

Prelate Johannes Schytt, Inspector of All Catholic Churches in South Russia, 1833-1857

Johannes Schytt, son of Felix Schytt, was born in 1789 on the estate of his parents, Tobolkach, province of Vitebsk, district of Dryzensk. Schytt began his career as a landowner. With his knowledge of agriculture and his rectitude, he soon earned for himself the confidence of his colleagues, who consequently chose him as district inspector. But he found no pleasure in the way of life as then led by the young noblemen of his homeland, and consequently turned over his office to another man and travelled abroad to become better acquainted with the world. But in his travels he had various experiences which developed within him the resolve to renounce the perfidy of the world completely, and to dedicate himself to the service of the church.

In the 29th year of his life he entered the clerical academy in Rome, finished there, and as he won the doctorate of theology and philosophy, he was ordained as priest in Rome in 1820.

In 1822 he left the Eternal City and returned to his homeland, where he was chaplain on his own estate until 1825. In 1825 he was named the honorary Canon of Kiev, and in 1828 the Prelate-Curator of the Archdiocese of Mohilev. During all this while, by establishing church discipline and order everywhere, he won considerable support for the church, which had been allowed to deteriorate completely under the administration of the unscrupulous Sestrinzevitch.

From 1825 to 1827 he was a member of the Mohilev consistory (diocesan senate); and from 1827 to 1829 sat as assistant judge in the Roman Catholic commission in Petersburg. Since Archbishop Ziezishevsky could not himself supervise the large archdiocese of Mohilev because of infirmities of age and total blindness, he therefore entrusted its administration to the learned and worthy prelate Schytt, (with the Russian government consenting), whom he designated concurrently as his co-adjutor in Rome, and requested the Pope for confirmation.

In 1831 Prelate Schytt received a costly ring and the Order of Anna, second-class, from the Russian government. But an event then interceded, compelling Schytt to show everyone whether the Spirit of God or that of the world animated him. In 1832 Secretary of State Bludov made the proposal to the Roman Catholic

74

commission of doing away with all Catholic monasteries. The assistant judges of the commission, mostly high-born and unscrupulous court chaplains, eager to surrender body and soul for a decoration, voted without opposition for the abolition of the monasteries. At this, Prelate Schytt arose, as presiding official, and gave an impressive speech to the unscrupulous assistant judges with the courage and eloquence of a Saint Paul, about the purpose and the necessity of the monasteries in the Catholic Church. This speech caused a great stir in government circles. Prelate Schytt was considered dangerous to the state, and his ban from Petersburg was sought, for otherwise he could awaken the conscience of the court prelates, and the whole project of getting rid of the monasteries would be defeated.

By a decree of 1833, Prelate Schytt was removed from the administration of the Mohilev archdiocese and designated in name only as inspector of New Russia. Soon afterward he received from the Minister of the Interior the mandate to inspect the Catholic churches in Moscow and in the colonies on the Volga. When he arrived in Saratov, he received through the Minister the order to make his residence in Saratov, pending further instructions. This was a sly way to ban someone. He lived in Saratov until 1857, living only with his books and by contributing benefits to his poor exiled compatriots. In 1829, Schytt was first temporarily assigned to New Russia as inspector, to bring orders into Odessa and the Catholic colonies. He lived in Odessa from the 28th of February until the 18th of June, 1829. From Odessa he was summoned to administer the archdiocese of Mohilev. His plenipotentiaries in the ecclesiastical duty were Canon Raphael Musnizsky (1830-1842) and Prelate Georg Rosutovitch (1842-1857). From 1857 to 1876 Rosutovitch remained only dean of the Cherson deanery.

Canon Raphael Musnizsky, Plenipotentiary
Inspector of All Catholic Churches
in South Russia, 1829-1842

Raphael Musnizsky was born in 1791. About his native homeland, his early years and educational career, I could find nothing in the source-material at my disposal. Since a number of ecclesiastics from various Orders had held the post of Inspector among themselves following the departure of the Jesuits and of Lindl from Odessa, but were not in the position to enforce good order and churchly discipline, especially upon the colonies, the aged archbishop Ziezishevsky decided to appoint the assistant judge of the Mohilev consistory, Canon Raphael Musnizsky, as temporary inspector of New Russia in the place of Prelate Schytt who was summoned to Petersburg.

Musnizsky was a very accomplished, active and worthy priest, who was very much occupied with the colonists' school. On his first trip of inspection in the Catholic colonies he had the sad experience of seeing how the situation was worsening in all respects among the colonists. He consequently attended to what was needed above all, and that was a supply of prayer books and school books. In 1832 he had a large number of these books printed in Vilna for the colonists, so as always to have a stock of them to spare. In 1833 he ruled that instruction in all Catholic schools take place from September 1 to May 1, and that the children he compelled to attend school, once they were over six years of age; likewise that the teachers were not to be appointed by the clergy without examination and were not to act as village secretaries simultaneously.

With the lax ecclesiastics he dealt strictly and required them to fulfil their religious duties conscientiously, to lead an edifying life, and light up the way ahead for their parishioners in all good qualities. With the colonists he was steadfastly very affable and kind, and thereby won their love and respect, which he earned no less by his constructive life. Universally mourned, he died in Odessa August 31, 1842, and was interred in the old Catholic churchyard, with Father Stankevitch presiding, along with five other ecclesiastics.

Prelate Georg Rosutovitch, Plenipotentiary Inspector of All Catholic Churches in South Russia, 1842-1857

George Rosutovitch was born in 1811 not far from the city of Vilna. Feeling the call of the ecclesiastical station, he entered the clerical seminary at Telshev. Finishing there, he entered the religious academy in Vilna, received the degree of M. Theology, and was ordained as priest in 1837. In 1842 he was appointed Instructor of Religion in the Lycee Richelieu in Odessa. When in 1842 the plenipotentiary inspector, Raphael Musnizsky, died, Rosutovitch was named to replace him. In this post, Rosutovitch was active for many years in Odessa.

Rosutovitch made himself memorable to the Catholic community in Odessa by building the handsome parish church there in 1853. Apart from the church building, Rosutovitch did not build much, but what existed he always kept in order and good condition, which was indeed no small service on his part. Rosutovitch did nothing noteworthy for the Catholic colonies other than strive to enlist a goodly number of colonists' sons for the Catholic seminary, which was opened in 1856 in Saratov. The local clergyman was usually his interpreter. Since he did not understand German, he was on rather formal terms with the colonists, and therefore could not be very influential. Yet he frequently made inspection trips to the colonies and looked after orderliness, and also sought to persuade the colonists to build attractive churches and schools everywhere. Indeed, he succeeded in many colonies where, especially in the sixties of the last century many beautiful churches were built. Also, he made many gifts to newly-built churches, particularly that of Kleinliebenthal, to which he bequeathed in his will, two houses, with a trellis garden into the bargain.

Rosutovitch was an educated man and was esteemed by the highest authorities of Odessa. He was on particularly good terms with the Governor-General, Count Stroganoff, who visited him daily in the last days of his life.

His life assumed a very tragic end. After he was retired, he had two colonial style houses built for himself next to the church in Kleinliebenthal, in order to live there and to pass his last days in peace and quiet prayer. Since the prelate was taken to be very rich, he was set upon by three plundering murderers during the night of October 1-2, 1877, robbed and mortally wounded by a shot through his right side, so that by the fourth of October he died in Odessa. The burial took place on October 10th, 1877, attended by Father R. Reichert, in company with many clergymen and a large crowd of the faithful.

The Cultural State of the German Colonies in South Russia

The System of Instruction

The primary school forms the first stage of the scheme of instruction imparting elementary instruction to children seven to fourteen years old, and thereby ushers in and begins the basis of child education. Accordingly, the elementary school is the child's first educational institution. As such, the primary school has the task of fostering, training, developing, strengthening and refining all physical, spiritual, moral and religious potentialities of which the child's nature and human dignity are capable, and assisting their development to full effectiveness. Through education the child is to be refined and equipped to learn how to know and practise his social duties, so as to be able to emerge into public view as an upright citizen of his country, and a useful member of human society. Finally, education aims at ennobling and glorifying contemporaneous life, and prepares one for eternal life in the hereafter through religion, the noblest agency in upbringing. Indeed, the religious school is therefore one of the primary and most important institutions of mankind, since the weal and woe of the world hinges upon it.

The village school of the German colonists was always, and is still, inadequately provided for. The colonists have never grasped its purpose and its importance. When something needs to be done for the schools, one has to drag them into cooperation by the hair, so to speak. They all want to be bright, clever and learned, but do not want to establish schools where these praiseworthy qualities can be acquired. People who have been in Germany and have seen there the beautifully equipped educational institutions, must have serious doubts that our German colonists, with their primitive schools, are really a branch of that great nation whose educational system is in such a splendid state.

Even though progress in the school system has been made recently in the German colonies, there nevertheless remains a great deal to do to have it compare at all with the schools in Germany.

And then, instruction in the colonist schools suffers from an evil that makes the basic teaching of the children impossible. It is simply the circumstance that instruction is given in the Russian language, which is unfamiliar to the children. Our colonists' children are in themselves slow enough in comprehending a clear and intelligible idea of a subject; how much more difficult it must be for them to grasp the idea first in a foreign language. This absurd situation ought to be done away with as soon as possible and the mother tongue re-introduced as the language of instruction.

Another consideration which speaks unfavorably of the colonist attitude toward education is that almost always the initiative for founding a school comes not from themselves, but from other persons. As evidence of this the following two school projects will serve.

School Project of Inspector Platzer, 1829

"The fervor with which I always wish to serve our benevolent Monarch and the State, creates in me the thought of providing the young in this country with a great advantage in reference to their upbringing. It surely has been necessary for a long time to teach the Russian language to the youth of the colonists. For what does a citizen amount to in the State if he does not understand the language of the country? . . . Haven't we examples showing that people with the best of talents reap no advantage at all from their knowledge because they do not understand the Russian language? . . ."

After bringing to bear various additional reasons for the founding of a district school, he presents his plan more specifically:

1. "It is accordingly my opinion that a public district school for the colonists' children should be established here under my superintendence, in which not only the Russian language is taught along with German, but also knowledge essential to mercantile life such as, for instance, arithmetic, world history, and geography, with all these subjects given in the Russian language, for which purpose a Russian teacher should be employed. The school would have only a single class in the first year (since the pupils do not yet understand Russian), in which fundamental grounding in Russian is developed. In the succeeding year the school is to have two classes: the first one for the beginners, the second for those who have advanced in the Russian language.

2. "In the first-year the Russian teacher, having only one class to look after, is to teach in the forenoon, and the German teacher in the afternoon. But in the second-year when there must already be two classes, both these teachers share the teaching between themselves, alternately.

3. "So that his holy obligation may always be fully realized, this school must have an overseer who not only completely understands both of these languages, but who also masters the above-named subjects of study. He must understand the teaching profession well enough on the whole to detect errors on the part of teachers and be in a position to correct them.

4. The German teacher will continue to receive his present pay, the Russian teacher five hundred rubles annually with lodging, and the school overseer, who must be responsible for the entire well-being of the school, six hundred rubles.

5. "In order to find the means to support this school easily, I think that every father who wants a good education for his son and have him acquire the Russian language thoroughly, should pay six rubles annually, two rubles per term paid in advance. And in order to give this school an assured success, it is permitted to admit girls also into the school, but only those not yet twelve years old.

6. "In pursuance of this I call upon each regional office to make known to all school officials the present report by circular, and to collect signatures from those who wish to transfer their children into this district school, thereby giving notice that whoever has once agreed by signature to send his son or daughter to this school, does not have the right to remove them before the end of the three-year course.

7. "However, should it occur upon the opening of this school, or some time in the future, that more subscribers sign it than would be needed for the stated pay of the Russian teacher and of the school overseer, along with school expenses, then a third teacher can of course be taken on to teach the French language and drawing.

8. "Seeing that the present schoolhouse located in Grossliebenthal is sufficiently roomy, this school can doubtless be accommodated there.

9. "The School will be responsible to the official school inspector and to His Excellency the head of the Welfare Committee. The teachers to be appointed must show their certificates of ability and right to teach to the school inspector, who will pass their application on to the Welfare Office for the attention of the head of the Welfare Committee."

There followed some other points of less significance. Two religious teachers, one Catholic, the other Lutheran were to be appointed. It was permitted also to accept in the school children from other districts.

The original is signed: Honorary Councillor PLATZER, Grossliebenthal, May, 1829.

This school project was distributed to all colonial communities for inspection, but the colonists wanted no such school, and hence the high-minded man had to abandon his well-intentioned scheme.

School Project of State Councillor von Hahn
of July, 16th, 1843.

"The German colonists of southern Russia, notwithstanding their settlement there many years ago, comprehend practically nothing of the Russian language.

With the exception of a minority of enlightened farmers they do not even feel the need of it. Only the knowledge of this language could bind them to their new homeland and would bring incalculable value into their commerce, in that they would be saved from the harmful mediation of Jewish brokers and other people; and it would help to some extent in simplification and acceleration of business. For disseminating knowledge of Russian, it is absolutely necessary that this language be given in the village schools along with German.

This goal will be attained only when schoolmasters knowing the Russian language will have been trained from among the colonists themselves. For this purpose there will be founded in the colonies of the Taurian and Jekaterinoslav provinces, as also in the provinces of Bessarabia, up to one or two schools in which the colonists' boys (once they will have successfully completed the usual course of study of the village school) can acquire such knowledge as is essential to investiture in the post of teacher in the colonies.

"The founding of similar schools in the Cherson province as well, to be training colleges for teachers and office clerks, would bring undeniable profit. As a consequence, the Welfare Committee has come to the conclusion:

1. "To open a similar teaching college in the colony of Grossliebenthal and another in the colony of Landau (in Beresan): the first for boys of the Lutheran faith, the second for Catholic boys.

2. "To permit all among the colonists so inclined to attend these schools, and in addition to accept into them regular boarders (up to ten in Liebenthal and up to eight in Landau), who must be selected from among homeless orphans. After completing the course of study, all are duty-bound to serve for ten years as teachers under colonial jurisdiction.

3. "The expenses attending the establishment and maintenance of these schools are to be drawn:

(a) "Those of the Liebenthaler from the revenue of the sheep-land fund of the Liebenthal, Kutschurgan and Glücksthal territories.

(b) Those of the Landauer from the sheep-land capital of the Beresan territory, where for this purpose a suitable part of these funds must then be set aside as an inviolable reserve.

4. "Since by this manner, all districts will share in this generally useful matter, the filling of the boarders' vacancies in the schools is to proceed along the following lines:

(a) In the Liebenthal school, from the group of ten boarder vacancies: four from the Lutheran colonies of the Liebenthal territory, three from the Lutheran colonies of the Beresan territory, and three such from the Glücksthal territory.

(b) In the Landau school, from the group of eight boarder vacancies: three from the Catholic colonies of the Beresan territory, three from the Catholic colonies of the Kutschurgan territory, and two from the Catholic colonies of the Liebenthal territory.

5. "The teachers appointed in both of these schools must thoroughly understand German and Russian, quite apart from their native language, and in this connection will submit to an examination in the Welfare Committee. On the other hand, the religious authorities will test them from the catechism and on church history, since these subjects must be counted."

Odessa, the 16th of July, 1843.

of the Colonists in South Russia
State Councillor von Hahn

The Central Schools in the German Colonies

As we see from the foregoing projects, we are indebted to the great friend and benefactor of the German colonies, State Councillor von Hahn, for the existence of the central schools. Even though many districts were slow about starting such an essential project, it was eventually set up almost everywhere. What would our colonies be today if they did not have the central schools which train teachers and secretaries for them? Surely in education they would not stand much above the Kaffirs and bushmen in Africa.

From this project we see also that a Catholic central school was to be founded, but that the Beresaner and particularly the Landauer believed that they were already sufficiently educated or could acquire their wisdom on their own and could consequently get along without the central schools. Because of this the Beresan central school went to Neufreudenthal, where it was opened in 1869.

Again, the Mennonites were the first to perceive the importance of founding central schools, and opened such a school in Chortitza as early as 1842. Next in order of age was the Werner central school. The following is the present make-up of the central schools, with figures for the year of their founding and the count of teachers and pupils.

	Year Founded	*Colony*	*Teachers*	*Pupils*
1.	1842	Chortitz	5	180
2.	1844	Sarata	4	106
3.	1869	Grossliebenthal	5	97
4.	1869	Neufreudenthal	3	60
5.	?	Neu-Schönsee	3	31
6.	1873	Prischib	9	114
7.	?	Halbstadt	3	93
8.	?	Neusatz	4	75
9.	1872	Gnadenfeld	3	29
10.	?	Grunau	4	60

In addition, there is a cooperative school in Orloff with three teachers and eighty-two pupils, and in Chortitz a model school with one teacher and thirty-eight children.

In this year also (1905), central schools were opened in Zürichthal, province of Tauria and in New-York (Jekaterinoslav province).

Rules for Attendance in the Village Schools and for Instruction in 1841
(which should be re-introduced today)

For the advancement of instruction in the colonies, the following rules are laid down by higher authority for conscientious observance and compliance by the village authorities, and family heads as a body.

1. Every father is duty-bound to send to school each day from the beginning of October to the end of March his children, pupils, apprentices, or attendants of either sex, and to have the same attend religious instruction or Sunday school on Sundays.

2. Every schoolmaster must keep a true list, by names, of all children who must attend school, including afternoon as well as morning school periods (including each Sunday school); must check the attendance and record the ones present in a special list which he hands over daily to the village authorities of the colony.

3. Having received the list, the village authorities get information from the families on the cause of absence of the pupils from school; and if they find pupils legitimately absent, they mark it down opposite the names. For those absent without sufficient cause, the village authorities get from the head of the family the stipulated fine noted below.

4. To be regarded as legal grounds for absence of pupils are: illness of the pupil himself; the necessity of caring for an ill member of the family; a death in the family (but only to the end of the funeral); and stormy weather when the school is remote.

Other grounds, no less important, can also count to prevent the pupils from attending school, for which the village authorities must be guided by their judgement under such circumstances as to whether these grounds appear sufficient for exoneration from fine.

5. For each and every absence of a pupil from school without valid reason, the parents or guardians must pay a fine of three silver kopecks.

6. As already said, the fine money will be collected through the village authorities and at the same time be delivered with the listing to the church elders, on receipt, for incorporation in the school treasury.

7. The school treasury will be administered on the same basis as any church property, and the fines levied will be utilized for

procuring the indispensable books for poor children, and of such books as will be allotted after examinations, to pupils known for diligence.

8. If those who are subject to the fine are not in a position to pay it, then they are to be punished by the village authorities with community work instead of the money fine, at the rate of half a day's work for each day's absence of a pupil from school.

ODESSA, December 7th, 1841
Deputy General-Guardian of the Colonists
State Councillor von Hahn.

A New School Project*

"Therefore have courage in the end . . . to arise, even listen to reason, and to kindle and inspire something great."—Göthe.

From the foregoing we gather that the German colonists in South Russia had founded schools, to be sure; but such a school as teaches their trade, namely, farming, they have not yet founded. It would be high time to make up for this omission and found such a school, a school of agricultural technology. For only such a school can clear the colonists' way for progress on an equal footing with other bearers of civilization on the pathway of universal cultural development.

According to the definitions of constitutional law, a modern civilized state consists of the following co-ordinated departments: a) an agricultural department; b) a business department; c) an industrial department. The mission of the agricultural department is to wrest the raw products from the soil rapidly and skillfully; that of the business department is seeing to the delivery of the raw products to the industrial department inexpensively and undamaged; the industrial department aims to manufacture genuinely, cheaply, and exemplarily the raw products assembled for it, for the urgent and convenient necessities of human life, in order to offer them for sale by trade in the market place.

When we apply this measure to our homeland, great and powerful Russia, we must therefore say: Russia is no such civilized state yet, but is in the position and process of becoming one. All conditions for it are at hand except for one minimum essential, namely, the necessary education.

By education I mean here the essential specialized technique of agriculture, of trade and of industry. Notable in Russia, which is

_____
*This project was proposed by the author in Grossliebenthal on February 27, 1904, at a meeting.

84

particularly cut out by Nature for being an agricultural state by virtue of its immense land mass, is the lack of knowledge on cultivation of the soil. Great, land-rich Russia has only three technical schools of agriculture: those of Novo-Alexandrovsk (Lublin province), Moscow, and Petersburg. How can that be sufficient for so many? So, more information must be amassed in respect to agriculture. And who is to do that? We German colonists, whom the Russian government called in for this purpose as much as a century ago, are obligated to supply this knowledge. And that we can do only if we are in possession of an agricultural school, whether it be a technical one or an academy. For only such a school imparts the knowledge of pursuing farming rationally and profitably.

We are, consequently, obliged to call such a school to life: first, out of a debt of duty to the Russian government; secondly, the duty of self-preservation forces this undertaking. We see in the manifesto of the Russian government, dated February 20, 1804, by which the German colonists were called to South Russia as model managers in agriculture, that between this government and the colonists, a formal contract was signed, following the axiom: "Because you give do I give." The Russian government said this, as it were:

"Germans, come to Russia! We will give you a good deal of land for cultivation and for other agricultural pursuits; we will support you financially and give you house and farm effects; we will accord you many freedoms and privileges.

"For all of this we require of you only your energetic work, your industry, and your knowledge of farming and other rural pursuits. You are expected to be helpful to other residents of South Russia as model farmers in all respects.

The German colonists said "yes" and came to Russia. The Russian Government faithfully kept its promise. It gave so much land to the colonists that the poor people had no idea what to do with it all; it gave them farm implements and seed grain in order to till and seed the land; it gave them money and provisions until they had gotten the first harvest in; it supported them for a number of years free from all bills and taxes. And when crop failures and instances of misfortune intruded in the first years, the government provided them again with the necessities.

The government appointed a special judicial authority for the colonists with the splendid and significant name of "Welfare Committee." The highest officials of this authority were mostly Germans. I name only Kantenius and Hahn, who have won for themselves enduring renown in the history of the colonists. These men always showed themselves to be full of devotion and good will toward the German colonists, and at all times strove to raise their well-being.

But we are now asking: Have the German colonists really exerted themselves, always, to become worthy of their assignment of being models of agricultural management? Anyone familiar with the colonial history of the hundred years now elapsed and the present desperate agricultural plight of our colonists must answer with an emphatic "NO." I do not wish to say thereby that our colonists have accomplished little or nothing at all. Rather, I maintain that isolated regions and farm owners have accomplished a great deal in agriculture. But this is not yet the model, the ideal which our colonists must accomplish as stipulated. To be model managers the German colonists must deliver the best which agriculture has produced in theory and practice. And our colonists absolutely cannot accomplish that before they have an advanced school of agriculture.

I said further: self-preservation requires us to found an advanced school of agriculture. A German proverb says: "Necessity is the mother of invention." But among the German colonists this saying does not appear to turn out to be true. For how often has necessity knocked on their doors during the past hundred years, without their yet having learned how to cultivate their farms well and correctly! The great philosopher Balmes* says: "The best farmer is he who best knows the characteristics of the soil, of the climate, of seeding and of plants, the best process of tillage; the one who extracts from the soil superior products at low cost in less time and greater quantity; in a word, the one who is in possession of the most truths relating to the practice of farming." And where can one thoroughly learn these truths having to do with farming? I answer with firm conviction: only at an advanced school of agriculture. The distressed condition of the German colonists worsens from year to year, and inevitably demands redress.

Who does not know the frightful, despairing cry for help which in the last bad years has been wrung from our colonists? This cry was so great that it echoed throughout Russia and even beyond. It was asked how it was possible for a single unproductive year to bring these richly praised colonists to the beggar's staff. The question is much in order and gives a great deal to think about to every reasoning colonist. The question demonstrates that the plight of our colonists is sad, indeed desperate. We face a serious and dangerous crisis, if not economic bankruptcy. Ways and means

*Balmes, "The Road to Knowledge of the Truth", p. 4.

must therefore be set up to prevent threatening disaster. And for that we need more light, more intelligence, more technical information in agriculture, and other rural occupations, and this only an advanced school of agriculture can give.

Or are we perhaps to hand over the founding of such a school to the other colonists in South Russia, perchance to the Jewish colonists? Oh, yes, they are already at it, for some years ago they founded a lower school of agriculture in Novo-Poltavka, and it is very easy for the moneyed Jews to convert this school into an advanced school of agriculture. Then what? Are the Jews, who are so despised by the Germans, then to become, as farmers, our instructors in agriculture? That would be an everlasting disgrace for the proud German colonists in South Russia. How would it be if, after the present ferment, the economic conditions were cleared up and regulated, and a regional agronomist appointed; and then all at once there came to Grossliebenthal, as a now-educated agronomist, a former town wine merchant or his son to teach agriculture to the German colonists? Would you not crawl into the ground from shame, you German colonists? What is not, can yet come about!

If you want to forestall this disgrace and other evils, lose no time and found such a school. By founding such a school, you repay to the Russian government the debt which your ancestors saddled you with, that is, to serve the dwellers in the country as model managers in agriculture. But such a school will also prevent bankruptcy, which is within sight, and guarantee the well-being of future generations.

Boldly on then, fellow members of that great people which is always grateful for benefits received, which always strives for great things and produces them, rise up out of your languor and pay back your debt of gratitude to your Russian homeland! Found an advanced school of agriculture which gives you the knowledge of how to manage agriculture rationally, exemplarily and profitably! And Almighty God will give it His blessing; and this educational institution will long endure, to the glory of the German colonists and the salvation of descendants from generation to generation.

The Colonists' Press

Like other factors which serve for the education and enlightenment of our German colonists, the press too is poorly developed. Yet the press is a great power today. Bishop Kettler of Mainz says: "The two great forces on earth are the press and the school; the matters of greatest concern therefore must be the press and the school. Anyone who is indifferent toward them has no right to call himself a true son of the Church, an enlightened Christian who knows and loves the cause of Christ."

These words are weighty and full of meaning and each of us must ask himself: Have you done everything up to now to raise the colonial press to a tolerable level, corresponding to the sad state of the colonists? It should be time, once and for all to remedy this evil. All priests, teachers and writers who still have a heart for our poor uneducated colonial people ought to get together to print a paper that would be suitable in every respect. Things would soon look different in our colonies.

The first colonial newspaper was the one founded in 1845 by the Welfare Committee in Odessa, "Unterhaltungsblatt für deutsche Ansiedler im südlichen Russland". This paper fulfilled its purpose fairly well. Mainly, it instructed the colonists in their agricultural occupations and frequently brought interesting, instructive and entertaining stories. The price was low, only 60 kopecks. Nevertheless, the paper had to cease publication in 1861 due to lack of subscriptions. In 1862 the "Odessaer deutsche Zeitung" began to appear. It published news about the activities and the life of the German colonists under the heading "Colonial Affairs".

At present the "Odessaer Zeitung" has over four thousand subscribers, the highest in its existence. The Catholics have had since 1897 a weekly, "Clemens", published in Saratov by Prelate Kruschinsky. This has lately increased its subscriber list significantly and also the variety of its contents. In Odessa there has been appearing for the last 35 years the "Christliche Volksbote", published by Father Becker. A new paper, the "Beobachter", began appearing this year (1905) in Jekaterinoslav. To be added to the list also is the "Friedensbote" published by Pastor Günther in Saratov. These are all the German press organs in South Russia and the Volga. Certainly a small number for half a million German colonists.

The almanac literature is also slim. The following exist: "Neuer Wirtschaftskalender" by L. Nitsche, "Hausfreund" by Schmidt (both in Odessa), the "Molotschnaerkalender" by Schaad, and a Mennonite almanac.

It is time, once and for all, for us to say to ourselves, "Who am I?" Konrad von Bollanden called to the church of today with the following words: "A clergy which, in abandoning the people themselves in the struggles of the present, shuts itself up inside the church with indifference, does not fulfill its duty before God, and loses esteem and influence among the people. How can people be attached to and love a clergy who coldly and unconcernedly ignore their holiest interests?" God grant that the new freedom leads to more light and progress in this also.

Agriculture

South Russia is included among the most fertile regions of Europe. In respect to quality and productiveness, its soil is suited to growing most cultivated plants in rich abundance. But systematic agriculture in South Russia is still a wish of the future, in spite of an abundance of machines. The German colonists who are supposed to be model managers still carry on agriculture after the old pattern, while others of different culture hurry ahead with giant strides. The German colonists lack even a higher school of agriculture, where they could acquire the knowledge needed for farming and other rural occupations. In South Russia, particularly in the Crimea, most tropical fruits would grow, but until now, no more than a few attempts have been made to cultivate them.

Farming

As in every other country practising farming, so too in South Russia the cultivation of grains stands preeminent, since they furnish the population with the most important article of food, namely, bread.

The foremost products of grain-growing for the German colonists are: wheat, rye, barley, oats, flax, maize and potatoes. Wheat is cultivated as summer and winter varieties.

1) Winter wheat comes from the Sandomierz district in the kingdom of Poland and hence is called Sandomirka. This wheat, abundantly grown in South Russia, is best sown in early August, and usually turns out well, if not damaged in the winter by glaze-ice and by strong March winds in the spring. Four to six pud (a pud equals forty pounds) are sown per dessatin. Winter wheat is exported especially to England, where it frequently is worth a very high price.

2) Hirka wheat is an excellent variety of unknown origin, whose name, however, points to the Caucasus. Hirka is very tender and sensitive, especially to frost. It is distinguishable from winter wheat by its dark red color and seemingly by its finer flour. This wheat wants early seeding, needs good, clean, firm soil, and ripens in 100 to 120 days. In former times a good deal of Hirka was sown but now it is done on a smaller scale.

3) Ulka wheat was not sown by the German colonists until 1889. It is said that this variety of wheat grows better in South Russia than the previously-named ones. I was told that Ulka was ordered from America by the Odessa Uprava district for the German colonists.

4) Arnaut (also Glass wheat) is the oldest variety of wheat in South Russia, and is much sown, especially in Greece and Bulgaria.

Arnaut has a hard grain, a longish form, and a very thin transparent skin. It is more tolerant of frost and wind than Hirka wheat, and it grows especially well in the district of Taganrog. This Arnaut of Taganrog is sold mainly to Greece, Italy and Spain, where it is consumed primarily in macaroni factories and fancy bakeries. Arnaut wheat can be sown later than Hirka and fully ripens in 110 days. This wheat is seldom sown at present among the German colonists.

5) Rye grows remarkably well in South Russia and was first grown here by the German colonists. The profit from rye is very good in Russia because of its use in large quantity in many whisky distilleries and also its considerable export to western Europe. In many places summer rye is sown.

6) Barley used to be raised among the German colonists mostly for their own requirements. But for a number of years a good deal of barley has been sown for selling, because it often commands a high price.

7) Oats are usually sown only for home use, for which the German colonists are to be strongly censured; for oats are the most undemanding variety of grain in respect to climate, soil and tilling; also, the grain recently has had a good price.

8) Flax is a plant which the Mennonites cultivated first in South Russia. In 1800 Privy-Councillor Kantenius ordered for them 150 puds of this seed. Flax was grown by the colonists mainly for its seed. Its fiber was not used for linen, but uselessly burned up. In modern times flax is little sown any more, because the firm soil (turf) needed has become scarce.

9) Welsh corn (maize) comes from Bessarabia, where it has constituted, since antiquity, the foremost edible grain for the inhabitants there. Just as the German cannot do without potato and the Russian without borsht, so too the Moldavian cannot do without mamaliga, which can be prepared only with maize flour. The German colonists used to plant maize only for hog fodder, but for some years a lot of it has been cultivated for sale as well, since the prices for it are climbing every year. In addition to those named, still other varieties of grain are planted, but not often.

10) The potato, a tuber plant, is liberally planted in the German colonies, because it constitutes a foremost food, especially for the poorer classes. Mostly early and late potatoes are grown, and near Odessa also the Polish potato. Besides potatoes, a large number of other tuber and root plants are cultivated among the German colonists, both for their own use and for sale.

Crop Systems

The ways in which the German colonists in South Russia have carried on agriculture was and is still today highly varied. At first farming with a rotation of four crops with black fallow ground was in use by the Mennonites, because it was suited for the most part to the local climate and quality of the soil. Experiments for many years demonstrated the merit of this system, especially since with the increased population and activity there was no more of the virgin steppe available. The four-crop rotation system of agriculture was introduced on the Molotschna and by the colonists of the Berdyansk, Mariupol and Chortitza regions almost universally. Later it was tried also in the Swedish and Kutschurgan districts. During the fifties of the last century experiments were also made with the three-crop rotation system in the Mariupol colonies and with good success.

With the Molotschna Mennonites, the soil was distributed for the purpose of a uniform rotation of crops at 22 5/8 dessatine per farmer and over and above that, each farmer had 4¾ dessatine more of land to cultivate in any way he wanted to. Also in other colonial districts where the four-crop agriculture was introduced, the procedure was similar. With the Mennonites, the following crop rotation was customary: the first year, barley, hemp, millet or potato; the second year, wheat; the third year, rye or oats; the fourth year the field lay fallow again, and at year's end was cultivated as much as four times, so that no weeds could grow.

In the Mariupol colonies a different rotation was preferred: the first year wheat was sown, the second year, rye, and the third year, barley or oats. Fertilizing of the fields is still not done among the German colonists. Only with the Mennonites and in the Crimea are there a few farmers who frequently spread fertilizer on their nearby fields. Also, growing fodder crops, and cultivation of meadows was first carried on in a few colonial districts, but with little active interest, hence with limited success. However, at present, increasing attention is apparently being accorded again to this branch of work.

That the German colonists were already raising a large amount of grain as long as fifty years ago is proved by the following figures. In the autumn of 1854 there was sown on the colonists' fields of 65,010 dessatine, some 39,060 tschetwert of winter crops; and in the spring of 1855, 275,531 dessatine were sown with 213,574 tschetwert of summer crops. The 1855 harvest was very limited; indeed, it can be called a complete crop failure, for the yield from crops, was: winter crops 79,990 tschetwert; summer crops, 382,476 tschetwert. In 1855 27,834 tschetwert of potatoes were planted for a harvest value of 76,844 tschetwert, that is, also a small yield from potatoes.

Garden, Vegetable and Forest Planting

Garden planting had been made a duty by State-Councillor Kantenius at the start of the settlement of the colonists, but until the founding of the Agricultural Association in 1851, was carried on very carelessly. This association, under whose custody were the gardens and plantations, exerted itself a good deal in several districts to bring about an increase, improvement and refinement of fruit-growing in the German colonies. In 1855 there were 3,099,000 fruit trees in the colonies, of which 127,000 were bearing fruit. Moreover, in the fruit-tree nurseries of the colonists there were over 22,600 grafted trees and more than 832,000 young trees. Most of these fine fruit gardens and plantations have come to an end, following the dissolution of the Welfare Committee, at least in the Cherson province.

The colonists busied themselves with the growing of vegetables for the most part only to satisfy domestic wants. Only those colonies situated near large cities raised vegetables for sale. And so in the colonies of Kleinliebenthal, Josephstal and Marienthal vegetables were planted in quantity and sold in the market in Odessa. In 1855, vegetables sold in the colonies amounted to 3,757 rubles.

Tree culture in the German colonies was limited to artificial laying-out of forest plantations, for there were really no natural forests in the colonies. Only in a few valleys and glens, were traces here and there of forest trees. The last ordinance relating to forest plots was issued by State-Councillor von Hahn in 1841, when he was still deputy to General Inzov. On every farm establishment one-half dessatin of forest had to be planted. In 1855, 279 forest plots could be counted in the colonies, in which, apart from mulberry trees, there were 480,300 forest trees, 2,044,000 in quickset hedges, and 1,307,000 forest trees in forestry nurseries.

Moreover, 573 pounds of seed of various forest trees were sown in order to enable the colonists to provide the various species of trees in the easiest and cheapest way. Since the Welfare Committee was discontinued, the forests in most of the colonies have been destroyed in a barbaric way. Since gardening and forestry, as well as silk culture and agriculture are interdependent, so it follows that these too, although not-assiduously-practiced branches of business, are among the first to perish from neglect. Bee-keeping is still carried on to some extent by only a few fanckers, mostly ecclesiastics and teachers.

Wine-Growing

Wine-growing was at first generally introduced among the colonists by the authorities. But afterward it was neglected in many colonies and even given up. Only in the Bessarabian colonies, and in a few in the Cherson and Taurian provinces, were vines regularly planted. In 1856 the vines belonging to the colonists numbered 9,707,882 in Bessarabia, 4,579,606 in Cherson, and 857,872 in Tauria. Wine could seldom be valued higher than one ruble a bucketful. In 1855, 535,637 pailsful of wine were made by the colonists. From this amount, 177,943 pailsful were sold at various prices, mostly to soldiers who were then located in the colonies. The wine harvest was rather good in 1855, especially in Bessarabia. The wine which the colonists make is of limited merit and spoils very soon. The Chabag (Schabo) colony near Akkermann is an exception, where the colonist Tardent has by selection done well in wine-growing. At present wine-growing is carried out more, once again, and even in such colonies where, as has been mentioned, it was formerly not grown at all, as in the Beresan colonies, excellent wine is now being produced, especially in Sulz.

Stock-Farming

1) *Horse Breeding* Many colonists brought horses along from Germany to their new homeland. But these horses seem not to have been of a particularly good breed, for State-Councillor Kantenius was anxious to improve the breed of horses of the colonists. Later, a number of stallions of Friesian and Norman breed were purchased from the Mennonites, to improve the native breed. In addition, stallions were made available by the government at appointed places for improvement in breeding. Equally, Russian noblemen contributed a good deal in South Russia to the improvement of horse breeding, and have given the colonists opportunity to provide themselves with the improved breed of horses.

2) *Cattle Breeding* At the beginning, the German colonists, excepting the Mennonites, had cows of the Podol or steppe breed. Later on, the Dutch breed was acquired by individual colonists. On the Molotschna, Swiss cows were kept, and such ones of the Frisian breed which then, when blended, got the name "Molotschna Cattle." Subsequently there was introduced by the Mennonite Johann Kornies on his manor "Jushanlee," the breed ordered by Peter the Great from Holland, and later called the Cholmogor breed, and blended in with the native one. The crossing of this breed created an excellent, strong, muscular, large breed of cattle which is eagerly bought in annual fairs. In modern times the Hungarian breed of cattle has been introduced among the colonists.

3) *Sheep Breeding* Sheep breeding was introduced among the colonists right from the beginning. In all districts sheep farms were established and the authorities went to great pains to make sheep breeders of the colonists. But it was successful only with a few prudent colonists, such as with Fein and Kornies, both of whom became millionaires through sheep breeding. Mostly, the Merino sheep were kept; these furnished, to be sure, very little, but nevertheless fine and expensive, wool. At the present time, only the rich colonists still have flocks of sheep on their purchased estates, the district sheep farms due to shortage of grazing land having long since come to an end.

4) *Hog Breeding* Hog breeding is widespread among the German colonists, because they are very fond of pork products. There is hardly a well-to-do colonist's house where every day in the winter something of pork is not stewed or roasted, with the exception of fast-days among Catholics. Apart from the local breed, the English, and a few mixed-breed, hogs are at present being raised among the colonists.

In 1856 the following livestock were on hand in the German colonies in South Russia: 97,836 horses, 63,133 oxen, 46,299 cows, 929,965 sheep (among these the herds of Fein and other wealthy sheep breeders are not included), 275 stallions and 803 bulls.

The present livestock numbers in the colonies is, regretfully, unknown to me, because statistics are now estimated on an overall basis.

Trades, Industry and Commerce

Handicrafts thrive in many colonies, especially on the Molotschna and among the Mennonites, whose artisans are sought out far and wide. Today almost all machines and farm implements used by the colonists are constructed in the factories and workshops of the colonists. In 1855 the number of master craftsmen in the colonies amounted to 4,899, of which 385 were masons, 447 carpenters, 680 smiths, 43 lathe workers, 333 wheelwrights, 249 coopers, 38 weavers, 661 cobblers, 581 tailors, 48 saddlers, 62 locksmiths, 319 cabinet-makers, 7 pewterers, 4 bookbinders, 100 dyers, 247 millers, 30 potters, 115 welders, 8 coppersmiths, and 493 various other artisans. The value of the products of these artisans were estimated at 332,000 rubles per annum.

In 1855 there existed in the colonies 46 factories and 342 manufacturing workshops, most of which were in Mennonite districts. Within the count are included: 2 cloth factories, 35 fulling-mills, 41 dye works, 2 cheese factories, 2 brandy distilleries, 10 breweries, 19 vinegar works, 8 soap-boiling plants, 11 candle

94

factories, 90 oil mills, 79 grist mills, 11 brick works, 16 tile and shingle works, 12 lime kilns, 10 pottery factories, and 154 silk-reel works. The production value of these establishments amounted to 608,000 rubles. In the Russian report, from which these estimates are taken, it says, word for word: "Referring to the factory work and handwork, the excellence belongs among the peasantry of South Russia incontestably to the colonists, and among these, to the Mennonites in particular."

Commerce among the colonists was always but little developed, because they simply have no technical training. They left commerce to the Jews, and let themselves be cheated by them on every occasion. It seems, at present, that this nuisance is being comprehended in many places, and co-operative stores are being set up, which is very praiseworthy. In 1855 nine annual fairs and 362 ordinary market-places were permitted in the colonies, whose turnover averaged 300,000 rubles a year. The markets dealt, above all, with horses, horned cattle, wool, bacon, grain, wine, leather, pottery wares, farm implements, linen, dry goods and groceries.

There were 22 inns and six ordinary taverns.

The Agricultural Association

In order to encourage agriculture among the colonists, a number of presidents of the Welfare Committee gave all possible assistance. As a significant means to successful development and improvement of all branches of agriculture, the founding of the associations, which took place in 1851 in all colonial districts, was useful. The members of the district associations were chosen from those colonists who possessed the most knowledge and experience. In the isolated colonies, the duties of these associations were assigned to the village mayor's office.

Under the direction of these associations, in respect to agriculture, were 202 colonies. The useful influence of these associations became more evident with every passing year, since the various branches of agriculture evolved in the colonies more each year. In many places the results were successful and gave evidence of the skills and efficacy of many association members. But that was not universally the case. In numerous places these associations existed in name only, and the members came to the district office only to smoke their large Hungarian pipes. After the Welfare Committee was done away with, these associations also came to an end. The voice of these associations was the Unterhaltungsblatt für deutsche Ansiedler im südlichen Russland founded in 1845.

Ethnography of the German Colonists in South Russia

A. *Character*

As the German colonists in South Russia are representatives of all districts of great and noble Germania in their good and bad traits, their character can not be of one kind only. I shall therefore present only the general features. The German colonist is usually good-natured, honest and faithful, but only so long as he is not put to the crucial test. He is somewhat dull, mostly serious, seldom friendly and cheerful, generous in small matters, neat in many respects, not usually agreeable and hospitable to strangers. He is sensual, as is shown by his lewd language in conversation. He is proud, ambitious, boastful, vengeful, stingy and superstitious. That goes for the general run of the German colonists, but there are a great many notable exceptions.

Distinctive intellectual characteristics of the colonists are: keen understanding, sagacity, good memory and rather slow but intensive power of comprehension. Among the colonists the ability to learn foreign languages is rare, for the Russian language is mostly incorrectly pronounced by them, even if well learned in school. The German colonist is not much good at associating with foreigners, at which time his behaviour is mostly unnatural and awkward. He adapts himself easily among other peoples, but clings to his own home village with devotion, and strains toward the possibility of visiting his relatives and friends there, on his vacation each year.

The German colonist is courageous, valiant and able, and has a taste for order and discipline, which makes him an excellent and serviceable soldier, openly recognized as such by even the Russian officers. The general aspiration of the German colonists is directed more toward material than spiritual riches of life, for which reason school affairs are generally neglected by them. "Money and land" is the cure-all cry among most German colonists.

B. *Outward Appearances*

The German colonists are, in the main, a handsome and healthily built race of men. Those originating from Alsace and Baden generally have blond hair, those from Swabia and the Palatinate are dark.

Their complexion is mostly fair, with gray, less often blue, or black eyes, accompanied for the most part by regular features and often a sharply-defined profile. The forehead is seldom high, and the eyes are moderately large with heavy eyebrows. The noses of blondes are usually pointed, and of brunettes, flat; the mouth and the ears are rather large. The facial expression is serious, frequently indifferent, and among many, crafty. The neck generally is short, the chest stately and broad, and the arms strong and muscular. The torso is mostly long, with broad shoulders, the legs short but solid, strong, and somewhat bowed. Body stature is mostly moderate, and bearing, slovenly or unnatural. In former times the colonists were all clean shaven, but today many, especially Lutherans, wear beards and mustaches.

After the age of forty, many of the colonists tend toward corpulence, which is especially true of the women, among whom there are many individuals weighing eight to ten Pud (Pud = 40 pounds). Whatever this has to do with health, the fact remains that no race of people in South Russia measure up to the German colonists, for epidemic diseases are rare in the colonies. That is also a reason for the large number of children among the colonists, there being in Kleinliebenthal alone ten families, each having ten to twelve lively and healthy children.

C. *Clothing*

Men's clothing used to be what was brought along from the old country. Leather shoes with buckles for Sunday and wooden shoes for weekdays; trousers and vest with silvery buttons and the coat, were of blue cloth; the shirt with stand-up collar; a felt hat . . . often a stovepipe hat among the well-to-do, but among the less well-off a blue cap with long visor; those were the articles of clothing of our great-grandfathers. Nowadays things are different with the colonists. They dress stylishly today, like a gentleman, and if they really have no money, the Jewish merchant lends some to them until the next harvest. The dress of an affluent colonist usually includes a suit of finely woven fabric, fine linen, a white or colored straw hat, neat laced boots. The poorer ones must cut their coats according to the cloth and wear buckskin cloth and other cheap fabrics, instead of fine weave. In the winter the rich ones add an overcoat or wolf skin to the clothes named above, the poor a sheepskin.

Much more varied and abundant is the clothing of the women colonists. The shoes, stockings, chemises, skirts, jackets, and aprons of the women and girls are mostly in brightly colored stripes and of a single pattern, which, however, changes nearly every year. The material is different each year. The more moneyed wear clothes of silk and other expensive fabrics; the poorer ones usually buy cottons for clothing. The head cloths, even among those lacking means, are mostly of silk. Also, the girls (especially in the Beresan) are already starting to wear hats, and stylishly. In many colonies there are daughters of rich colonists who have sixty to seventy dresses in their wardrobes. Among the Catholic women and girls, silver or gold crosses and medallions are worn as necklaces.

D. *Dwellings*

Even at first glance the German colonies very advantageously distinguish themselves from of all the rest of the settled places in South Russia. The villages are compact, even though each house is adequately spaced from the adjoining one; mostly the buildings have retained the old-country form and appearance. If the little old crown-houses of clay, such as one still remaining in Kleinliebenthal, are compared to the massive, attractive colonists' stone houses of the present time, it must be acknowledged that the German colonists have made the greatest progress in this matter.

What greatly facilitates house-building by the colonists is the fortunate circumstance that in most of the colonial regions there are strata of good rock which can often be hewed to shape. The cut stones are used largely for wall corners and door-and-window openings. The most expensive material for a colonist's house is usually wood, which even yet is often transported a long distance.

Viewed from the outside, the colonist's house looks different; depending upon whether it faces the street with its front or its gable side. In the first case the main door is in the middle; and to the right and left side of it are two large windows with good clear panes, often of Bohemian glass. In the other case, the main entrance opens to the spacious yard; and the gable facing toward the street has two or three windows.

On the gable is the family coat-of-arms, with the house number and the family name.* Above the gable rises a stately roof of reeds or tile, which protects the house from wind and weather, and whose gable-ends are decorated with two heads of horses carved out of wood and mounted crosswise, facing each other. Every house is enclosed within a stone wall, behind which a row of attractive acacias is planted.

Upon entering the house, you step through a small anteroom directly into the kitchen. On both sides are the entrances into the living room. The main pieces of furniture of the colonist's house is the sometimes-open bed, more often concealed with curtains, in which the pillows and coverlets are not infrequently heaped up high, to the great pride of the housewife. In addition, there stands in the right-hand room, or front room, a large, massive table with a few chairs and benches, and a cupboard whose glass doors let you see cups, plates, spoons, all set up in an attractive arrangement.

*Many houses have so-called fire-gables too.

Farther on, a clothes-closet, a wall clock and a mirror, and on the wall a row of pictures of saints,** constitute the principal decoration of a colonist's house.

In the room to the left, also called the back room, are the beds for the children and domestic servants; and the furnishings of these are more scanty, and simpler than those in the front room.

E. *Foodstuffs*

The most important food of the colonists is baked bread of wheat or rye. Equally, the potato is everywhere an article of food among them. Foods made with flour among the colonists are mostly: dumplings, pinched noodles, cream noodles, sliced noodles, cheese noodles, cheese buttons, egg muffins and pancakes. Meat dishes are prepared with potato, sauerkraut and pork, roast pork, roast beef, roast veal, sausage, head cheese, and ham. Soups are boiled up with flour, rice, groats, beans, lentils, peas, and potatoes. Salad is made of various kinds of vegetables. There are also many and various milk diets, but I find it superfluous to enumerate all of these.

As far as is known to me, the colonists have taken to only three dishes of other peoples: borsht, plazinta, and mamaliga. In the summer many fruits are eaten, especially strawberries, melons, cucumbers, grapes, apples, pears and others.

Among the colonists the drinks are wine and less often beer; but they are much more fond of the Russian national drink, vodka. A good deal of Russian kvass is drunk in the summer, too. Likewise not a little tea and coffee are drunk in the colonists' homes. Nowadays a samovar is to be found in nearly every colonist's house, usually prepared in the evenings for all members of the family.

Information on the Contributions of the German Colonists of South Russia in the Russo-Turkish War of 1828

On the 14th of April, 1828, a manifesto of Emperor Nicholas I of Russia declared war on Turkey. An army of 130,000 Russians drew near the south in the spring of 1828, when all orders for the war's campaigns had already been decided upon. The Welfare Committee issued orders to all German colonists in the south to maintain a certain number of conveyances in readiness so that they could come into action at the first summons. On the 10th of February, 1828, there was a gathering in Grossliebenthal of all mayoral officials of the entire Liebenthal region. This meeting drew up the following resolutions:

**In Catholic homes.

1. "Every man must lay in a stock of whatever quantity of oats and barley is possible, and have at his disposal not less than 1 tschetwert of one of these.

2. "The Liebenthal district must supply 18 two-horse wagons, which must be ready at the first summons. Regarding the horses and wagons, the following is requested: The horses irrespective of color must be ordinary farm horses of this region; must be of strong constitution; must be shod on the front hoofs; must not be blind or have similar deficiencies and infirmities; must not be younger than four and not over eight years old; must be 2 arschine (1 arschine equals 28.0 inches) tall, or even a few werschock (1 werschock equals 1.75 inches) less. Collars and bridles must be of strong, untanned leather and be smeared with pure tar; the driving lines, side ropes and remaining ropes must be new hemp. The wagons must be similar to those typical of this region, strong and fit for carrying 1400-pound loads on a long journey. Along with each and every wagon is to be one large, or two small, untanned thick skins for covering of provisions. Both axles on the wagon must be covered with steel plate, and the wheel-hubs on all four wheels must be secured with iron.

The price of each horse is set at 70 rubles, the harness of each horse 5 rubles, and the skins for covering 8 rubles. The two-horse wagon, a grease cask and everything that goes with it is set at 20 rubles. For every wagon a driver is stipulated who should be of healthy constitution, but heights may vary. Drivers should be no younger than twenty-five and no older than forty-five years of age. Each driver, at his send-off, is to be presented with a sheepskin coat, a robe, a cap, a whip, three shirts and two pair of boots, by the community. All these articles of wearing apparel must be new. Also, every driver must be provided with provisions for fifteen days. If the vehicles travel to the assigned place without provisions loaded on, the community must provide each transport with 20 pud of hay for feeding the horses, free of charge.

His Majesty, the Emperor, has authorized the request of the Minister with regard to participation of the German colonists for general aid that may be needed in the case of troop movements and has been pleased to order:

1. That the collection of payments from the colonists is not to occur otherwise than under the sole charge of their colonial authorities.

2. That receipts for supplies and vehicles shall be issued to them through their authorities.

3. That the colonists be assured that they will be given credit through their taxes for the horses and wagons taken from them, according to rates set by the government.

4. That, in doing so, all oppressions and offences to the colonists shall be avoided, under pain of strict and certain punishments of the culprits.

The eighteen vehicles which the Liebenthal district was to furnish were apportioned as follows: Grossliebenthal, with 167 householders, furnished four and one-half vehicles; Kleinliebenthal, with 82 householders, two vehicles; Alexanderhilf, with 62 householders, one and one-half vehicles; Neuburg, with 60 householders, one and one-half vehicles; Marienthal, with 60 householders, one and one-half vehicles; Josephstal, with 68 householders, one and three quarter vehicles; Petersthal, with 61 householders, one and one-half vehicles; Freudenthal, with 78 householders, two vehicles; Franzfeld, with 43 householders, one vehicle; and Lustdorf, with 40 householders, one vehicle.

The mayoral officials were ordered to prepare as quickly as possible the needed wagons and supply of provisions, so that everything would be ready when asked for. On February 20, 1828, all vehicles were required to appear at the military review in Grossliebenthal, ready to go. The Kleinliebenthal colony paid out 485 rubles and 90 kopecks* for their two vehicles.

Contributions of the German Colonists in South Russia During the Crimean War, 1853-56

On the 2nd of March, 1855, Baron Mestmacher, the Chairman of the Welfare Committee, prepared the following decree:

"For prompt evacuation of the hospitals overfilled with patients in the Crimean peninsula, bases will be set up at various places at which a certain number of vehicles will be stationed to transport the patients from base to base to their final destination. The colonists are asked to supply this transportation because they have good horses and the most comfortable wagons. Having determined that 30 vehicles for this purpose are to be supplied by the Liebenthal district, the Welfare Committee proclaims the following:

1. These vehicles must be equipped without the least delay, and on each vehicle there must be a canvas covering on hoops for the protection of the patients against bad weather and heat.

2. With each group of vehicles an elder must be appointed, who is responsible for the arrangement as well as for the suitable maintenance of the vehicles.

3. These vehicles are assigned to the garrisons of the bases in the towns of Cherson and Berislav, according to needs; but for now they must be dispatched directly to Berislav.

*According to documents of the Kleinliebenthal Community, 1828, No. 16.

4. For a given vehicle with driver a monthly payment of 75 rubles is stipulated, with the stipulation that the colonists are responsible for the continuing durability of thirty vehicles.

5. After arriving at the spot, the vehicles come under the management of the hospital director with the duty of obeying the officers accompanying the transport of patients; but in all their emergencies they must apply to the Colonial Inspector, Tshernavsky, permanently stationed in Cherson, to whom the necessary mandates have been given."

The vehicles were outfitted and assigned, according to the population, to the colonies of the Liebenthal district; and as an inspector for them, an official committee member was chosen. Equipping two of the vehicles cost the Josephstal community 290 silver rubles.

Early in March, the vehicles with the sick aboard came to Odessa, and from there the caravan drove on the broad highway via Nikolaev to Cherson, arriving there on the 21st of March. In Cherson Inspector Tshernavsky introduced the entire transport, along with the drivers, to the Governor. The Governor appeared, gave friendly greetings, and after he had inspected everything and had deemed it good, he said: "Your conveyances are excellent, and everything is in order; I thank you!"

At the same time the Kutschurgan and Beresan colonists brought sick soldiers to Cherson on forty vehicles. The other German colonists also had to provide vehicles for the sick and provisions at this time. So for a whole month in all colonies near Odessa, biscuits were baked for the militia. It was a strenuous time for the German colonists. Scarcely a day passed without the bailiff bidding every father to some sort of free service, or another contribution to the military. In the Beresan colonies it came about that those who gave all the asked-for services and contributions during this frightful war were rewarded with a village landholding.

To complete the picture I am giving here the count of vehicles and services which the Josephstal colony on the Baraboi contributed in the war years 1854 and 1855: for militia passing through, 34 vehicles; for militia stationed at other locations, 404 vehicles; for the wounded and sick, 155 vehicles; for transporting heavy baggage, 67 vehicles; for transporting of provisions, 317 vehicles; for transportation of flour from which biscuits were baked in the colonies, 46 vehicles; for building materials and bridge-work, 238 vehicles, 365 workmen who were 28 days at work; and 1,769 lodgings with heating. Five hundred and eighty-two pud (23,280 pounds) of biscuit were baked in Josephstal. In addition, the

Josephstl district presented 60 pud (2,400 pounds) more of biscuit to the Crown.*

That the Russian government valued and prized the services and contributions of the German colonists, on the basis of merit, is quite clear from the list given below of the written commendations and rewards given to the colonists by the government.

The Very Highest Written Commendation to the German Colonists of the Chortitza, Mariupol, and Berdyansk Districts

"When the emperor learned from a report submitted to him that the Mennonite and Colonist communities of the Chortitza, Mariupol and Berdyansk districts had shown their devotion, in connection with the present war conditions, through money contributions and generous hospitality to wounded soldiers, by caring for these soldiers at community expense, His Majesty ordered that, to commemorate the exemplary zeal of these communities, they were to be rewarded in the name of the emperor through a special document which will serve forever as a record of their praiseworthy deeds.

In fulfillment of this highest wish, the Ministry of Imperial Domains sent to the Welfare Committee written statements of praise, No. 511 of the 26th of November, 1855, concerning the foreign settlers in South Russia. One was for the communities of the Chortitz Mennonites, one for those of the Mariupol Mennonites, a third for those of the Colonists of this district, and a fourth for those of the Berdyansk district. It was the intention to have these documents delivered to the district officials concerned for preservation and for publicity within the local district.

The original has as signatory: Minister of the Imperial Domains, Count Kisselev (St. Petersburg, November, 1856).

Name List of Those Colonists Who Were Commended Most Highly for Their Services in the Crimean War and Other Occasions

On the recommendation of the commanding officer of the former southern army, Prince Gortshakov, and subsequent presentation by the Minister of the Imperial Domains and approval of the Ministerial Council, His Majesty the Emperor has taken supreme pleasure in bestowing upon the following persons for zeal displayed in fulfillment of various wartime requirements, a silver medal with the inscription: "For Zeal."

*From the documents of Josephstal community archives 1855, No. 83.

To colonist Friedrich Fein of the Molotschna district; to district Mayor Christian Klassen of Mariupol district, to the assistant mayor of Molotschna, colonist Jacob Schefer of Prischib; to colonist Christian Glöckner of Wasserau; to colonist Nikolaus Haag of Rundewiese; to colonist Gottfried Stach of Grunau; to colonist Martin Glöckner of Prischib; to Mayor Johann Prieb of Hoffenthal; to colonist Jakob Hermin of Tiegenort; to colonist Michael Zerf of Göttland; to colonist Johann Findler of Ludwigsthal; to Mayor Johann Koch of Grunau; to colonist George Zeiger of Grunau; to Mayor Johann Schröder of Kronsdorf, to Mayor Konrad Masgold of Grosswerder; to Mayor Valentin Seib of Elisabethdorf; to colonist Johann Schmidt of Rosenberg; to Mayor Paul Haag of Rundewiese; to colonist Michael Maier of Rundewiese; to colonist David Pelz of Rosenberg; to the district Mayor of the Berdyansk colonial district, colonist Friedrich Meister of Rosenfeld; to colonist Konrad Kurtz of Rosenfeld; to colonist Johann Scheib of Neuhoffnung.

Commendatory letters were received by colonist Johann Fischer of Kaiserthal; colonist Adam Herth of Darmstadt; colonist Johann Zeller of Reichenfeld; and colonist Johann Zarnikel of Neumonthal. A golden tobacco-box, worth 100 rubles, was received by the Mennonite Johann Cornis of Orloff.

Gold watches valued at 150 rubles were received by: headmayor David Friesen of the Mennonite district of Molotschna, and Mennonite Johann Wiens of Altona, Mennonite Peter Wiebe of Tiegerweide, the head-mayor of Mariupol Mennonite district Jakob Peters, Mennonite Peter Unger of Bergthal, Mennonite Abraham Hobert of Schönthal, head-mayor M. Johann Siemens of the Chortitz district. A gold watch worth 100 rubles was received by Phillip Wiebe of Orloff.

Gold watches valued at 80 rubles were received by: Mennonite David Kornis of Orloff, Mennonite Johann Tews of Tiege, Mennonite Samuel Kleinsasser of Hutterthal, Mennonite Franz Klassen of Ladekop, Mennonite Abraham Tissen of Neuosterwick, mayor Abraham Neustädter of Einlage, mayor Abraham Dridger of Halbstadt, mayor Kornelius Lepp of Muntau, mayor Heinrich Teichgreb of Blumstem, mayor Christian Waldner of Hutterthal, secretary Wilhelm Penner of the Mennonite district of Chortitz, Mennonite Johann Neufeld of Halbstadt and Mennonite Heinrich Wilms of the same colony (The last two received watches worth 72 rubles). Gold Medals with the inscription"For Zeal" were received by: Head-Mayor and Freudenthal colonist Johann Kraus of the Liebenthal district, head-mayor Georg Biegler of Kutschurgan, head-mayor Christian Kirschmann of Glücksthal, head-mayor Christian Feigel of Sarata, assistant mayor Samuel Rossmann of the same district, mayor Jakob Bolle of Lustdorf, colonist Peter Black of Josephsthal and colonist Ignaz Fischer of Baden. A silver medal, inscribed with "For Zeal", was received by: colonists Adam Schnurr and Philipp Mantel of Zürichthal and colonists Jakob Walz and Matthaus Oelwein of Heilbrunn, as well as by colonist Joseph Wenster of Speier.

On 2 January, 1858, the colonists of the Swedish district received a most gracious letter of thanks for services in the Crimean War; and the head-mayor of this district, Gottfried Werle, received a medal with the inscription "For Zeal". For wartime services colonists Ignaz Kass and Adam Jordan of Rastadt received the most exalted thanks.

In recognition of the services of the Landau colonist, Johann Dukart, in the matter of distributing preserved smallpox vaccine, he was rewarded with the silver medal by the exalted decree of 4 September, 1856.

On the Presence of Colonial Deputies at the Solemn Coronation of Emperor Alexander II in Moscow

Through an ordinance of the 7th of July, 1856, the Welfare Committee informed the German colonists subordinate to it, that from their midst representatives were most graciously summoned to the solemn coronation of their Imperial Majesties in Moscow; and designated as such the head-mayors, Johann Kraus from Liebenthal, David Friesen of the Molotschna Mennonites, and Maichaila Malina of Bolgrad.

Right after the arrival in Moscow, these deputies had the honor of being introduced personally, on July 29, to the Director of the Moscow Imperial Area, Mr. Wishneffsky, who looked after them throughout their stay.

On August 13, the presentation of the assembled deputies from the village communities took place before the Minister of the Imperial Domains, Count Kisselev. On this occasion, the Minister expressed his thanks in particular to the German settlers in South Russia for the regular discharge of duties, as well as for the perseverance and devotion during the last war, adding to his thanks the meaningful words: "His Majesty, Emperor Nicholas, reposing in God, thought about you before his end, and said he lacked words enough to express to you his thanks for your services."

On August 26, on the coronation day of their Majesties, so highly important for all Russia, the head-mayors, as representatives of the German settlers, formed the first row of persons chosen in conformity with the highest established coronation ceremonial.

The next day it fell to the great good fortune of the assembled community deputies to be introduced personally to the Emperor and Empress in the Andrew Hall of the Kremlin. In the course of this introduction Their Imperial Majesties by questions directed at individual deputies showed their exalted interest in even the most humble of their subjects.

The gracious reception closed with the words of the Emperor, unforgettable to all dwellers in the country: "Accept commendation. I thank you sincerely for your devotion and zeal; you have given proof of both, particularly during the period of the last war. I am convinced that you will demonstrate to me your future loyalty. Pray to God that He will stand by me and my toils, and I shall pray for you. Convey this to your colleagues: and to all Crown farmers and colonists."

On September 1, the assembled deputies of the rural communities were presented to Her Majesty, the Empress-Mother, and were received with affable generosity. A similarly gracious reception occurred on the same day in the presence of Grand-Duchess Helena Pavlovna and Grand-Duke Constantine Nikolaevitch. Likewise there took place on the same day in the Hall of Justice the ceremonious presentation of gold and silver medals to the assembled head-mayors and district elders, on which occasion mayor Kraus was honored with a gold Vladimir stripe, Malina with a silver medal on a neck ribbon and Friesen with a silver medal cast expressly for the occasion of the coronation.

On the 6th of September all the village deputies of the colonies were granted a 4-day leave for a trip to St. Petersburg, where they had the rare fortune of seeing and wondering at all the sights of this beautiful capital with their own eyes, including the Imperial Villas of Zarskoje-Selo, Peterhof, Oranienbaum and the vast sea fortress, Kronstadt.

On the 11 September the deputies of the colonies, along with the other district elders, found themselves in one of the salons of the Kremlin, at an Imperial mid-day meal. When designated places had been shown to them, His Imperial Majesty, accompanied by the Grand-Duke Nikolai Nikolaievitch, entered the room and proposed a standing toast to the health of his loyal subjects. The assembled deputies of the rural communities replied to the good wishes with a triple hearty "Hurrah", whereupon His Majesty and the Grand-Duke left again and all deputies sat down. In the course of the noon dinner, a similar triple hearty "Hurrah" followed the toast of the President to the health of the newly-crowned Emperor.

With this festive reception the brilliant series of Imperial acts of graciousness came to a close and the deputies of the rural communities returned to the circle of their colleagues and their professional businesses, deeply touched by the gracious reception of the noble monarch. So may the remembrance of the colonial deputation about these great festive days, remain an unforgettable memorial for the most distant descendants of the German colonists in South Russia.

(From the Reports of the head-mayors Kraus
and Friesen)

THE GERMAN COLONIES IN SOUTH RUSSIA
SECOND PART

The Liebenthal
Colony District

"We should know everything that our forefathers did, so that we may unerringly learn the truth". Oppius

Through imperial decree of 17 October 1803, Count Richelieu was permitted to buy land in the Odessa region, upon which to settle German Colonists. In the neighbourhood of Odessa there were two good estates owned by Count Vinzenz Potozsky and General Kislinksy. The total land in these estates amounted to 17,835 dessatine. Just to the west of this there was some additional good land owned by the noble Knjaschewitsch, amounting to 8000 dessatine. Richelieu bought these three estates to settle the Liebenthal colonists thereon. Since this amount of land was not enough he took 8000 dessatine from the Russians at Majaki, Galiklei and Belaewka and made up the deficiency with crown land. The land of the district extended from the colony of Lustdorf on the Black Sea as far as Franzfeld on the Dniester. It is for the most part level, with the exception of the areas through which the rivers Dalnek, Little-Akerscha, Big-Akerscha and Baraboi pass. These run from a northerly to a southerly direction.

MAP showing the LIEBENTHAL COLONIES near ODESSA

The land under cultivation is quite productive, the surface soil for the most part being composed of black earth (humus).

At this point I had intended to describe briefly the industrial development of the Liebenthal colonists during their first years of settlement, but the documents of the archives of the Liebenthal districts were not placed at my disposal. I will give instead a summary of the account of the above named districts as contained in the Welfare Committee report in the year 1859, according to Dr. W. Hamm's newspaper printed in 1860.

The General State Of Affairs

The Liebenthal district consists of eleven colonies, of which seven profess the Protestant faith and four the Roman Catholic. . . . In these eleven colonies there are 811 full landholdings, but 1527 families. There are 6108 males and 5954 females, totaling 12,062. In 1858, births were: 271 males and 274 females, totalling 545. Deaths were: 132 males and 134 females, a total of 266.

The state of health of the settlers for the year was a satisfactory one, except for the first and the last months. In the first months a rather general whooping-cough prevailed and in the two last months of the year there appeared the present-day hoarse cough, or croup, in various colonies and families; the victims who succumbed to this illness were not very numerous. Epidemic or other significant illnesses were not prevalent. Looked at in individual departments, the following results stand out in the Liebenthal district, which give a brief picture of the state of this district as of 1 January, 1859.

Territories

The settlers of the Liebenthal district used the following land areas as of 1 January, 1859:

1) Crown lands:
   a) houses and yards, 486 dessatine at 4 morgen per lot
   b) Church and parish land, 480 dessatine
   c) Garden land, 1342 dessatine
   d) Vineyard land, 953 dessatine 406 faden
   e) Agricultural land 18,017 dessatine 1473 faden
   f) Hayfields, 6906 dessatine 1404 faden
   g) Pasture-land, 12,500 dessatine 53 faden
   h) Roads and embankments, 2013 dessatine 177 faden
   i) Forest lands, 408 dessatine

Total: 43,105¾

2) Private land owned by colonists:
   a) Agricultural land, 16,506 dessatine
   b) Woodland, 32½ dessatine
   c) Sheep ranch belonging to the entire district, 537 dessatine

   Total: 17075½ dessatines.

3) Additionally, the colonists rent 27,740 dessatines of land from various country dwellers and estate owners, for which they pay 78,211.95 rubles annually.

All in all, the colonists make use of 87,921¼ dessatines. The prices for rentable land are increasing each year, so that it is becoming very difficult for the poor people to afford the high rents. Only at a great distance from this district is land to be rented at moderate prices, but near the colony, the high rent nearly nullifies the benefit which the farmer could realize. For these reasons, agriculture will become limited in the future.

Fees and Taxes

In fees, Crown debts and community taxes the Liebenthal district in 1858 had to pay: 1) Crown fees, 19,919.18 rubles. 2) Land assessment, 3,610.405 rubles. 3) Administrative taxes for the colony, 1,200.96 rubles. 4) Crown debts, 5671.43 rubles. Total 30,401.98 rubles.

Community taxes assessed were

1) For the clergy, 899.89 rubles. 2) For the support of the Government Inspection Office, 142.73 rubles. 3) For the salaries of the district mayor and councillors, 244.9 rubles. 4) For the salaries of the village mayors, 368.20 rubles. 5) For the district secretary, 521.93 rubles. 6) For the community clerks, 1,562.385 rubles. 7) For the district office messengers, 608.51 rubles. 8) For the bailiffs, field and forest rangers, 1,078.155 rubles. 9) for the herdsmen, 6,344.10 rubles. 10) For the schoolteachers, 2,094.305 rubles. 11) For improvement in cattle breeding, 173.325 rubles. 12) For insurance of houses in the fire-insurance office, 2,026.325 rubles. 13) For repayment of debt of the Josephsthal fire-insurance office, 305.51 rubles. 14) For maintenance of community buildings, 117.52 rubles. 15) For assistance to a fire casualty in Güldendorf, 100 rubles. Altogether, 16,581.9875 rubles. Not only were all taxes and fees paid without arrears, but, on auditing of fees for 1859, they were paid in advance by 4,836.1725 rubles. In this respect the Liebenthal district will scarcely trail behind the best German settlements.

Items Rented and Revenue Therefrom

1) The revenue from items that are rented out came in regularly during the year 1858. In addition to the community items mentioned below, there are 7 items rented out. These should have brought a revenue of 3276.82 rubles, but brought only 2475.90 rubles, because the lease renewals for the fishing rights in the Dniester near Franzfeld and in the Sea at Lustdorf only come due in 1859.

2) In the year 1858 there were 28 items rented out which are under the economic administration of the mayoral offices. In the course of the year 2 of these were cancelled, leaving only 26 items for the year 1859.

The two rent items: the fishing in the dam at Peterstal and the restaurant at Peterstal had to be abandoned, because during the year 1858 no one came forward to rent them. The items rented out in 1858 brought a revenue of 1767.90 rubles. All rents were received regularly and were used for the purposes for which they were intended.

Orphans and Guardianships

On the 1st of January, 1859, there were in the Liebenthal district 286 guardianships for under-age orphans and 19 for delinquents and for bankrupts: a total of 305. These guardianships are for 657 orphans of both sexes and for 19 delinquents and bankrupts, a total of 676 persons. The orphans of the Liebenthal district as at the 1st January, 1859, owned the following property: (a) in notes of credit institutions 2000 rubles; (b) in the community orphans' bank and in the hands of private individuals in Güldendorf 111,640.28 rubles; and (c) other property in the colonies worth 40,105.03 rubles, a total of 153,745.31 rubles. On the average therefore each orphan owns 242.60 rubles. This sum is obviously not very large, but is nevertheless significant. Viewed in itself it is not large, but, considering the fact that there is probably not that much for every other person in the district, it is a significant sum. In looking after its orphans and their property the Liebenthal district behaves in a way that compares favorably with any other area and probably no other district can show better results for its orphans.

The Liebenthal district has a community orphans' bank, which is administered by two men, elected for life, who enjoy universal trust. Every bit of the orphans' money must be deposited in this bank, and accumulates in this place at 5½% compound interest. No orphan can rightfully claim to have been wronged by even a kopeck in this bank, as long as the orphans' money has existed. On the contrary, every fund in it is administered with care, and watched over so that in due time it can be refunded to the orphans with accumulated interest. As soon as an orphan comes of age, he receives his money in full immediately on his first request.

If instead the money is administered by a trustee, satisfaction for the orphans concerned cannot accrue so promptly, for in case the guardian to whom the money is entrusted wants to increase it, he can do none other than lend it to private individuals, with the result that he cannot demand its return at just any time at all, but has to await the time-limit of the loan. This means that either the orphan must wait for his money, or the money must wait for the orphan, whereby in either event there is disadvantage to the orphan. This is not true of the Liebenthal orphans' bank. It always pays out cash on first demand, and the deposits in it are as secure as anywhere. Rightfully, therefore, this institution will and must be looked upon as a true benefit for the settlers of this district.

Savings Bank

Closely allied to the orphans' bank is the community savings bank of the Liebenthal district. As the orphans' bank is beneficial to the orphans, so too is the savings bank a benefit to the better-off class of the people of the district. There, any colonist can safely deposit his larger or smaller funds, and just as with the orphans' funds, these too are secure, bearing 5% annually. Neither the deposit nor the withdrawal of such funds is limited. This bank enjoys so great a confidence among the settlers of the Liebenthal district that the colonists would just as soon deposit their funds in it as in the Odessa office of The Imperial Bank of Commerce. This bank possesses the sum of 62,526.5725 rubles, adequately demonstrating that the settlers know their savings are safe in this bank.

Through the orphans' and the savings bank, things are adequately looked after for the orphans and the well-to-do, but it is fair to ask, "Why not for others too?" To this the answer is given by the following.

Although the rural lending-bank does not yet exist by that name in the Liebenthal district, it does exist in fact and reality. The funds of the orphans' and the savings-bank must not lie idle if they are not to be harmful to the banks, and are consequently loaned out at a fixed rate of 6%.

For instance, as soon as a colonist comes to the point of needing some capital for furtherance of his agriculture or his trade, or for both, he has access at once to the lending-bank, fully knowing that he does not have to pay exorbitant interest there and is not going to be cheated.

Certainly, no colonist can receive a loan from the bank without permission of, and agreement with, his local mayor's office; but as soon as he is recognized as reliable by this office (and) produces two trustworthy warrantors for the desired loan, a promissory note printed for this purpose is presented to him for his and his warrantors' signatures. Once this is signed and witnessed by the mayor's office, it is sent to the lending-bank from which the loan, in its turn, is sent back to the mayoral office for issuing to the one concerned.

Because of this measure it becomes possible for the person without means to rise, and for the person with means to increase his wealth. Every one is benefited, no one has to fear falling into the hands of a usurer and having to pay exorbitant interest. On the contrary, each one knows just what to expect. To be sure, it is true that the man who incurs no debts has none to repay, and every uninitiated one will say that what is said here may all be well and good except for the catch, and that is that the repayment can ruin the debtor. This is true: he who incurs debts and does not want to go bankrupt must pay for them; and such people who like to borrow and not to repay cannot partake of the benefit of assistance in a money emergency.

But no one will be ruined by repayment of loans, and indeed, nobody has been. The reimbursements do not take place in accordance with a previously-set time limit, but are paid entirely according to business and circumstances. Rule 1) is that: No debt may become larger than it was; hence the running 6 per cent must be paid annually. 2) Apart from this interest, no other payment is required in the event of crop failure or other adverse fates affecting the settlers. But with good growing years and copious harvests, 6 to 10 per cent is retired from the capital debt annually, so that it decreases year by year and will ultimately come to an end. The debtor remains free to pay his debt at any time, partially or in full. So, through the orphans' bank, the property of orphans is safely administered; through the savings bank the surplus capital of the well-to-do is safely invested; and through both the whole district is provided with the means of increasing its prosperity through loans at reasonable rates of interest. In this way, these banks work together, hand in hand, one supporting and assisting the other, uniting us all and making us strong.

From what has been said up to now, it can be seen that the bank pays 5½ per cent annually to the orphans and 5 per cent to the wealthy, but collects 6 per cent from debtors. About this, it should be said that both from the orphans' funds as well as from the funds invested in the savings bank, one-half of 1 per cent is applied to administrative expenses in the form of salary for the accountants. The half per cent remaining from the capital of the savings bank is devoted to a fund against possible bank losses.

This reserve fund, on January 1, 1859, amounted to: (a) 278 rubles in notes of credit institutions; (b) 722.96 rubles in cash; (c) 2013 rubles invested at interest in the savings bank. The total was 3014.16 rubles.

Religious Census

On 1 January, 1859, the Liebenthal district numbers, in all, 12,063 souls: 6,109 males, 5,954 females.

a) Greek-Russian religion:	49 males,	84 females	Total	133
b) Evangelical-Lutheran:	4,059 males,	3,882 females.	Total	7,041
c) Evangelical-Reformed:	215 males,	208 females.	Total	423
d) Roman Catholics:	1,786 males,	1,780 females.	Total	3,566
			Total	12,063

The Liebenthal district has only three churches and six chapels, and in the colonies of Lustdorf and Güldendorf, the church service is held in the schoolhouses. At the present time there are five parishes here, all except Franzfeld being provided with clergy.

The Gross-Liebenthal parish is the largest and most populous, and as of January, 1859, counts 4,563 souls. The colonies of Lustdorf and Güldendorf are counted in with the Odessa Evangelical-Lutheran parish.

The churches and chapels are in good condition, except for the church in Josephsthal. This one was completely dismantled by eccleciastic order. The community of Josephsthal has intended for a good many years to build a new church which, until now, could not be started because of insufficient means. Also, the community of Lustdorf is planning to build a church. In this colony the means are more adequate so that it may be possible to start and to complete the building with the aid of a small loan.

Schools

On 1 January, 1859, every colony had its own school building. The classrooms in the Grossliebenthal and Freudenthal colonies are spacious and in good condition. In Grossliebenthal there are three classrooms and in Freudenthal, two and additionally, partitioned-off living quarters for the teachers.

The number of pupils includes 977 boys and 954 girls, totalling 1,931. In 1858 there graduated from the schools at the end of the course of instruction: 86 boys and 125 girls, totalling 211.

In 1858 there were rewarded:

a) with books: 49 boys, 82 girls, total. 131
b) with commendatory letters: 136 boys and 172 girls. 308

In all 439

The pupils' attendance in schools in compulsory and absence from school is subject to fine stipulated in school regulations, the money being remitted to the school bank for providing help to the support of instruction. In all the schools there are appointed: 11 teachers, 4 assistants; 15 in all.

An unsatisfactory situation prevails in the schools. The Catholics are permitted to leave school too early and the Protestants have to stay too long. Particularly it should be seen to that girls do not have to attend school beyond the age of 14. The Catholic young people should be induced to attend school longer so as to become at least a little more educated. However, the district office can not deal with the matter because it has too little information about the inner organization of the schools. Some years ago the district office was prevailed upon to visit the schools repeatedly, in conformity with various invitations. But from this came no sort of regulations at all, apart from recommending cleanliness to dirty children and exhorting all pupils to be obedient to their teachers and to strive to make themselves agreeable to them and (be) deserving. The result of this was a complaint by different clergymen against the intrusion of the civic authorities into their own prerogatives. In order not to come into dissension with the worthy clergy no further visits have been made and hence it is not known which measures the clergy enacted for improvement of the schools, or are going to enact. Only so much is known, that the teachers in the Protestant schools are to be made over into sextons, the reason for which is easy to understand.

School Property

The eleven schools of the Liebenthal district own:

a) Books: 349 readers, 1763 writing books, 32 religious books, 4 arithmetics, 33 books for teachers' use, 255 books for sale.

b) Teaching aids: 537 slates, 9 abaci.

c) Furnishings: 26 blackboards, 278 tables with seats, 8 bookcases, 13 chairs.

The teachers are paid from community taxes and other community revenue. 2094.30 rubles were used for this purpose. The fuel needed for heating the classrooms and living quarters of the teachers is contributed in kind by the communities.

House Construction

In the colonies of the Liebental district there are the following buildings:

1) Colonist houses: of stone 1262, rammed earth 67, adobe huts 33, total 1362, which is 40 houses more than in 1857.

2) Community buildings there are 44, apart from churches and prayer halls.

With regard to house building remarkable progress was made in 1858. No only were 40 new houses built, but a significant number of older houses were repaired and rebuilt. The new construction was not only done in an orderly way, but was according to plan and purpose, so that the colonies, where they are not handicapped by the site chosen at their founding, are presenting an ever better and more attractive appearance, until they reach the goal that was intended for them. Only in the matter of mayoral office buildings is there still much to be desired. But there is hope even here that a change will come and that suitable accommodation will be constructed. The parsonages, in all colonies in which they exist, are all well-planned and well-built.

Accidents

In 1858 there occurred in the Liebenthal district:

a) Five fires. Five colonist houses burned down, causing damage amounting to 3254.98 rubles, which is 2479.76 rubles more than in 1857. The fire victims were compensated with 2804.98 rubles from the fire insurance fund of the Liebenthal district. A fire victim in Güldendorf received 100 rubles from that village's community funds, making a total of 2904.98 rubles compensation. Those in the old colonies of the Liebenthal district who were burned out were compensated for the entire damage they suffered, but the Güldendorf victim received only 100 rubles from local community funds, because that community is not as yet a participant in the joint fire insurance fund.

b) Six persons died through various accidents, two of them being children from Mariental. Two were killed in accidents due to fast driving, one child died as a result of its clothes catching fire, a woman lost her life as a result of a cave-in in a sand pit, and a Josephstal colonist lost his life as a result of a fight. In all, four males and two females died.

Community Granaries, Grain Supplies, Supply of Capital

There are community granaries in the Liebenthal district, one in each colony, but only three of them built according to plan. The rest are actually in very poor shape. Special attention has to be given to those in Kleinliebethal, Mariental, Josephstal and Güldendorf. These are in the worst condition and larger and roomier ones are needed. Kleinliebenthal and Güldendorf have petitioned for permission to build new granaries and the Liebenthal district office has made a proposal on the matter to the Welfare Committee, but as yet has not received a decision. Peterstal already has a small amount of capital for this purpose and will soon begin the building of a granary. For Mariental and Josephstal the solution of this problem appears to be pushed into the background more than ever. Mariental is too poor to be able to build on its own and Josephstal is planning to build a church, as already mentioned, and if this happens a granary can not be undertaken for a long time to come.

The supply of grain found in the community granaries on 1 January 1859: winter grain 2734 tschetwert,* summer grain 3737 tschwtwert, a total of 6471 tschetwert. The supply of grain had increased in 1858 due to good crops in some colonies and the per capita contribution by a total of 730 tschetwert. There was sold during the year from the grain supply in Peterstal 80 tschetwert of winter grain and 200 tschetwert of summer grain for the sum of 848.37 rubles.

The following communities own the capital sums indicated: Grossliebenthal 5254 rubles, Kleinliebental 2382.25 rubles, Alexanderhilf 135 rubles, Neuburg 373.79 rubles, Mariental 315 rubles, Peterstal 1262.12 rubles, Freudental 881.15 rubles, Franzfeld 972.36 rubles, Lustdorf 534.17 rubles, Güldendorf 1797.56 rubles, a total of 13,907.40 rubles.

The reserve capital of Neuburg has been deposited with the Welfare Committee at compound interest, but that of Freudental and Mariental is kept in the savings bank of the Liebenthal community.

As late as ten years ago there were no significant amounts of grain in reserve and now all reserve stocks are fairly full. A significant reserve of capital is also on hand — a fresh demonstration of progress.

Doctors, Hospitals and Smallpox Vaccination

There are no formally appointed physicians in the Liebenthal district. This is an obvious deficiency. As yet the district government sees no way to help this.

*1 tschetwert = 10 pud = 360 lbs. Can. = 6 bu. (for wheat).

There are two hospitals in the Liebenthal district, the previously mentioned hydropathic establishments in Gross- and Kleinliebenthal.

In 1858 there were in the Liebenthal district 152 colonists' children who had not yet been inoculated against smallpox. Through births in 1858, another 550 were added, making the total 702. Of these, 552 were inoculated in 1858, leaving 150 children without inoculation for 1959: 18 because of illness, 34 because they were not yet of suitable age, 24 because of death right after birth, and 74 because of absence of the inoculator. Most of the non-inoculated children are in Mariental, Freudental and Güldendorf. In the first two of these colonies the Odessa inoculator Versebe has been given the job, but in Güldendorf no particular persons have been appointed. In 1858 the district paid out 92.1 rubles for inoculations.

Sowing and Crops

In 1858 the following was sown:

a)	Winter grain	4,599	tschetwert on 8,766 dessatine
b)	Summer grain	14,780 3/8	tschetwert on 23,401 dessatine
	Total	19,379 3/8	tschetwert on 32,167 dessatine

This was more than in 1857 by the following amounts:

a)	Winter grain	2,918 7/8	tschetwert on 5,759 dessatine
b)	Summer grain	1,146 2/8	tschetwert on 4,441 dessatine
	Total	4,065 1/8	tschetwert on 10,200 dessatine

Harvested in 1858 were:

Winter grain	10,394	tschetwert
Summer grain	78,771	tschetwert
Total	89,065	tschetwert

On the average, harvest results were: From the winter grain, 2 3/10; from the summer grain, 5 3/10. More winter grain was harvested in 1858 than in 1857, but summer grain was 47,251 ½ tschetwert less. From the whole harvest there is 7 2/6 tschetwert for every person in the district.

In 1858 up to 623 dessatine of grain were damaged by bad weather: 60 tschetwert of winter grain and 2,945 tschetwert of summer grain, a total of 3,005 tschetwert, worth 12,500 rubles. Of the entire crop, 36,307 tschetwert were sold for the sum of 158,192 rubles. Although in 1858 a far greater seeding was arranged than in 1857, the success of the harvest was, nevertheless, far more limited. As the cause of this decrease, only the unfavorable weather can be considered. This is to say, there was a lack of rain as is frequently the case in this region, unfortunately, and of course at the very time when it was needed the most.

Cultivation of Potatoes and Vegetables

In 1858, on 1491 dessatine, 5,040½ tschetwert of potatoes were planted, 76 6/8 tschetwert less than in 1857, yielding 12,770 tschetwert, 3,159 tschetwert less than in 1857. Three-quarter tschetwert of millet was sown in 1858 on 3 dessatine, yielding 19 tschetwert; 62 tschetwert of maize were seeded on 402 dessatine, and yielded 2,030 tschetwert. On the whole the yield of garden vegetables in 1858 was less than in 1857. Vegetable gardening is important only in Kleinliebenthal, Lustdorf and Güldendorf. It is mostly highly developed in Kleinliebenthal, where it is a source of considerable revenue. In places where water is in short supply, growing vegetables is very difficult. If the place in question is also remote from a market, then it is not worth while. For this reason in most other colonies vegetables are grown only for home use.

From the sale of potatoes and of vegetables the colonies had an income, in 1858, of 10,463 rubles.

Crop of Hay and Straw

In 1858, 415,670 pud of hay were gathered, 36,270 pud more than in 1857. Straw gathered amounted to 598,472 pud, which was 30,943 more than in 1857. From the sale of the hay and straw, the colonists had an income of 5,885 rubles. Feed for cattle was consequently harvested in a more abundant way, so that there was no lack of it, but even a surplus.

General Economic Situation

1) The settlers of the Liebenthal district had, on January 1, 1859: 1,563 plows, 2,918 harrows, 2,613 vehicles, 80 stone rollers.

2) Among the 811 land-owning families on the 1st of January, 1859, 692 owned more than four head of draught-animals; 86 of them owned four head; and 33 owned fewer.

3) Industrial concerns that can be found in the colonies of the Liebenthal district are: 2 potteries, 7 oil mills, 4 weaver's looms, 1 lime kiln, 47 windmills, and 5 horse-powered mills. In all these concerns 66 persons are employed, whose income in 1858 reached 6,000 rubles.

4) Of families engaged in handicrafts and trades there are 432. Artisans to be found are: 16 carpenters, 38 cabinet-makers, 9 coopers, 37 cart-wrights, 7 tanners, 2 potters, 2 weavers, 24

butchers, 58 blacksmiths, 35 millers, 22 masons, 2 coppersmiths, 3 harness-makers, 11 bakers, 4 confectioners, 32 locksmiths, 3 soap-boilers, 15 shepherds, 2 glaziers, 27 gardeners, 2 bookbinders, 7 oil-millers, 7 wood-turners, 3 sieve-makers, 80 shoemakers, and 22 tailors. In 1858, articles made by these artisans had a value of approximately 39,132 rubles—422 rubles more than in 1857.

The artisans in the Liebenthal district have already exercised a significant influence upon their neighbors, the remaining inhabitants. In the adjacent Crown villages, the German colonist's wagon is becoming indigenous. The better-off class of Crown farmers must, so it seems, have reached the view that horses and a wagon with iron axles are worth more to the farmer than oxen and a wagon on which there is not enough iron to be able to make even a single nail. The plow devised by the Freudenthal colonist, Konrad Bechtold, and now named after him, is finding widespread use, and for a long time has been popular among people near and far, both Russians and Germans; experience has taught that this plow is the most practical one for the farmer of South Russia.

The German artisans of the Molotschna (in the Tauric province) have long been famous and not infrequently have been recommended as an example to the tradesmen of the Liebenthal district. In the past year, 1858, however, a considerable number of Bechtold plows have been dispatched to the Molotschna. In other branches of trade, too, the colonists have furnished a good example and have thereby fulfilled the purpose of their calling.

Breeding of Cattle and Sheep

1) As of January 1, 1859, the colonists of the Liebenthal district own:

a) Draught-animals: 6636 horses, 365 more than in 1857; 177 oxen, 55 more than in 1857.

b) Animals for direct profit: 6682 cows, 211 more than in 1857; 5253 sheep, 230 fewer than in 1857; 1555 hogs, 291 more than in 1857.

And so there are found, on the whole, 815 head more than in 1857.

This might be a good sign. However, it is to be observed that draught-animals have increased the most, and this is due to the fact that the cultivation of fields in 1857 has increased. But cattle breeding in the Liebenthal district can no longer expand very much, since pasture land is no longer adequate for doing so. Grain-farming is gaining in area every year, and cattle-breeding must therefore be curtailed. Sheep-breeding cannot be carried on in the colonies of the Liebenthal district. Those colonists of the

Freudenthal and Güldendorf colonies, who do significant sheep-raising, do it on rented land.

2) Community draught-animals include: 17 stallions, 61 bulls.

With respect to improvement of the communal draught-animals, a few small curtailments were made in recent years; which, however, are now lifted, and significant grants of money are being allowed to the local officials.

3) In 1858, livestock died: 188 horses, 454 horned cattle, 208 sheep, 66 hogs; 916 in all. There was foot-and-mouth disease in the colony of Alexanderhilf in 1858, but not much livestock succumbed.

4) In 1858 the colonists had an income from their cattle-breeding totalling:

a) 18,191.10 rubles for butter and cheese sold.

b) 128 rubles for ham sold.

c) 3794 rubles for wool.

Total: 22,113.10 rubles.

The little wool that is sold in the Liebenthal district is paid for in sweat.

Forestry and Horticulture

1) *Forestry* In the colonies of the Liebenthal district there are 13 forest plantations, and in these as of the 1st of January, 1859, the trees are:

a) In the plantations, 270,387 forest trees and 18,566 mulberry trees.

b) In growing hedges, 23,164 mulberry trees and 26,264 other forest plantings.

c) In the tree and plant nurseries, 460,031 forest trees and 16,211 mulberry trees.

Total: 824,623

In 1858 the following trees were set out: 10,351 forest trees and 2,064 mulberry trees.

2) *Horticulture* As of January 1, 1859, there are 624 colonists' orchards. Fruit trees in these: 60,301 bearing, 12,809 non-bearing, 32,521 cultivated ones, 19,178 wild ones.

Total: 124,809

In 1858, 3,733 fruit trees were planted and 325 were improved.

3) *Wine-growing* In the colonies of the Liebenthal district there are, as of January 1, 1859, some 787 vineyards and 2,160,646 vines in them. In 1858, 4,400 vines were planted. In the same year, 6,203 pails of wine (17 bottles each) were prepared, and of these, 2,278 pails were sold for 88 kopecks per pail.

Relative to forestry, horticulture and wine-growing, only very little took place in the Liebenthal district during 1858. The agricultural association set a poor example, or, better said, none at all. In the past years the war stood hinderingly in the way, and so a great deal is to be done in this regard. Since another president is to be elected for the agricultural association, it is to be expected that something more will happen of concern to forestry, horticulture, and wine-growing than was hitherto the case.

Litigation

In 1858, litigation came up for settlement before the officials:
a) 105 to the district court;
b) 128 to the mayoral courts.
Total: 233
Of these, 229 were settled, and four were committed to decision by higher authority.
In 1858, colonists were sentenced:
a) In the district court: 80 males, 3 females; 83 in all.
b) In the mayoral courts: 688 males, 16 females; 704 in all.
Total: 787
Punishments by the courts of justice were undertaken.
a) Fines: 551 males, 7 females; 558 in all.
b) Punishments with communal work: 55 males, 6 females; 61 in all.
c) Penal arrests: 36 males, 3 females; 39 in all.
d) Penal flogging: 46 males.
Total: 704

Summary

What has been said thus far gives an indication of all that the Liebenthal district had to show for the year 1858. To sum up, if we now observe the whole again, two very different things appear before our eyes. First, that the settlers of this district already have many a good thing to show, but that they are lacking in others. The Liebenthal district was, years ago (indeed, not so many years ago), a sinful district. The inhabitants liked nothing better than expensive, time-and-health-robbing pursuits. Heavy drinking was common; eight-day church festivals and three to four-day wedding and christening celebrations were the order of the day.

This is changed; indeed it has already progressed so far that these disorders have ended. It is so far along that the communities have decided in favor of having anyone publicly punished who gets intoxicated in a tavern. In offices, in which dawdling was previously common, and not infrequently coupled with injustices, order and rectitude have taken over. Churches and schools are attended; clergymen and teachers are honored because they deserve to be; whoever does not qualify has only himself to blame. And so we can say it has become better: better in morality; better in civilization; better in church and school; better in upbringing of children; and hence, better also in well-being.

But whatever was bad and became better, is not yet good, at least, not completely good. It is really that way in the Liebenthal district. We, the natives, see deficiencies and defects still, still wrongs to heal, still improvements to be made, which are not only beneficial, but indispensable; and a judge from outside would surely find even more.

Since we have had many successes, we have unshaken faith that we will have many more. The march for good, along the previously laid out path, is still short of its goal. The number of good wishes ushered in with the new year, urges us to try something new. So at last we will see what the Liebenthal district has brought here to Russia, with the best German settlers marching together to bring about the well-being and noble wishes of the Government.

To be sure, there will be some difficulties in 1859; doubtless these adverse conditions are for our purification. Particularly the innumberable great green grasshoppers which appear with the warm season of the year, will make the prospects for the farmers appear gloomy and dark. We are afraid, but we do not despair in fear of devastation, for in union there is strenth, and with determination and good will, much is possible. The Lord will never refuse His blessing to those who work hard.

SHORT CHRONICLE OF

Kleinliebenthal

in commemoration
of the hundred year existence
of the colony
1804-1904

> We do not wish to appear better
> than we are, but we wish to
> strive to improve ourselves;
> therefore let the truth speak out!
> —The Author

Kleinliebenthal

Kleinliebenthal, also called Kseniewka and Malaja Ackerscha, is located in the Odessa district, province of Cherson, twelve versts from the railway and seaport of Odessa, on the river Malaja Ackerscha. The Malaja Ackerscha has its origin fifteen versts north-west of the colony, near the main road, winds its way across the boundary of the Kleinliebenthal fields, from the north to the south. It flows through the middle of the colony dividing it into two parallel streets. It is joined by two tributaries and flows in a three faden wide river bed below the colony into the Liman (estuary).

The banks on both sides of the little river are approximately one faden high. The flat land extending from the river banks to the higher ground is divided into vegetable gardens. Each of these gardens has one or two wells for watering the plants. The location of the gardens and vineyards on both sides of the colony makes it an attractive sight. The soil in the valley is rather stony, but very productive; higher up the black earth begins. The two streets are joined to each other by small bridges built across the river.

The eastern street, in which the church is located, called the Russian street, runs from north to south, is 2 versts long and has 115 houses in 2 rows. The western street, which has the bathing establishment, called the Jewish street, is 2 versts and 40 faden long and has 140 houses in 2 rows. The number of people in the village is 2347. The most common occupations of the inhabitants are grain-farming, wine-growing, livestock-raising, and vegetable gardening. The important buildings in the colony are a church, two schoolhouses, a parsonage, a municipal office and a bathing establishment.

The houses in the colony are all built according to the same plan, usually with the gable to the street. They generally have two rooms and a kitchen, along with an entrance or porch.* The front room with the window facing the street is the parlor. The back room is the bedroom. The house is usually 8 faden long, 4 faden wide and 1½ faden high up to the roof. The roof is usually covered with reeds, which are skillfully flattened. Behind the house, commonly under the same roof, are the barns for the livestock and farther back, near the threshing place, the barns for chicken and geese. Opposite the house there is a cellar and often also a well or cistern and a baking kitchen. The farmyard is surrounded by a stone wall about 5 feet high. Behind the farmyards, on both sides of the village, are the vineyards, of which 1 dessiatin belongs to each farmer. On the east side the vineyards stretch about 300 faden down to the liman. In front of the white-washed walls along the street side there is a beautiful row of acacia trees, extending from one end of the village to the other, which gives the colony an exceptionally picturesque appearance.

Kleinliebenthal was settled in 1804 by immigrants from various regions of Germany. When the settlers first arrived at the site where the colony now is, there were five houses and four clay huts, owned by a Russian nobleman. Sixteen families destined for this colony had arrived in Russia in 1803, but because the land had not yet been purchased for them, they had to be quartered in Odessa. Two families, Johann Senger and Adam Schleich, came to this site in 1803 and can therefore be called the founders of Kleinliebenthal.

In March 1804, 48 families arrived and settlement was begun. There were 50 lots measured out, 25 on the east side and 25 on the west side of the river. The lots were all in a row from the site where the hydrotherapy institute is now located northwards to the Kunanz lot. On every lot a reed hut was built as a shelter for the people and the meagre belongings that they had brought with them. So Kleinliebenthal came into existence. In 1805, 20 more

*Some houses have eight or more rooms.

families arrived; in 1807, one; in 1808, four; and in 1809, seven, making a total of 82 households. The plan for the colony of Kleinliebenthal was made by Duke Richelieu, who also gave it its name.

List of Names of the First Settlers and Homesteaders of Kleinliebenthal

House Number.

1. Franz Däschle
2. Lorenz Heinzmann
3. Johann Senger—the estate went to the son-in-law, Jacob Stein
4. Adam Schleich—the estate was taken over by Wendel Wolf
5. Johann Kretzner
6. Jacob Sperle—the estate went to the son-in-law, Joseph Brauer
7. Joseph Baumann
8. Peter Stein
9. Johann Paulo—the estate went to the step-son, Johann Steiert
10. Adam Grad
11. Michael Brünster—the estate went to the son-in-law, Johann Ochs
12. Christian Gesell
13. Philipp Lutz
14. Magdalena Maffenbaier—the estate went to the son, Herrmann
15. Franz Wendler—the heir unknown
16. Johann Klein
17. Peter Prawo—estate to son-in-law, Andreas Steiert
18. Johann Herzog
19. Joseph Kraft
20. Franz Maier
21. Martin Klausz
22. Andreas Faszbinder—the estate went to Johann Schlick
23. Jacob Hurrbein—the estate went to the step-son, Peter Nieder
24. Sebastian Sahly
25. Margaretha Fetsch—the estate went to the son-in-law, Joseph Paris
26. Jakob Weberbauer—the estate went to the son-in-law, Johann Gretz
27. Peter Streicher—the estate went to the son-in-law, Michael Kunanz

28. Michael Roszany—the estate went to the step-son, Martin Daniel
29. Johann Fix
30. Andreas Schnurr
31. Michael Schneider—the estate went to the son-in-law, George Bürk
32. Johann Baumstark—the estate went to the son-in-law, Anton Kocher
33. Peter Wolf—the estate went to son, Stefan
34. Anton Löwenstein
35. Cyriak Sahly
36. Katharina Warther—estate went to son-in-law, Franz Mayer
37. Xaverius Fix
38. Franz Walz
39. Nikolaus Schumacher—the estate went to Philipp Kraft
40. Johann Malsam
41. Franz Spiesz—the estate went to stepson, Johann Hartmann
42. Johann Peter Jean—the estate went to stepson, Konrad Mock?
43. Ignaz Jehle—the estate went to stepson, Gabriel Götz
44. Valentin Dieringer
45. Lorenz Dieringer
46. Joseph Sahly
47. Georg Imbery
48. Sebastian Adler
49. Anton Krämer—the estate went to the son-in-law, Friedrich Malsam
50. Anton Wolf
51. Jacob Hartmann
52. Peter Dörrhe—the estate went to son-in-law, Joseph Holzmann?
53. Christian Heier
54. Johann Merklinger
55. Anton Wagner
56. Anton Wagner II
57. Mathäus Tschan—the estate went to Ignaz Waldmann?
58. Adam Moser
59. Jacob Braunstein—the estate went to the stepson, Joseph Binder
60. Michael Walter—the estate went to the stepson, Thomas Renschler
61. Georg Kocher
62. Jakob Hell—the estate went to stepson, Ignaz Leppert
63. Ignaz Binfait
64. Joseph Dobler

65. Joseph Leppert—the estate went to Heinrich Schüler?
66. Joseph Gander—the estate went to Johann Kirchgäszner
67. Johann Paris
68. Joseph Götz
69. Franz Gresz
70. Valentin Eisenkirch
71. Adam Erk
72. Ignaz Most
73. Gottlieb Haag
74. Michael Wolf
75. Johann Wagner
76. Sebastian Wildemann
77. Ignatz Götz
78. Joseph Ott
79. Jakob Wetsch
80. Johann Merklinger
81. Theobald Werner
82. Jakob Steiner

The Kleinliebenthal Community Land

The quantity of land owned by the Kleinliebenthal community was 4,073¾ dessatine. This included 130 dessatine of pasture land (grass) near Franzfeld on the Dniester (river) and 120 dessatine parish land. The outline of the land formed a long quadrangle which extended from the south to the north for a distance of 15 versts. The boundary on the south was formed by the liman (estuary) and the land of the Greek village of Alexandrovka, on the west the Grossliebenthal community land, on the north the colony of Dalnek and surroundings, towards the east the land of the city of Odessa and the liman (estuary).

The contour of the land is almost level, the only deviations being the depression which carries the Little Akersha and to the east the upward slope towards the hills of the Dalnek river. The upper layer of the soil consists of saltpetre-containing black earth up to a foot and a half in depth, with a subsoil of white clay and in many places of red clay and marl. In favorable weather the soil is very productive and is suitable for most varieties of grain.

The Present Wealth and Condition
of the
Colony Kleinliebenthal

The land in the community is divided approximately as follows: (house) lots 58¾ dessatine; for colony streets, 12 dessatine; for cattle range, 100 dessatine; for vegetable garden, 25 dessatine; forest and shrubs, 17 dessatine; for water (ponds, etc.) 140 dessatine; vineyards, 120 dessatine; stone quarry 30 dessatine; clay pits, one dessatine; slopes, 207 dessatine; trails, 50 dessatine; agricultural land, 2481 dessatine; hay-land, 10 dessatine; pasture land, 821 dessatine. In addition to the community land Kleinliebenthal seeded more than 1500 dessatine which they rented from the Alexandrov Greeks, at 12 rubles per dessatin per year.

In the year 1905, the seeding was done as follows:

In the community land,

Summer wheat	6¾	dessatine
Winter wheat	823½	dessatine
Rye	171¾	dessatine
Barley	622	dessatine
Oats	284½	dessatine
Corn	157½	dessatine
Potatoes	162½	dessatine
Onions	47¼	dessatine

On bought and rented land,

Winter wheat	752½	dessatine
Rye	102	dessatine
Barley	425	dessatine
Oats	236	dessatine
Corn	85¾	dessatine
Potatoes	92½	dessatine
Onions	34	dessatine

The grain crop in Kleinliebenthal was a failure this year, most of the farmers harvesting little more than their seed.

The teachers, public officials and municipal workers received the following remuneration: the school principal 425 rubles; the two Russian teachers 400 rubles and 330 rubles; the German teacher, who is also parish sexton, 660 rubles; the mayor 100 rubles; the village secretary 550 rubles; the village treasurer 30 rubles; the bailiff 175 rubles; the horse-herder 150 kopecks per head; the cowherder 60 kopecks per head; the cowherder for night herding 88 kopecks per head; the calf-herder one ruble per head. The number of animals in the village were: 880 horses, 872 cows, 205 pigs, and 5 community bulls.

There are in Kleinliebenthal 12 booths and retail shops, a whiskey and wine tavern, a hotel, two windmills, a steam-powered flour mill, a pharmacy, and a hydrotherapy institute which has not been too well looked after in recent years. There are about 29 craftsmen in the village. The people of Kleinliebenthal have some special sources of income. The guests at the hydrotherapy institute, mainly Jews from Odessa, increasing in number every year, bring in more than 10,000 rubles annually. The vegetable gardens also yield a good income, particularly when the prices are good in Odessa.

The community paid the following taxes: crown taxes, 411 rubles, 5 kopecks; property tax, 1661 rubles, 50 kopecks; community taxes, 2148 rubles.

Kleinliebenthal Parish

Kleinliebenthal has 255 houses with 2397 people, all of the Roman Catholic faith. People of other faiths live here only temporarily. The parish belongs to the Odessa deanery of the diocese of Tiraspol. To this parish belong also the Catholics in neighboring non-Catholic communities. The post office at Mariinskoje (Grossliebenthal) is 3 versts distant.

Parish History

In March 1804 Father Alois Löffler S.J., along with lay-brother Lieb, arrived in the new settlements just founded near Odessa to provide religious services for the Catholics. At first he chose newly-founded Kleinliebenthal for his residence and called the new parish "Parochia Kleinliebenthalensis", that is, "Kleinliebenthal Parish". But after a year and a half he found this village not suitably located to be the centre of the parish and moved over to the colony of Josephstal, which was more centrally located for the new Catholic settlers. From this time on Kleinliebenthal was affiliated with the parish of Josephstal, until 1840 when it again became a separate parish. From 1824, Kleinliebenthal had its own church records, in affiliation with the Josephstal parish.

In 1828, Father Dominik Sibini came to Kleinliebenthal, and lived there from the 17th February to the 15th October. As a result of the expulsion of the infamous Ignaz Lindl by the Bishop in Kamenez-Podolsk, Father Sibini was sent to Sarata to live there and to win back those people, who were mostly Catholics, to the

Mother Church. But all of the pains of the Father were fruitless and he had to leave these perverted people to their own destiny. In 1828, the community of Kleinliebenthal gave a written petition to the Welfare Committee and asked that they might have a priest for their own parish, and requested Father Sibini as parish priest.

But the Mohilev Archdiocesan Consistory* was not willing for the following reasons:

1) The community of Kleinliebenthal is too small to be a separate parish and have its own priest, particularly since they have substantial arrears in the crown debts.

2) The colonies of Josephstal, Marienthal and Franzfeld, requested that it not be permitted for Kleinliebenthal to withdraw from the mother parish at Josephstal, since it was too heavy a burden for themselves to support a priest and parish alone.

Father Sibini was then sent to Jamburg near Jekaterinoslav, and the priest from there, Father Petraschevsky, since he was a restless fellow, was to be sent as helper to Father Eybel, in Josephstal, if and when the parishoners provided an increase in remuneration, for the priest and his curate. But the parishioners did not wish to hear anything about paying an extra stipend, and therefore no curate came to the Josephstal parish. So the situation remained until 1835.

The Community of Kleinliebenthal Again Requested a Priest

In 1835 the community of Kleinliebenthal held a meeting and submitted the following resolution to the Welfare Committee:

"The community of Kleinliebenthal, which because of existing arrangements regarding religious affairs is part of the parish of Josephstal, has on many occasions asked the authorities for a change from its present status of an affiliate to that of full parish rank and for the appointment of its own parish priest, but so far this plea has not been successful.

"Confident that our righteous request will receive a favorable hearing, we present it again in all humility to the revered Welfare Committee and support it with the following arguments:

"The necessity of converting Kleinliebenthal from its present status of daughter church to full parish rank with its own parish priest is apparent from the following:

(a) Since the time of settlement of our colony, our population has increased considerably, upwards of 804 people are now living in 105 houses, comprising 146 families.

*According to the documents of Kleinliebenthal Council Archives, No. 19, lit 1.

(b) Can the ukase of 1795 be applied here, which orders that a priest should not have more than 100 farms with an average of four souls each at not to great a distance from one another?

"In order to comply with this edict Kleinliebenthal must be in a position to pay its own priest, in addition to having its own church and other buildings such as a rectory and annex, required by the parish.

"A church provided with an organ is at hand, and everything necessary to serve God has been accumulated. The rectory will be completed this year. For the maintenance of these buildings, we will pay the church dues as well as the remuneration of the priest in the following manner:-

"On our community land there is more low land and small islands, which because of their distance from the colony and irregular shape, were not divided among the householders for their own use. This land is rented to outside vegetable growers. From this rent which yearly amounts to about 1500 rubles, the church was built in earlier years. From this rent it can be supported in the future, the rectory completed and the priest paid.

"In order to insure this undertaking, we promise that the above mentioned rent will not be used for any other community purpose. In addition, the community promises to offset any deficiency in funds, through voluntary donations of money.

"The salary of the priest we settled temporarily at 500 rubles per year, pending agreement of the highest ruling church authority. We promise to pay this in divided portions per term without even the smallest arrears. Any additional income of the priests (deaths, marriages and baptims) will be paid separately as has been the custom in the past. Also we will immediately commit ourselves to measure off 120 dessatine from our community land to be given to the priest. (This will be done) according to the plan of division of the land surveyor, Mr. Niedzwinsky. If this (recommendation) is approved by the highest ruling body, the benefits to the community of having a priest of their own will be:-

1. Divine service will be held on Sundays and Holy days, according to the custom of the Holy Roman Catholic religion.

2. Sermons and Christian teaching will take place regularly for the youth.

3. In the school also, our dear children will receive the necessary instruction and knowledge of our holy religion.

4. Through the presence of a priest in our colony, all these things will be improved and elevated. In a word, the education and morals of all inhabitants will be strengthened and improved through the benefits of a priest.

"If the priest does not live here, and if our community does not create its own church, then the previous disadvantages will remain: The mother parish in Josephstal is 16 versts away. For every divine service the priest must be brought from there, which in a year's time happens very frequently. As many as are sent to transport the priest, so much time must be calculated as a loss; particularly during seeding and harvesting time, this results in considerable damage. Often the weather is bad when one needs the priest for someone seriously ill, then one must first drive 16 versts by bad roads, only to find that the priest is away visiting another sick person. Consequently the sick person dies without receiving the last sacrament; through this there is considerable grief and sadness among the relatives left behind.

"If under the present circumstances, your most gracious Excellency willing, for the basic reasons stated above, considers it important enough to change our affiliation to a mother parish and approve the appointment of our own priest, so we add another humble request, if your highness may be so disposed, we ask you to appoint Prior Eybel, who has served us faithfully since 1833 and whom we all love. We are convinced that his wish is to spend his last days with us in peace and tranquility."

There are 78 signatures attached.

Mayor Schüler
First Assistant Ott
Second Assistant Bürk
Secretary Ochs

Kleinliebenthal,
22 June, 1835.

Kleinliebenthal Requested a Priest for the Third Time, This Time With Success

Prior Eybel died on the 8th of September, 1835, and was buried by Father Kaspar Borowsky, in the churchyard at Kleinliebenthal.* After the death of Prior Eybel, the community of Kleinliebenthal again sent a request to the Welfare Committee and asked for a priest, who could understand German well. This time the president of the Welfare Committee, General Inzov, looked favourably on the request of the Kleinliebenthal people, and granted permission for their own parish. In a letter dated the 29th of October, 1835, he (General Inzov) asked Inspector Musnizsky whether a priest who understood German well could be sent to Kleinliebenthal. Inspector

*Father Jager had a cross placed on the grave some time ago.

136

Musnizsky answered General Inzov on the 23rd of November, 1835, (number 264), that he considered it essential that Kleinliebenthal should have its own parish, but unfortunately there was no priest available who understood the German language well enough to be sent there. However, he (suggested) that they turn this proposition over to the Minister of the Interior, who will send it to the Administrator of the Archdiocese of Mohilev, to Bishop Valerianus Komjunko. On the 4th of November, 1835, General Inzov sent the request of Kleinliebenthal to the Minister of the Interior, with the explanation that there were sufficient reasons for Kleinliebenthal to have its own parish.

On the 16th of May, 1840, Inspector Musnizsky reported to the Welfare Committee that Metropolitan Pavlovsky had sent a request to the provincials of various orders to find a priest for Kleinliebenthal able to understand the German language well.

Order of Succession of the Priests of Kleinliebenthal

FATHER JOHANNES GARTZ, a Franciscan, was the first priest in Kleinliebenthal, from the 2nd of July 1840 to the 24th of June 1841. He was born in 1800 and ordained a priest in 1832. He came from a Polish monastery. He was a big, strong man, a good speaker, and from the beginning very conscientious. He visited the schools, taught religion there and diligently preached the word of God. Since he was in Kleinliebenthal only a short time, his good work had no particular effect. Much more was accomplished by his successor.

FATHER GABRIEL GRIZEWITSCH was parish priest from the 24th of June, 1841, until the 17th of February, 1848.

Father Gabriel Grizewitsch was of medium build, heavy stature, a good speaker and spoke German reasonably well. In his parish duties he was accurate and punctual. He was strict with himself and expected his parishioners to be conscientious in fulfilling their duties. In the pulpit and in the confessional, he was extremely energetic, explaining to the people the sacred truths, so that they might lead a good Christian life. He visited the school every day where he would often punish the lazy and disobedient children himself with a little whip which he carried with him in his boot tops. He held Christian instruction the whole year around. First he taught a lesson out of the mission manual that he had published himself and corrected assigned written work; then he took the children to church for catechism instruction. In the year 1848 he was transferred to Mannheim, where he died of cholera the following year.

FATHER LEOPOLD FRANZ BORIA (also Borgia), Parish Priest from the 24th of March, 1848 to the 1st of January, 1851.

Father Leopold Franz Boria was born on the 15th of November, 1811, in the Hungarian district of Ostrau, near the city of Olmütz, receiving his priestly education in the seminary there. In 1836 he was ordained priest and sent as chaplain to the parish church of Märisch-Ostrau. In 1842 he came as an apostolic missionary to Russia and was posted to Mariupol, on the Sea of Azov. When he got as far as Odessa he was stopped and then sent as parish priest to the colony of Mannheim, where he worked diligently until 1848.

Through an order of the Vicar General of the Archdiocese of Mohilov, Father Boria was sent to Kleinliebenthal on the 6th of October, 1847. Father Boria came to Kleinliebenthal from Mannheim in a wagon caravan formed by his previous parishioners from Mannheim and Elsass, on the 24th of March, 1848. In Kleinliebenthal, Father Boria performed his duties as priest with considerable fervour. He frequently visited the schools and held Christian instruction. He also worked hard in the pulpit through his fiery, vehement sermons. However, this type of blessed work did not continue long. An enemy came and "sowed weeds among the wheat". This enemy was the discord between himself and his parishioners.

When Father Boria arrived in Kleinliebenthal, Joseph Rissling was the teacher there. When he resigned shortly after, Father Boria appointed Joseph Baraneck, who had a teacher's diploma from Moravia, as teacher and sexton in Kleinliebenthal. Many did not like the new teacher; in particular his methods of singing and praying were not to the people's taste. At first the dissatisfied ones mocked him, later they became more and more insolent. They were very rude to Father Boria and spread the ugliest slanders about him, until he found it necessary to lay charges against them before the Welfare Committee. According to the decisions of this body on 18 December 1848 (sub. no. 7519) all those who had participated in the slanders and other excesses had to pay heavy fines and one man who had insulted Father Boria personally was condemned to 10 lashes.

But that was only adding fuel to the fire. Those who had been punished now became even more malicious. Hatred, enmity, factionalism reared their heads everywhere. Mayor Nikolaus Kraft, who did not agree with the agitators, was insulted and maligned in his office and decided to resign. Father Boria began to defend himself from the pulpit, but with words that were not appropriate for a preacher of peace and Christian love. Matters grew steadily worse, especially because Father Boria gave scandal in his personal life. He was therefore forced to ask for transference to another post.

He was sent to Odessa as German preacher, where he was soon in difficulty with Prelate Rosutowitsch, the sequel of which was, that in 1858 he left Russia and return to his homeland. He was there in a monastery, during the 1870's, when he wrote a letter to teacher Benesch, which was filled with complaints about the bad food, which consisted only of beans, peas and stale beer.

So the most famous preacher in our colonies, as he was generally considered, had a shiny beginning but a lustreless finish to his career. The whole cause for this misfortune was that he did not practice what he preached.

FATHER DIDAK SAMBOR Parish Priest from the 1st of January, 1851 to the 22nd of January, 1854.

Father Didak Sambor came from Lithuania and was born in 1798. As a youth he attended the Bernardine monastery near Druick, where he completed his studies in the monastery school and was ordained a priest in 1828. Through an order dated the 23rd of July, 1838, he was sent to Eichwald; in 1851, he was transferred to Kleinliebenthal.

He was a good devout priest and conscientiously performed his duties.

From Kleinliebenthal Father Sambor was sent to Landau where he continued the work of the church till 1862 and left the memory of a devout and faithful priest. If I am not mistaken, he died a short time later in Heidelberg.

FATHER MICHAEL STANKEWITSCH Parish Priest from January 22, 1854 to the 24th of June, 1861.

Father Michael Stankewitsch was born in 1798 and ordained a priest in 1828. He was a very devout and well educated man. His favourite subjects were astronomy and physics. In Kleinliebenthal he worked for a long time on an apparatus which was to bring rain. However when the machine was erected on the liman, one waited in vain for the rain which this machine was to bring. He was very strict in fulfilling his priestly duties and also in the confessional. Those who did not have faith, hope and love would be dismissed without further ado. In some respects he was very scrupulous. For instance he used only mass wine which he pressed himself.

FATHER ZENO KALINOWSKY Dominican, was the Parish Priest from the 4th of July, 1861 to the 12th of June, 1862.

Father Kalinowsky was born in 1809 and was ordained a priest in 1843. He was a very well educated man and spoke German well; in his rounds among the parishioners he was very amiable. He died in the 1880's, in a monastery of his order.

From the 19th of June 1862 to the 27th of October, 1866, the parish was supervised alternately by Prelate Rosutowitsch and Father Schamne.

FATHER ANTON SIMNOCH Parish Priest from the 27th of October, 1866 to the 3rd of November, 1867.

Father Anton Simnoch came as cleric from Volhynia in 1864 to the Catholic seminary in Saratov, where, on the 21st of June of the same year he was ordained a priest by Bishop Helanus Kahn. Father Simnoch made himself unforgetable in the parish of Kleinliebenthal in that he built the lovely, imposing parish church. Because of his friendliness, Father Simnoch gave the people the impression that the rectory should be carefully watched, and if a woman drove up to it, they would immediately ask if she was Father Simnoch's sister.

Later he returned to his home in Volhynia, where I heard he died a few years later.

FATHER JOHANNES GARTZ, Parish priest from the 10th of November, 1867 to October 1st, 1873.

Father Gartz was in Kleinliebenthal a second time, serving also as military chaplain for Odessa and the surrounding garrisons.

From the 8th of October, 1873, until the 1st of August, 1878, Kleinliebenthal was alternately supervised from Odessa and Josephstal.

FATHER KYPRIAN GINTILLO Parish Priest from the 1st of August, 1878 until the 8th of December, 1882.

Father Kyprian Gintillo was born in 1817 and ordained a priest in 1843. He served as a priest for a long time in Eichwald, where he managed land on a large scale and through this, accumulated a large fortune. In Kleinliebenthal his activity was not edifying; consequently the people were glad that he was soon moved to Elisabethgrad, where he died soon thereafter.

There was an interval from the 9th of December, 1882 until the 4th of April, 1883, when the parish was supervised by Father Wanner from Josephstal.

FATHER JULIAN MICHALSKY Administrator from the 4th of April, 1883, to the 25th of June, 1884.

Father Julian Michalsky was born in 1837 and ordained to the priesthood in 1860. During the Polish revolt he was exiled, as a result of which he suffered considerably. In 1870, he came to Sulz, where he came under the guardianship of the devoted Father Balthasar Kraft, the priest who had taken over the newly founded parish. At first he understood very little German. But after one month, because of his indefatigable energy, he understood the language sufficiently well that he could preach freely. Father Michalsky worked in Kleinliebenthal with considerable devotion, and started the Rosary brotherhood.

In addition to many other praiseworthy qualities and virtues, Father Michalsky possesses those connected with works of mercy, especially the visiting of the sick, which is truly the most fertile field for a priest's work. For when the poor sinner lies there helpless, forsaken by his passions, forsaken by the deceptive joys of this cheating world, forsaken by everything that has so far alienated him from his Creator and Redeemer, and when he finally realizes that self-deception is now at an end and that at the next moment he must appear before the strict judgment seat of God, then, I believe, a light dawns once more and for the last time in the depths of the sinner's soul and he hears for the last time the words of a merciful Father through the mouth of His priest, resulting in either light through repentance or darkness through obduracy for ever and ever.

FATHER KASPAR JÄGER Parish Priest from the 26th of June, 1884 until now.

Father Kasper Jäger was born on the 18th of April, 1857 in the Colony of Landau in Beresan, studied in the clerical seminary in Saratov, where after completing his studies on the 27th of April, 1880, he was ordained a priest by Bishop Zottmann. He was immediately sent to Katharinenthal as administrator, where, for four years he performed the duties of priest with diligence and zeal, to the general satisfaction of his parishioners.

In 1884 the church authorities transferred Father Jäger to Kleinliebenthal. Here he acquired great merit for his work in connection with the parish school. He recruited excellent teachers and by 1885 had brought the school to such a flourishing state that there was no other like it in the whole area. The decoration of the church too was always his special concern. He bought new pictures for the stations of the cross, a picture of the patron saint of the parish, a new side altar, a fine new organ and many other objects, so that the inner furnishings of the Kleinliebenthal church can be described as among the most beautiful in the whole diocese.

Parish Endowment

The parish is endowed with 120 dessatine of land, the parish field and vineyard behind the church towards the liman, and in addition 400 rubles for the priest's salary. It appears that the Kleinliebenthal parish land was divided off from the community land, by the first settlers. As has been previously described, the priests of the Society of Jesus had first founded a parish in Kleinliebenthal. Whether these priests utilized this land, then considered worthless, is not clear from the records.

The first mention in the records is in 1824, when Father Eybel made a claim on the earnings of the Kleinliebenthal parish land. On 27 May 1824, at the direction of Inspector von Löwen, the community of Kleinliebenthal was asked why this parish land was not given to Father Eybel for his use. The community answered: "The priest comes to Kleinliebenthal seldom, only once or twice a year. The people of this community have to drive to Josephstal for baptisms, marriages and other church services, and on each occasion the priest is paid for those services."

Thereupon the Welfare Committee ordered that the parish land in Kleinliebenthal be rented each year, and the money from the proceeds be deposited with the Welfare Committee, for unforeseen expenses in the school-house and in the church in Kleinliebenthal.

Until 1824, the parish land had brought no returns; the Tshumaks and Russians from Dalnek utilized it for pasture land. Whether any of the money from the proceeds of the parish land was deposited to the Welfare Committee, and how large this sum was at the founding of the parish in 1840, or whether the money was squandered, I can find no information in the archives.

The Parish Church — the First Church

Where the Kleinliebenthal people worshipped before they built their first church (1819), I have been unable to find out.

In the Kleinliebenthal file in the community archives (1818) one finds the following document:

Binding Agreement, 24 August 1818

We, the undersigned colonists of Kleinliebenthal, herewith testify that we have agreed among ourselves, in the presence of our community officials, to build a church in this village. It is to be located on the street between Joseph Götz and Johann Paris up on the hill in the direction of the liman. Every householder promises to pay 30 rubles for this purpose and also deliver a faden of good stone before 1 April 1819. All of us also promise to contribute the hauling

142

of wood, sand, water and other materials needed during the construction. The mason's wages for the building of the walls are to be paid out of the money collected.

Then follow the signatures, sixty-five in all. The official personnel at that time were: Mayor Peter Stein, first assistant Franz Maier, second assistant Adam Grad, town clerk Adam Erk. The community then had the following resources for building the church:

Rent money for the islands near Dalnek.	1181 rubles
Loan from the Welfare Committee	1500 rubles
Community contributions.	1950 rubles
Total	4631 rubles

On 13 May 1819 the Kleinliebenthal community presented the plan for the new church to the district government office and reported: "The total cost of building the church will be 11,060 rubles, without finishing the interior. A contract has been signed with Michael Röhmer on the following basis: Röhmer has to supply stone, wood, lumber, lime, iron and nails; has to build the church, stucco and whitewash it; erect the framework of the roof and enclose it; lay the floor; construct and enclose the steeple; and supply the labor needed for all this. The community itself has to transport the needed materials. For this Röhmer will receive 6400 rubles. The work had to be finished by 29 September 1819."

On 27 August 1819 the Kleinliebenthal community reported to the district office that the church building was enclosed and roofed in; that the steeple was boarded in, but that the tin for covering it was lacking. It was requested that some sheets of tin on hand in Grossliebenthal be made available to complete the construction. An additional loan of 1500 rubles was requested from the Welfare Committee to complete the building. The church was finished in October 1819 and was blessed by Father Pierling S.J.

The length of the church, apart from the steeple, was 10 faden, its width 4½ faden, its height to the roof 2½ faden, and the height of the steeple 8 faden. The roof was covered with shingles and the steeple with tin plate.

Inside the church there were three altars: the main altar dedicated to the parish patron, St. Wendelin; the side altar to the right dedicated to the Blessed Virgin; and the side altar to the left dedicated to the Holy Knight, St. George.

To give a picture of the furnishings of the interior of the church and of the spirit of sacrifice of the people of Kleinliebenthal for the decoration of their church, I give herewith an inventory of the new church for the year 1820.

List of Church Furnishings

Those bought from Collections, those donated to the Kleinliebenthal Church in 1820.

Name of Object	Price Rubles	Kopecks
1. Eucharistic vestments with surplice, maniple, sash and shoulder—cape	100	—
2. An alb	—	—
3. A corporal	—	—
4. A surplice for the priest	—	—
5. Two surplices with shirts and collars for the altar boys	13	40
6. Three altar cloths	—	—
7. Coffin cloth from Achilles in Odessa	32	—
8. Confessional	—	—
9. Communion rail—presented by P. Petre	—	—
10. A bell	—	40
11. A lantern	2	—
12. Wine and water glasses with plate—presented by Gress	—	—
13. Holy water container	4	—
14. Two German hymn books	6	—
15. Three painted pictures—St. Wendelin, St. Rochus, St. Sebastian	60	—
16. Red Damascus flag with pole	160	—
17. Eight standards—presented by Dobler, Stein and Eisenkirch	—	—
18. A bell weighing 80 lbs.	—	—
19. A large bell weighing 120 lbs.	—	—
20. A ritual presented by Father Jann, S.J.	—	—
21. A church cupboard	35	—
22. A crucifix presented by Father Jann, S.J.	—	—
23. Scripture tablet—presented by Father Andrew Pierling, S.J.	—	—
24. Antipendium—presented by Father Jann, S.J.	—	—
25. New Testament (2 copies)	16	—
26. Monstrance, chalice and tabernacle	240	—
27. Missal, altar stone, Eucharistic vestments	110	—
28. Two brass candle sticks—presented by Joseph Sahly	—	—
29. Two candle sticks from Luis Duriele	—	—
30. Two candle sticks from Anton Kramer	—	—
31. Two candle sticks from Franz Maier	—	—
32. A lamp for the everlasting light—presented by J. Sahli	—	—
33. Censer with vessel	10	—
34. Two lanterns—presented by Peter Stein	—	—
35. A portable statue of Mary—presented by Eisenkirch, which he himself brought from Germany in 1821. The statue is now located in the chapel in the cemetery.	—	—

In 1824 a collection was started for church pews and this brought in 104 rubles, 20 kopecks. In 1828 when Father Sibini was in Kleinliebenthal, there was a further collection to decorate the interior of the church. The request for donations was given in German, French, Italian, Polish, Russian and Greek, for it was hoped to get some collections from Odessa. The collections totalled the sum of 949 rubles, 45 kopecks.

The New Parish Church

The old church, which was built in 1819, was large enough for the Kleinliebenthal community until 1849, when it became too small for the number of parishioners. In view of this crowding, the community, on the 22nd of December, 1849, decided to lengthen the old church by 5 faden, to cover the roof with sheet-metal as well as other improvements. The total cost of this renovation was approximately 3,079 rubles. The permission for this undertaking had already been obtained from the highest authorities, and the material for the extension was already at hand. However now the Kleinliebenthal people realized that the undertaking of lengthening the church by 5 faden conflicted with all rules of architecture, in that the length, to the width, to the height, resulted in complete asymmetry, and the building would look more like a sheep barn than a church.

As a result of this information, the project of enlarging the church was stopped, and the thought was entertained, that instead of enlarging the old church, they should build a new, larger church. At this time a depression occurred, so that the community was not able to proceed with this project until 1861. On the 18th of April, 1861, the community of Kleinliebenthal had a meeting and made the following resolution: "We request from the highest authority permission to build a new church in Kleinliebenthal."

Permission to build the new church was received from both the highest church and lay authority without difficulty. Now it became necessary to find the means wherewith to build the church. The community at this time had 3,079 rubles and 10,000 stones and through community pledges expected to collect another 3,079 rubles at the end of the year.

With the consent of the Welfare Committee and all colonies of the Liebenthal and Kutschurgan districts, 6000 rubles at 3 percent, to be repaid in 6 years, were borrowed from the sheepland fund. Later the Kleinliebenthal community made another loan of 3000 rubles from the sheepland fund and on 30 November 1875 a loan of 2684 rubles, 75 kopecks, from the fund accumulated from the leasing of liquor sale rights.

145

The inhabitants of Neuliebenthal (Wolchov) donated 180 rubles toward building the church in Kleinliebenthal. Through a community decree it was ordered that every land owner would haul two tons of sand and every landless household, one ton. Also the community obligates itself to provide all wagons to transport the building materials.

The plan for the new church was completed by the colonial architect Schukovsky, and in 1865 submitted to the minister of state domains for approval. The building committee was appointed from among the colonists: Ludwig Häuser, Johann Dobler, Peter Malsam, Andreas Wolf, Philipp Kraft and Lorenz Adler. On the 24th of February, 1865, the Kleinliebenthal community concluded an agreement with the merchant Laurenzius Sacharov, contractor from Odessa. He undertook to provide the building, masonry, sheet-metal work and stuccoing for the new church for the sum of 5,770 rubles. The work was to start on the 16th of April, 1865, and to be completed by the 15th of August of the same year.

On the 18th of April, 1865, Prelate Rosutowitsch laid the corner stone for the new church, and the building was successfully started and completed. The building committee, zealous about fulfilling its duty, earned worthy praise from fellow citizens and superiors. In the fall of 1866, the imposing church was completed and on the 23rd of October, 1866 it was solemnly blessed by Prelate Rosutowitsch. The act of consecrating the church was performed by the Right Reverend Bishop Antonius Zerr, in the presence of many priests and a very large crowd of devoted people, on the 22nd of November, 1892.

The cost of the rough building of the Kleinliebenthal church, without completing the interior, was approximately 17,339 rubles, 63.5 kopecks.

The patron of the church is St. Wendelin.

Description of the Church

The church is located in the centre of the colony on the eastern or Russian street, 10 faden upwards from the street on the liman hill. The church yard is 38 (?) faden long, 18 (?) faden wide and is surrounded by a stone wall measuring 2 arschine high. The church sits high on the slope of the liman hill and has a stately and majestic appearance. On directions of the church authorities, it was built from the west towards the east.

The length of the church is 22 faden, the width 9 faden, the height to the rafters is 7 faden; the height of the steeple is 19 faden. The style of architecture is Gothic. The building material, hard yellow fieldstone, is found not far from Kleinliebenthal. The church

146

has two entrances. The main door is situated under the steeple and framed by a fine Gothic arch, with thirteen steps leading up to it. The second door is at the back, suitably added onto the right side of the sacristy. On either side of the church there are five windows, 2 faden high, adorned with a matchwork. Around the church under the roof there are 3 divisions adorned with pretty ornaments, which are interrupted by pillars, and subdivided by these into small areas. The roof of the church is covered with sheet metal and is painted green. The steeple is built into the church and is two storeys high, appearing slender and delicate above the church. The bottom storey which rests on the church roof has four half-round windows and is supported on each of the four corners by a pillar. These extend upwards in small steeples, with three cornered roofs, crowned by small crosses. The steeple roof is 4 faden high, and is crowned by a cupola and an iron cross. In the steeple there are three melodious bells, which resound in loud harmony. Surrounding the church there are two rows of lovely acacia trees. The wall toward the street is decorated by iron railings. When a visitor first enters the inside of the church, he is overcome by a pleasing brightness, which comes from the five windows on either side and is diffusely distributed. The church has the appearance of a ship; the choir loft is supported on three massive Roman arches. On the right of the entrance, the visitor sees the fine drawings of the Stations of the Cross, attached to the pillars between the windows. These Stations of the Cross were obtained by Father Jäger from the H. Chunadsky Art Gallery and cost 500 rubles. Under the third station is the confessional. Three steps forward one finds the lovely marble side altar, blessed in the name of the holy knight, St. George; his picture was painted by an artist in a niche above the altar. The altar is surrounded by a rail of imitation marble with sculptures of a dove, the symbol of the Holy Spirit, and a bust of "Ecce Homo" (Christ) and "Mater dolorosa" (Virgin Mary).

The altar was presented to the church by Prelate Rosutowitsch in 1866. Between the altar and the communion rail there is a statue of the Sacred Heart of Jesus enclosed in glass, which cost 200 rubles, obtained from the Art Gallery of Stuflesser by Father Jäger. Only three steps up one finds himself in the presbytery, which is illuminated by two stained glass windows, giving a twilight appearance. The length of the presbytery is 3 faden, the same as its width. On either side of this there is a sacristy room, each with one window facing to the east. The marble main altar is set on two steps with a platform and is surrounded by ten sliver candlesticks and six bouquets of artificial flowers, giving the appearance of a very ornamental altar. The tabernacle also is made of marble, in the form of an ornamental sacrificial house, composed of four small pillars, the front two each decorated with three-armed hanging chandeliers.

Above the altar hangs the beautiful picture of St. Wendelin. The design and the expression of the picture are excellent. The holy Wendelin, the rich king's son, stands with the shepherd's staff in his hand, in the midst of a harmless herd of grazing sheep. The sceptre and crown, the sign of his princely rank, are under his feet. His expression is tender, his bright blue eyes have the expression of a god-filled soul, displaying heavenly peace. Over his head, two angels hold the bishop's mitre, which shows his dignity. The picture frame is 2 faden high and 2 yards wide and is decorated with golden carved wood. The picture is very stately and stimulates devotion. The picture cost 350 rubles, and was drawn by the Odessa artist, Wenzev. On both sides of the altar there are a few small but very lovely pictures. If one returns to the center of the church and turns right, one stands before the beautiful statue of the Blessed Virgin Mary with the Child Jesus, which came from Paris and cost 400 rubles, a gift from Georg Malsam.

Immediately to the left of this statue is the second side altar, blessed in the name of the most Holy Virgin. This altar can be dismantled; below, it contains the replica of the holy grave and above, the Christmas crib, along with lovely cutout figurines. The altar was bought by Father Jäger from the art gallery of Stuflesser, and cost 800 rubles. Above the altar is a picture of the Blessed Virgin Mary, a copy of the "Sistine Madonna". Over this altar there is also a marble arch covered with lovely sculpture work, on the flat area there are three round niches. In the niche above the picture of the Madonna there is an eye, symbol of God's omniscience. To the right is a picture of the bust of St. Louis, and in the left niche is a picture of the bust of St. Philomena. One step to the left is the marble baptismal font. Beside this is a statue of Mary holding Jesus, a Pieta, artistic wood carving from the art gallery of Stuflesser, price 200 rubles.

One step westward, one finds the entrance to the lovely pulpit with the picture of the four evangelists. In the centre of the church hang two impressive crystalline chandeliers of which the larger cost 350 rubles. The organ is new, bought from the firm of Sauer at a price of 400 rubles.

The Church Yard with the Chapel

The churchyard was set aside by the original settlers and has been enlarged repeatedly as required. At the present time the length of the yard is 150 faden, the width 210 faden. In this church yard two priests are buried: Father P. Eybel died on the 9th of

September, 1835, and Father Joseph Matery died on the 1st of March, 1888. The chapel in the church yard was built by Father Jäger in 1892 and cost 1500 rubles. The chapel with the round tower is 4 faden long, and 3 faden wide, and 2 faden high. The altar is lovely. Above the altar the lovely and remarkable statue of the mother of God shines in a glass shrine*. This statue was brought from Lower Alsace by Eisenkirch in 1821 and presented to the Kleinliebenthal church. The same statue has for many years been carried in processions by girls dressed in white, but later was deposited in the storage room and replaced by a picture. Father Jäger found the statue there, recognized the artistry in it, and had it placed in the chapel. Besides this statue and the fourteen Stations of the Cross, there is one additional picture in the chapel. The chapel is lighted by four windows, two on one side, and two coloured windows above the altar. The steeple of the chapel is lovely and rises thin and elegant, five feet in height.

Church Bequests

1. On the 7th of October, 1826, Ciriak Sahly, Kleinliebenthal colonist, donated 25 rubles to this church. Signed—Mayor Nieder.

2. On the 15th of December, 1827, widow Katharina Ott of this colony, donated the sum of 25 rubles to this church. Signed—Mayor Nieder.

3. On the 5th of December, 1840, the colonist Peter Nieder donated 16 rubles to the holy parish church, which was owed to him by Joseph Bienfait. Signed—Mayor Ott.

A Short Review

of the Collections and Expenses of the Church Treasury in Kleinliebenthal,—during the pastorate of Father Kaspar Jäger, 1884-1905. Father Jäger took over the church on the 26th of June, 1884—with 112 rubles and 33 kopecks in the treasury.

No.	Year	COLLECTIONS		EXPENSES		REMAINING	
		Rubles	Kopecks	Rubles	Kopecks	Rubles	Kopecks
1	1884	447	51	359	68	117	83
2	1885	391	10	376	70	14	40
3	1886	447	63	259	39	188	24
4	1887	1,067	76	865	63	202	13
5	1888	839	25	692	99	146	26
6	1889	660	89	615	97	44	92
7	1890	855	04	828	77	26	27
8	1891	375	44	344	—	31	44

*Presently there is another statue in this shrine.

No.	Year						
9	1892	358	93	418	43	59	50
10	1893	373	07	312	09	60	98
11	1894	594	47	379	60	214	87
12	1895	607	27	112	78	494	49
13	1896	1,310	21	1,238	15	72	06
14	1897	1,163	69	883	18	280	51
15	1898	846	68	671	42	175	26
16	1899	897	87	502	79	395	08
17	1900	955	40	463	50	491	90
18	1901	1,513	—	1,407	62	105	38
19	1902	3,463	44	3,127	54	335	90
20	1903	1,673	21	1,511	18	162	03
21	1904	1,050	60	1,000	91	49	69
	TOTALS	19,932	45	16,372	32	3,609	64

Vital Statistics for the Parish 1884 to 1905

No.	Year	Births	Marriages	Deaths	Sickness
1	1884	107	14	38	
2	1885	77	19	40	
3	1886	109	15	42	
4	1887	103	14	50	
5	1888	91	33	33	
6	1889	104	15	46	
7	1890	91	21	23	
8	1891	113	18	37	
9	1892	96	11	37	scarlet fever diphtheria
10	1893	93	24	116	
11	1894	117	24	49	
12	1895	99	22	44	
13	1896	119	12	36	
14	1897	104	8	45	
15	1898	108	20	34	
16	1899	94	18	44	
17	1900	87	20	37	
18	1901	107	24	34	
19	1902	98	18	30	
20	1903	99	13	50	
21	1904	105	17	72	scarlet fever diphtheria
	TOTALS:	2,121	380	837	

The accuracy confirmed by K. Jäger—
priest of Kleinliebenthal and the

Church Elders—Anton Dewald
—Bernhardt Klaus

A Charity Fund was formed in 1897 in Kleinliebenthal. The following sums were collected, and through the church administration, were distributed among the poor, sick people.

No.	Year	Collections Rubles	Kopecks	Distributions Rubles	Kopecks	Remaining Rubles	Kopecks
1	1897	14	20	10	50	3	70
2	1898	18	33	7	70	10	63
3	1899	17	—	9	—	8	—
4	1900	21	79	11	25	10	54
5	1901	26	69	19	50	7	19
6	1902	45	10	33	50	11	60
7	1903	21	75	21	16	—	59
8	1904	8	21	8	50	—	(25)
		173	11	121	71	52	25

Every donation is signed for by the receiver in his own handwriting.

K. Jäger, Parish Priest.

Church Elders, Anton Dewald
Bernhardt Klaus.

From June, 1896 until the 12th of July, 1905, 176 rubles, 98 kopecks was collected in the Kleinliebenthal parish church to help the Red Cross. The money was sent to the Dean of the Odessa Deanery and each time, a receipt was sent to the Kleinliebenthal parish office from the receiver.—Kleinliebenthal, 20 August, 1905.

Parish office of Kleinliebenthal,
K. Jäger
Church Elders—Anton Dewald
—Bernhardt Klaus

Location of Rectory

The first rectory was built in a small separate yard immediately adjacent to the church. It contained four rooms and a kitchen, and at the present time provides living quarters for the sexton. The new rectory, built in 1883 by Father Michalsky is just to the left beside the church; it is a solid building containing six rooms and a kitchen. The lot where the new rectory is built, along with two houses, a garden and vineyard were presented to the Kleinlieben-thal church by prelate Rosutowitsch.

School Affairs in Kleinliebenthal

It would seem that the first school house was built in Kleinliebenthal in 1809. It stood where the present community government office is now located, and had the appearance of an ordinary colonist's house with two rooms. In the room nearest the street, the school master lived, as the teacher at that time was called. In the back room the classes were held. In 1843 the community build the present school house on Church Street. It is 10.5 faden long; 4 faden wide; the school hall contains 15.5 square faden. The new school beside the church yard was built in 1863 and until 1881 was used as a storage depot. It is 12 faden long and 4.5 faden wide and contains three wide, bright class rooms.

The School Master, Now Called the Sexton Teacher

The first school master in Kleinliebenthal was apparently Adam Erk. He was well educated and came to Kleinliebenthal from Germany in 1807; he was taken on as a colonist and became a land owner. Before 1819 the files are missing from the Kleinliebenthal Community Archives. The first contract with a school teacher in the archives files was made with Adam Erk in that same year (1819). Because of its originality, I will reproduce the contract word for word:

School Contract of the Communty of Kleinliebenthal with the school master, Adam Erk, for the year 1819. Adam Erk, chosen by the Community of Kleinliebenthal, with the permission of the clergy, must adhere to the following agreement.

1. He must keep school for this year, 1819 until the 31st of August, 1820, 3 hours in the morning and 3 hours in the afternoon.

2. To teach Sunday school for 1 hour every Sunday.

3. To ring the prayer bell 3 times daily.

4. To teach the children to read and write German and Latin and also Arithmetic.

5. To teach four boys how to serve Mass and instruct at least six boys in choral singing.

6. To assist the priest in the customary manner.

7. To conduct an hour of prayer on Saturdays and the usual services on Sunday and Holydays.

8. Under penalty of dismissal, the teacher Adam Erk is not permitted to visit the local tavern during the school year. He must promise also, in view of his position, to behave discreetly at all times.

9. He must not associate with people who read forbidden books, nor read such books himself.

10. If he should use scandalous language, he shall be assessed a church penalty of a payment for three pounds of wax, to be taken out of his salary.

152

11. He is to receive politely the school inspectors appointed by the clergy and in their presence examine the children on what they have learned.

12. With the consent of the clergy, for important and proved causes, the teacher may be dismissed during the year.

For this, A. Erk will receive the sum of 300 rubles; from each child 1 ruble; for assisting the priest at baptisms, marriages and deaths 40 kopecks and in addition 4 lots of hay like every citizen.

Now follow the names of the school masters:

Benedikt Thidick	1820-1821
Konrad Busch	1821-1822
Johannes Ochs	1822-1823
Kaspar Matery	1823-1824
The latter was school master until 1827	
Peter Aberle	1827-1829
Ludwig Weber	1829-1832
For half a year, Johann Mirschinsky replaced Weber	
Adam Erk	1832-1838
Michael Matery	1838-1841
Josef Riszling	1841-1848
Josef Baranak	1848-1858
Johannes Riszling	1858-1869
Franz Benesch	1869-1872
Johannes Riszling	1872-1873
(Died in Kleinliebenthal)	
Michael Riszling	1873-1883
Josef Lang	1883-1897
Gottlieb Tauberger	1897-1898
Josef Lang	1898-1903
Laurentius Adler	1903-

Persons who Became Priests from the Parish of Kleinliebenthal

FATHER GEORG DOBROWOLSKY, Died in 1894.

Father Georg Dobrowolsky was born in 1843 in Odessa, in 1857 he entered the seminary in Saratov. At the end of his theological studies on the 11th of June, 1867, he was ordained a priest by Bishop Lipsky, in Saratov. He worked in various parishes in the diocese of Tiraspol, but mostly in the region of the Volga. After 24 years of labour in the vineyards of the Lord, he contracted an illness, which made him unfit to carry on the duties of a priest. He asked for his dismissal and went to live with his brother Jakob Dobrowolsky, who at that time was parish priest in Landau, in Beresan. There he lived for 10 more years, and helped his brother a great deal with the duties of saving souls. He died of a lung disease in 1894 in Landau, and was buried in the churchyard there.

FATHER MICHAEL HAAG, Died in Luzern, 1878.

Michael Haag was born in 1848 in Kleinliebenthal. In 1861 he entered the Catholic Seminary in Saratov, where he studied diligently, and completed his seminarian studies as a "good dogmatitian." He was ordained a priest on the 22nd of June, 1869 by Bishop Lipsky. His first parish was Pfeifer where he worked very diligently for some years. Later he was entrusted with the administration of the deanery at Kamenka. In 1877 he exchanged with Father J. Beilmann, and was transferred to Luzern, where, however, he arrived already ill. He disregarded his illness and clung to performing his duties, regardless of the exertion. His strength broken, he became seriously ill and died after a few weeks in Luzern in 1878, and was buried there beside the church.

FATHER JAKOB DOBROWOLSKY, Priest at Mannheim and Dean of the Odessa Deanery.

Father Jakob Dobrowolsky, son of the Kleinliebenthal settlers Johann Dobrowolsky and wife Katharina (maiden name Pazernik), was born on the 8th of August, 1854, in the colony of Marienthal, Province of Cherson, Odessa region. He was baptised by Father Christofor Pietkewitsch in the parish church of Josephstal. His father was a poor, but upright master-shoemaker. The parents died when Jakob was still small and he was left a poor orphan. Through support from his older brother Georg, who shortly after the death of his parents was ordained to the priesthood, little Jakob came to the seminary at Saratov in 1868. After nine years of diligent studies, he left the seminary. He was ordained a priest on the 4th of September, 1877 by Bishop Zottmann. He began his priestly duties in Rohleder, where he worked diligently for 2 years, and with (considerable) success. In 1879 he was sent as parish priest to Landau in Beresan, by Bishop Franz Zottmann, where he performed the heavy duties of pastor for almost 20 years, under many difficulties. In 1899 he was sent as parish priest to Marienthal on the Karaman from where he transferred to Mannheim after 2 years. In 1903 he was made Dean of the Odessa Deanery by Bishop Ropp; which position he still holds.

Father Nickolaus Kraft, Posted as Vicar in Christina Parish Katharinenthal

Father Nikolaus Kraft was born on the 6th of December, 1875 in the Kleinliebenthal colony near Odessa. His parents were Leopold Kraft and Elizabeth, born Götz; they are presently enjoying good health. Of five brothers and sisters still living, he is the second oldest. In the school he was a witty little fellow with a thirst for knowledge, therefore the priest and teacher advised his parents to let little Nikolaus continue his studies. Although he was just a small school boy, he had a great love for books, and so would have given away everything for these silent friends. In manual labour he had no pleasure or pride, therefore his parents concluded that they should make a student of him. In 1890 they sent him to Catholic Seminary in Saratov. He entered the first class for boy seminarians and completed it in 1895, and then went over to the clerical seminary. His desire to learn the truth and clarity about God in his student years brought him more thorns than roses. He had the quality, in our time no longer considered desirable, of always expressing his views frankly, clearly and unhesitatingly. Consequently he was frequently misunderstood, hated and slandered. There are many people who cannot endure the truth, like one with sore eyes cannot endure the light. These same people will cry aloud and ask for a certificate from the individual concerned to see whether he has the right to tell the truth. These poor creatures do not know that one must hear the truth just exactly as the truth is, even if the truth is given by a gypsy. On the 2nd of May, 1899, he was fortunate enough to be ordained a priest in Saratov by His Grace Bishop Antonius Zerr. On the 31st of May of the same year, he held his first holy mass in his birthplace. Soon thereafter he was sent as Vicar to Christina, where he still works diligently in the vineyard of the Lord. The community at Christina, in addition to three colonies, includes 60 widely scattered hamlets and single farms with plenty of work.

Presently Father Kraft is building a small church in his Christina residence, which will soon be completed.

FATHER LAURENTIUS WOLF, Acting parish priest in München.

Father L. Wolf saw the light of day on the 10th of December, 1871, in the Kleinliebenthal Colony. He spent his childhood in the house of his poor parents Laurentius Wolf and Petronilla, maiden name Heier. On the advice of the priest from Josephstal, Father Joseph Wanner, he entered the Catholic Seminary in Saratov without any particular preparation. After five years of studying he felt weak and sickly; therefore he left the seminary so that he might recover and regain his health. In 1893 he returned to the seminary and after completing the courses in theology, he was ordained a priest on the 8th of September by his Excellency, Bishop Antonius Zerr. He was first posted as vicar to the Cathedral parish in

Saratov, where he remained for three months, and then was sent in the same capacity to the parish in Kostheim. After eight months in Kostheim he was sent to München as locum tenens, where he still works today, looking after the hamlets and villages.

Deacon Joseph Dieringer

Joseph Dieringer was born in Kleinliebenthal in 1861. He entered the Catholic Seminary in Saratov in 1877, where he studied very hard. After he was ordained as deacon, he came to his home village on holidays, where he preached his first sermon on the feast of the Ascension. After he returned to the Seminary he became ill and died in Saratov, and was buried in the Catholic churchyard there.

George Schütt, was born in Kleinliebenthal on the 28th of January, 1876. He went to America in 1900, where he worked for one year as a hired man. Then he felt the call to devote the rest of his life to the service of God. Our dear Lord gave him the proper spirit. In 1905 he entered as lay brother in the Capuchin monastery in Pittsburgh.

PAST EVENTS AND CONDITIONS IN THE KLEINLIEBENTHAL COLONY

April 1808—Johannes Malsam received a silver medallion from Tsar Alexander I.

1812—Through a glove the plague spread from Odessa to Kleinliebenthal, and 29 people died.

April 29, 1814—In 1814 the community of Kleinliebenthal had only 40 dessatine of land per family and they had to pay 15 kopecks per dessatine land tax; they promised to pay 18 kopecks if the government would give 60 dessatine to each family.

May 17, 1814—Through Inspector Hippius the first wolf hunt was organized.

June 9, 1814—Mayor Anton Wolf died on the 16th of June; Joseph Baumann was chosen in his place.

July 28, 1814—Mayor J. Baumann resigned because M. Wolf and J. Sahly accused him of drinking up the money of the community treasury. He (Baumann) demanded satisfaction.

Sept., 1815—Peter Stein built an oil press. The necessary parts for its construction he obtained from Kiev.

Oct. 9, 1815—J. Paulo was suspected of keeping company with thieves. He had, despite a poor harvest, bought three pair of óxen. The mayor's office requested to see the lawful transaction.

156

This offended Paulo, and he started to quarrel and insult and called the mayor a turkey thief. The mayor turned him over to higher authorities and asked for help and satisfaction.

Dec. 11, 1815—The debtors of Franz Brittner (formerly district mayor) are supposed to pay their debt; but the municipality said no, because Brittner's sheep ate half the haystack of the community of Kleinliebenthal, and they requested that Brittner pay 20 kopeck damages for each of the 900 sheep.

Dec. 30, 1815—The Kleinliebenthal people received verbal authority from Duke Richelieu to sleep their cattle in their pastures.

Dec. 31, 1815—School teacher Adam Erk had some sacred books for sale. The community land of Kleinliebenthal was surveyed for the first time in 1807.

Jan. 5, 1816—The Kleinliebenthal wine merchant Jacob Hurrbein informed the community that the price of brandy was as follows:

Prostoi—brandy	7 rubles per litre
Anis	14 rubles per litre
Wischnovka	14 rubles per litre
Bitters	14 rubles per litre

The Kleinliebenthal community complained about the high price and requested a new contract from the innkeeper.

March 1, 1816—The Kleinliebenthal Community accused Inspector Hippius on the following grounds:

1. He became drunk on punch.
2. On the 26th of February, he had requested that butter and eggs be collected from the community for himself.
3. He requested that every landowner plant 20 pounds of summer wheat for him.
4. Every time he came to the colony, he wanted his purse filled.
5. He requested 12 bushels of wheat from J. Däschle, in return for not punishing him for a misdemeanor.

April 2, 1816—For the year 1815, the Kleinliebenthal community paid 1,001 rubles, 15 kopecks for land taxes and head taxes.

May 19, 1816—In 1816 the number of animals in Kleinliebenthal were as follows: 300 horses; 320 oxen; 490 cows; 361 calves; 10 sheep; 335 pigs. In the fall of 1816 there was an epidemic of foot and mouth disease.

Oct. 15, 1816—The nobleman Schosdak was looking for apprentices for his clothing factory.

1816—The Kleinliebenthal mayor received 30 rubles, the secretary 150 rubles, the midwife 24 rubles.

Jan. 18, 1817—Alois Aquin, from the Rastadt colony, accused Ignace Bienfait of using abusive language toward him in Odessa. Bienfait said to Aquin in the tavern: "I have no respect for the people who once lived on the land and then move to the city. When they again return to the land, oxen and horses are stolen every time." The mayor's office fined Bienfait 2 rubles, 40 kopecks, payable to the church.

Jan. 17, 1817—Johann Wolf, son of Anton Wolf, was married on the 22nd of January, 1817, to Catharine Fix; moved to Franzfeld. (That's where the Franzfelder Wolfs came from.)

Jan. 17, 1817—Spinning wheels were offered for sale in the district office.

Jan. 24, 1817—The bridegroom and bride, Johann Krezner and Barbara Seiler from Kleinliebenthal, went to Father Franz Hoffman, S.J., at Josephstal (Father Jann was away), to be married. However, since the bride was poorly prepared, she had to remain in Josephstal 14 days to receive instruction from the school teacher; only then could she be married. (If a priest carried on like that today, the colonists would stone him.)

May 8, 1817—The Kleinliebenthal community complained to the liquor board because there was no ice cellar in the village to store their beer and mead in. It was therefore necessary to drink the bad, tasteless wine at "1 ruble a quart." Also, the liquor board did not give the full value for the silver rubel. In addition, the inn-keeper was charging too much per drink, e.g., for the Anis, Bitters and Wischnovka, 1 rubel 40 kopecks for a drink; for French wine, 3 rubles per drink. (Apparently the inn had good variety for our forefathers.)

May, 1817—The single man Thomas Däschle, 20 years old, married the single Elizabeth Adler, 18 years old. Franz Daschle gave to his son Thomas the following: a pair of oxen; 2 cows; 100 rubles in cash and half a farm. Sebastian Adler gave his daughter Elizabeth: 2 cows, 2 year-old steers, and 240 bushels of each of rye, winter wheat, summer wheat, oats and barley.

June 4, 1817—The ministry ordered that a pharmacy be established at Grossliebenthal for the colonists, and to be supported by them. One thousand rubles were to be taken from the community treasury for this purpose.

July 12, 1817—Andreas Wildemann, 20 years old, was struck by lightning in the field.

July 17, 1817—The Kl. community accused Inspector Sultanov:
1. Because he did not understand German, he was giving a bad reputation to the Kleinliebenthal people, in that he was accusing them of being revolutionaries.
2. He listened only to the complainant and not to the accused.
3. The community paid him yearly per family 1 ruble and 40 pounds of oats, so that they would not have to work for him, and still they had to work for him.

4. In his order of the 31st of March, 1817, number 278, he worded the instructions just as though he wished to make slaves of all those under his jurisdiction.

5. He said that the colonists were to report all their taxes paid to the community, but not to report any money expended on his behalf. They wished another inspector who could speak German.

July 28, 1817—In this year Kleinliebenthal rented land for 2,000 rubles.

Aug. 3, 1817—The new community granary was completed except for the roof.

Oct. 30, 1817—There were many new colonists from Würtemberg quartered in Kleinliebenthal, but since nearly all were ill, they were taken to the hospital in Grossliebenthal.

Nov. 7, 1817—New colonists from Würtemberg were also quartered in Beresan and Kutschurgan colonies.

No. 24, 1817—The new settler (Würtemberger) Mathias Richle, his son and daughter had leprosy and were taken to the hospital in Grossliebenthal. Four other people developed leprosy. Würtemburg colonists were quartered in every house, including those of the village officials.

Dec. 8, 1817—An order by the authorities was read to the Würtemberg people, that there was no land available for them in Caucasia, and the proposal was made for them to settle on the land of noblemen; but they did not wish this.

1817—In Kleinliebenthal there were 236 men and 251 women (among them five Lutherans).

March 1, 1818—The Würtemberg people were offered work in Odessa digging ditches for the newly finished free harbor, but they did not wish to do this.

1818—The orders for fire prevention were as follows:

1. A watch must be kept at all times.

2. To sound the alarm.

3. Every householder must have a full barrel of water.

4. In the community house there must be a water wagon with a barrel and fire axes and fire ladders.

5. Each householder must keep iron pitchforks and horses in readiness.

March 10, 1819—When the colony of Kleinliebenthal was surveyed, it was divided into 82 lots; by 1819 there were houses on 80 lots.

Jan. 7, 1819—Crown spinning wheels were offered for sale, but no one desired this type.

1819—There was already a Jewish wine merchant in Kleinliebenthal.

Feb. 13, 1819—Wendel Wolf bought the farm of Johann Paulo and paid him 1700 rubles in cash.

March 27, 1819—The community of Kleinliebenthal requested a loan of 1500 rubles from the district office so that they could start the church building.

April 14, 1819—Mayor P. Stein came into the tavern at 2 o'clock at night and found the drinking companions B. Dieringer, J. Hurrbein and R. Lang; he gave them time to leave but the three did not listen and insulted the Mayor. The mayor sued them in the district office and demanded satisfaction.

In the year 1819 two houses in Kleinliebenthal were burned, as people with the plague had died there.

July 30, 1819—General Inzov donated 100 rubles to the Kleinliebenthal church fund.

Sept. 4, 1819—It was ordered that trees were to be planted in front of the houses. Those who did not have any cuttings could get them from the master forester, Radoloff, in Slobodse. Those who did not follow this order would be punished with eight days of community work.

Circular — Bulletin

On the 24th of August the colonist F. Deschner from Marienthal stole a silver-mounted tobacco pipe from K.J. Tersch of Freudenthal, in the tavern at Karlsthal. As a result of this the community of Marienthal was insulted and enraged and ordered by community decree:

"The thief shall, in the sight of the whole community and the youth, have an iron collar placed around his neck for one hour, and the crime written on a slate and placed on his chest. The colonist A. Steininger in Odessa, is also to be placed in the iron collar for two hours. And lastly, M. Stahl from E, because he stole a lady's hat from the Phillippow cellar, is to be tied onto the same collar with a rope, next to Wenz, and each is to have his crime written on a slate and placed on his chest."

Signed: District mayor Wolf

This order was read out to the whole assembled community as a warning that no one should commit such a shameful deed.
(One notices from this event that there was a strong feeling of honour among the colonists.)

Sept. 1819—Joseph Wild married Theresa Ochs who had just arrived from Germany. J. Wild received the following dowry: two horses and two oxen. His step-father, Joseph Braun gave him his landholding. The bride's dowry was: 1600 rubles, one horse and furniture worth 200 rubles. (A very rich bride at that time.)

Dec. 21, 1819—It was strickly forbidden to shoot on New Year's Eve, the penalty for shooting was 10 rubles.

1819—A Crown windmill was erected in Kleinliebenthal.

1820—A frightful judgement of God: Johannes (Hanz) Heinzmann, a bachelor, saw Mrs. Theresa Wildemann digging potatoes in her field. He thought that she was Marie Gsell, who was very similar in appearance to Theresa Wildemann, and reported the Gsell woman as having stolen potatoes. The woman was brought to court where she swore high and low that she was not responsible for the robbery. Theresa Wildemann was also brought before the court as witness for the defence; she asserted that Marie Gsell did not steal the potatoes. On the contrary, she, Mrs. Wildemann, had been digging potatoes in her own field. The judges began to doubt the accusation of Marie Gsell. Then Hanz Heinzmann stood up and uttered these frightful words: "If my story is not true, the first lightning which appears in heaven shall strike me dead." On this dreadful vow the judges decreed that Marie Gsell was to thread some potatoes on a string and to hang them around her neck, and carry them around the whole colony. And what came to pass as a result of this false oath? Harvesting had already begun, when Hanz Heinzmann, along with his brothers and other people not far from the Grossliebenthal road, sat down beside the wagon during the noon hour. Their lunch consisted of cakes. There arose in the sky a dreadful thunderstorm that came close to those eating lunch. Hanz Heinzmann stood up and walked a few steps from the wagon, when there suddenly occurred a streak of lightning followed by a roll of thunder. Then one heard a dreadful scream. Hanz Heinzmann lay dead on the ground; he still had a piece of egg cake in his mouth. The spot where this frightful judgement occurred is still called the "Cross Field," because earlier there was a cross erected there, so that people would remember this spot.

1820—There were 72 stone and 10 wooden houses in Kleinliebenthal.

Feb. 3, 1820—Notice was given that a market would be held in Grossliebenthal twice a year, in May and October.

Feb. 4, 1820—The district government office had learned that some Kleinliebenthal men were spending the whole night long in the tavern, drinking and not observing the closing time of 10 o'clock It was ordered that the innkeeper observe the proper closing time every evening, that he should not sell any drinks after ten o'clock, and that a written promise be obtained from the innkeeper and sent into the district office.

Feb. 4, 1820—Promise of the innkeeper of Kleinliebenthal: "I, the undersigned Kleinliebenthal wine merchant, acknowledge the highly esteemed order. Now that the district office has clarified and has made known to me the order for closing, I promise to comply with the order, and under no circumstance to break it. I promise from now on, not to dispense any drinks at night after 10 o'clock, or permit anyone in the tavern after the above noted time. If I should break this order I will surrender myself to the harshness of the law, which I affirm with my undersigned signature.—Mendel Kreschnobalsky, innkeeper."

Dec. 22, 1820—Nikolaus Schüler accused Adam E. that he had insulted him, and had called the district mayor W. and the mayor St., "Common-thieves."

1820—In the fall of 1820 there were 128 dessatine planted with rye and 168 dessatine with winter wheat, in Kleinliebenthal.

1821—There were 10 Bibles in Kleinliebenthal. In each house there was a biblical history.

1821—Martin Malsam was horse herdsman in Kleinliebenthal; he received 2 rubel and 80 kopeck per horse.

1821—Johannes Merklinger was made cow herder and received 1 rubel 20 kopecks. When he brings a calf home he receives 60 kopecks.

1823—In Kleinliebenthal there is a common shepherd, P. Johannes Domarshausen. He took over the job of herding the sheep for the whole colony except those of the colonist Michael Wolf. For one year as herder, he received the sum of 150 rubles together with 5½ tschetwert of grain, half of wheat and half rye, along with free residence in the community shepherds' house. He also received a piece of land, and ½ tschetwert of rye to plant it. If a wolf killed a sheep the shepherd had to bring the hide to the owner.

1823—School master Johannes Ochs received the following salary: from each family, 4 rubles; from each school child 1 ruble and 4 lots of hay, and was free from any extra work for the community.

1827—An unheard of storm arose from the south moving north; it took off the roofs of many houses and barns, destroyed haystacks in Kleinliebenthal, blew over windmills, and even tore trees out of the ground.

March 8, 1828—The Beresan colonist Georg Kitzel, was hired as cook for Father Sibini. He had to cook, keep the rooms clean and do everything that the priest asked him. For this he received 40 rubles a year.

1828—The Kleinliebenthal secretary was a Pole, named Johann Mierschinsky; he received 350 ruble. When he was removed from the secretary's office, he took over the place of a colony innkeeper in Kleinliebenthal. One time he invited his previous office comrades, the mayor, the assistants and his other friends to a banquet of roast hare. When the roast hare was nearly eaten by the guests, one heard from behind the oven "meow, meow." Everyone looked up and at the host. From his roguish look they all concluded that instead of hare, they had eaten roast cat. This naturally caused considerable nausea for some, but the fact could not be altered. All went home cursing and swearing. This Mierschinsky married the maiden Elizabeth Walz in Kleinliebenthal, and she bore him two children. One day he left his wife and children and has not been seen to this day. His wife was cook for Father Grizewitsch and became married later in Baden. His son Henry is apparently still living in Cherson, and his daughter Barbara is married in Odessa. When I was the military chaplain in Caucasia, I buried an old Pole in Deschlagar, who earlier had been a steward there, named Johannes Mierschinsky. One wonders if he was not the missing man.

1829—There was a strong earthquake, but other than fright, it caused no damage.

1831—There were many people sick in Kleinliebenthal with cholera; only one died. The others drank peppermint extract and from this they again became well.

1833—It was a poor year, but still the peopled harvested enough for seed and bread. In the Beresan colonies this year there was a complete failure.

1834—The richest farmers in Kleinliebenthal were Ignaz Most and Georg Leppert; each this year seeded wheat, 14 dessatine, oats 7 dessatine, rye 5 dessatine, potatoes 3 dessatine. The land at that time was ploughed as far as the road to Josephstal. (The work was done mostly with oxen, up until 1850.)

1838—There were strong earthquakes, but no damage was done.

January, 1842—The single young men, J. Kirchgassner and J. Konnanz were fined 1 ruble, 42 kopecks for shooting on New Year's Eve, which was prohibited.

January, 1842—Joseph W. was given 10 cane blows for loitering around and squandering.

April, 1842—The colonist Johann M. was punished with 15 blows with the rod, for drinking and fighting. His two younger single brothers each received 10 lashes. (A handsome trio!)

July, 1842—S. Dieringer was fined 5 kopeck for smoking in the street, which was prohibited.

July 22, 1842—The wife of Joseph M., first name being J., was tried and fined with 10 cane blows. The district office, in co-operation with the office of the mayor and a jury of ten men from the community, investigated the case. She had wilfully and without cause accused her fellow citizens and so damaged their reputation.

July 22, 1842—Michael M., because of unbecoming conduct and insults in front of the parish rectory, was punished with 10 cane blows.

November, 1842—The women, Katharina D., Carolina R., Maria S. and Magdalena G., because of fighting and bad language were fined; the first three, 30 kopecks; the last 15 kopecks.

March, 1843—Martin S., single, received 15 cane blows for fighting.

April 15, 1843—The bachelor Wendelin E. received 20 cane blows for instigating a fight on the wolf hunt, when he seized the Franzfeld mayor, Merdian, and offended the Josephstal mayor, Scherer and the member of the Economic Association, named Amon.

May 26—Andreas A. received 15 cane blows for having music and dancing in his house on Easter Monday, during which time fighting occurred.

May, 1844—Stefan W. was punished with 20 days arrest for coarse insults to Father Griezewitsch.

June, 1844—A severe wind storm accompanied by lightning and hail arose in the west and moved to the east over a part of the Kleinliebenthal fields, doing about 320 tschetwert damage in the fields of nearly ripe wheat, which was severely damaged by the hail.

July, 1844—Martin S. was fined 5 rubles, to be paid to the church treasury for breaking the Sabbath by hauling wheat to his home on the Lord's Day.

November, 1844—In November the mayor's office went about the colony to check whether everything was in order. There were 35 householders fined because of disorder in their homes. I provide hereof only a few names:

1. Joseph Bienfait, since he had a poor fence around the yard and had no trees in the yard, had to clear 10 square faden.*

2. Stephan Wolf, for having a bad chimney, had to clear 5 square faden.

3. G. Bürk had a bad fence, for punishment he had to clear 3 square faden.

4. G. Stein had only half a fence, he had to clear 3 square faden.

*This clearing was usually done in the forest.

5. G. Fischer had a poor roof, no yard fence and no trees, for punishment he had to clear 12 square faden.

6. A. Sahly had no garden fence, he had to clear 5 square faden.

May, 1845—The bachelor Michael O. received 50 cane blows from the legal office for rudely insulting and ridiculing his parents and leaving home.

The two single sisters, Elizabeth and Mariana, because of the same matter, each received 10 cane blows.

1846—The single youths, Valentine M., Wendelin M., Peter M., and Philipp L., because they all stole meat and wine, each received 30 cane blows.

(One sees from above that there was much crime in Kleinliebenthal, but one sees also that at that time there was much right and righteousness in the community, and the crime was punished accordingly. But today there is a great deal more mischief, and the perpetrators walk the streets unpunished, as for instance one saw during the past summer.)

1850—Bishop Ignazius Holowinsky was in Kleinliebenthal.

1864—Bishop Vinzens Lipsky was in Kleinliebenthal.

1878—A maiden was killed, and the body thrown in Nieder's well. Some people hanged themselves, some drowned and more children drowned in the liman.

1885—Aloysius Erk was killed by lightning.

1886—Bishop Franz Zottmann was in Kleinliebenthal and lived here until the spring of 1887. Every morning after mass he gave a short address. On a few occasions he also preached the sermon on Sunday.

1895—Through an imperial government decree, the colony of Kleinliebenthal was renamed "Kseniewka."

1899—There was a complete crop failure in Kleinliebenthal.

1905—The harvest was very small.

A SHORT CHRONICLE OF

Josephstal

on the River Baraboi

from 1804 to 1904

The colony of Josephstal, also called Sergiewka, is under the jurisdiction of the Cherson Provincial Government, Odessa district, municipality of Marjinskoe. It is located 25 versts (1 verst is equal to 7/10 of a mile) from the seaport of Odessa and 20 versts from the main railway station of Tiraspolskaja Sastawa, on the small river Baraboi.

The Baraboi was called "Burjuboin;" that is, wolf's neck (collum lupinum) by the Turks, and is 90 versts long. It originates in the hills of the colony of Kapokleewka, on the southwest railway; it flows in a southerly direction through the whole Odessa region. On the right it is joined by the small rivers, Haidomazskaja and Gessel, joins with the Woltschaja and Krinitschka, and flows with them through Belayevka directly into the Black Sea.

For thirty years the Baraboi contained water to the edge of the Josephstal forest, and was rich in fish. Now, in the summer, it is mostly dry throughout its length. Only in the spring when the snow melts does it contain water, and occasionally overflows its banks, causing serious damage by its flooding.

Near Josephstal the valley of the Baraboi is flat, about 100 Faden (1 Faden is equal to 6 feet) wide, and planted with numerous lovely gardens. The colony is located on the left (east) side of the river and contains a single street, 2 versts long, with two rows of houses from north to south.

In the north end there is a small street—called the Chutor of the upper village as distinguished from the Chutor of the lower village, which is located on the other side of the valley. Josephstal has at present 162 houses, with 1,116 souls. The occupations of the inhabitants are agriculture, cattle raising, wine growing, and vegetable gardening. The most important buildings are the church, the school, the rectory, and community office. On either side of the colony there is a lovely row of acacia trees, picturesque in appearance. The stone walls on either side of the street are whitewashed, and the houses are mostly blue. The cleanliness of the yards and the streets is very obvious, when compared with the nearby colonies. The houses and other buildings here are similar to those in Kleinliebenthal.

The founding of the colony Josephstal began in 1804 and was completed in 1810. The settlers were from various provinces.

1. Lower Palatinate (Part of Rhineland) .... 6 families
2. Upper Palatinate .... 11 families
3. Duchy of Baden .... 9 families
4. Kingdom of Würtenberg .... 4 families
5. Hungary .... 7 families
6. Lower Alsace .... 11 families
7. Upper Alsace .... 14 families
8. Lorraine .... 1 family
9. Silesia................................ 2 families
10. Bohemia .... 1 family
11. Switzerland .... 2 families

In March, 1804, thirty-two families came with their few belongings to this place, where the colony is now located. But this place then was waste and desert; on both sides of the Baraboi were reeds and shrubs of every kind, which stood as high as trees. They were so high and thick it was only with considerable effort that one could get through. There were no traces of human habitation or any kind of cultivation to be found.

Only wolves, foxes, jackals and other wild animals made their homes here. How discouraged the poor settlers must have been! But there was no use complaining. They immediately had to get to work to provide themselves with a much-needed shelter. In one day under the instruction and supervision of the first Colonial Inspector, Joseph Schimiot, 32 huts were built of wicker work; in them the settlers lived and the "Colony of Josephstal" was founded. In the following years more settlers came. In 1805, five families

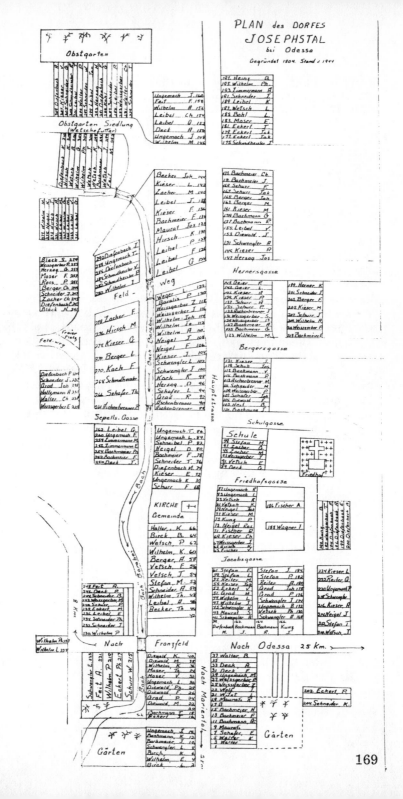

THE JOSEPHSTAL COLONY

PLAN des DORFES
JOSEPHSTAL
bei Odessa
Gegründet 1804. Stand 1944

169

arrived; in 1807, four families; in 1808, fifteen families; in 1809, ten families; in 1810, two families.

In the summer of 1804, the Crown built a small clay adobe* house for each of the first settlers. The colony was started by the Duke of Richelieu, and the name Josephstal was given to the colony by Inspector Schimiot.

The Josephstal Community Land

The landholding of Josephstal contains 3,126¾ dessatine (1 dessatin is equal to 2¾ acres), of which 181 dessatine are meadow land located near Franzfeld on the Dniester, and 120 dessatin are Parish Land. Bought land is occupied by only a few individuals altogether amounting to approximately 100 dessatine.

The community land is bounded on the south by Marienthal, on the west by Franzfeld and Petersthal, on the north by Freudenthal, on the east by the sheepland and Grossliebenthal Land. The number of household establishments or homesteads is sixty-eight.

Most of the land is level. Only the Baraboi and a few lakes break the level plain. The surface soil contains good, thick, black earth. two to three feet thick. The subsoil is clay and marl.** Near the colony, on the banks of the right edge of the river, are profitable stone quarries. The stones are hard and are used to build houses and other buildings. The soil is fertile, and with favorable weather furnishes the whole region with rich crops.

List of Names of the First Settlers and Homesteaders of the Colony Josephstal on the Baraboi

House
No.
1. Michael Ekert
2. Johann Fischer
3. Michael Grad
4. Jakob Simon
5. Johann Riener, estate inherited by his son-in-law Michael Bachmeier
6. Joseph Ekert
7. Philipp Deis, estate inherited by Christian Bürk
8. Johann Kunz
9. Johann Boll, estate inherited by Franz Neigel
10. Friedrich Gabel, the estate to Jakob Kunanz

*Adobe—unburnt brick dried in the sun.
**marl, a carbonate of lime, a valuable fertilizer.

11. Andreas Kunz, the estate to stepson Franz Heinz
12. Martin Weisgerber
13. Heinrich Moser
14. Georg Black
15. Jacob Roh, estate to his son-in-law George Bachmann
16. Peter Schäfer
17. Franz Stumpf, estate to stepson Franz Bachmann
18. Georg Stegmann, estate inherited by stepson Peter Hartmann
19. Johann Bachmann
20. Anton Schuh
21. Georg Zink
22. Michael Veigel, the estate went to Sebastin Wolf
23. Wilhelm Koch
24. Martin Herzog
25. Simon Goehringer
26. Joseph Aschenbrenner
27. Johann Ungemach
28. Georg Gse'l, estate inherited by stepson Nickolaus Ibach
29. Peter Mann, estate went to Johann Deck from Franzfeld
30. Georg Weisgerber, inherited by Philipp Ros
31. Andreas Maurath
32. Philipp Herbach
33. Johan Rössler, estate went to Joseph Wilhelm.
34. Georg Bachmann
35. Kasimir Walter, estate inherited by Johann Schnaible
36. Johann Maurath
37. Johann Deck
38. Phillip Epp, estate inherited by stepson Michael Kell
39. Sebastian Hettler
40. Heinrich Acker, went to Mannheim
41. Johann Hirsch
42. Christian Kieffer
43. Joseph Schwengler
44. Ludwig Diewald
45. Michael Hentsch
46. Ludwig Vetsch (also spelled Fetsch)
47. Paul Diewald
48. Balthasar Wüst
49. Sebastin Leibel, estate inherited by Johann Bachmeier
50. Jacob Weger
51. Kaspar Reich (is said to have died without progeny)
52. Georg Sacher
53. Michael Wilhelm

54. Franz Neugel (?)
55. Dittrich Erbach, estate inherited by his son-in-law Jakob Stefan
56. Leonard Wolf
57. Peter Geier
58. Heinrich Weisgerber
59. Martin Steiner, estate went to Johann Ekert
60. Philipp Schmidt
61. Adam Fleischmann
62. Karl Weiss, estate went to Philipp Ros
63. Leonhard Scherrer
64. Johan Werner
65. Georg Becker
66. Adam Schweizer
67. Peter Schmiedheissler
68. Michael Brünster

The following also settled in Josephstal: Stefan Stein, Joseph Schmidt, Jakob Geister, Martin Rauf, Joseph Moser, Xaverius Wacker, Franz Becker, Michael Junkert, Franz Wolf, Joseph Vetter, George Kolmer, Balthasar Erbach, Nicholaus Derschan (his wife Marie left him), George Ludwig, Johann Mergel, Jakob Sanger, Joseph Maul, Jakob Greiner (came from Grossliebenthal in 1815), Joseph Schnurr.

The Present Wealth and Welfare of the Colony Josephstal

The land in the community is divided approximately as follows: for the buildings, 20 dessatine; cattle range, 5 dessatine; vegetable garden, 30 dessatine; fruit garden, 10 dessatine; vineyard, 23 dessatine; forest and shrubs, 15 dessatine; ponds, 2 dessatine; clay hillock, 1 dessatine; hay meadow, 90 dessatine; stone quarry, 17¾ dessatine; roads, 51 dessatine; threshing place, 90 dessatine; pasture, 320 dessatine; cultivation, 2,537 dessatine; rented land, over 500 dessatine. The harvest in 1905 was only moderate.

The municipal officers and congregational attendant receive the following salaries. The mayor receives 50 rubles; the secretary, 400 rubles; the treasurer, 25 rubles; the bailiff, 170 rubles; the horse herder, 1 ruble and 20 kopecks per head; the cow herder, 46 kopecks; the calf herder, 60 kopecks; the field guard, 90 rubles per year; the school attendant, (janitor) 40 rubles per year.

Livestock in the colony include 178 horses, with 2 Voronezh stallions, 595 cows and calves with 7 bulls of the Molotschna breed, and 538 pigs.

In Josephstal there are two stores and one liquor store (monopoly). There are approximately ten tradesmen. The colony earned a considerable income by growing vegetables and fruit. The vineyards are not very profitable, for the wine is of poor quality. The people of Josephstal do not have their vineyards in the right place, and hence their wine is not worth very much. The vineyard should be on a hill in the valley, since it requires more sun. (Therefore, you people of Josephstal, find yourself such a hill, and your wine will taste better.) The people of Josephstal deserve special praise because they still have a beautiful piece of the original forest, which is absent in most colonies.

Josephstal pays the following taxes: Crown taxes, 323 rubles 28 kopecks; Land taxes, 1,364 rubles 29 kopecks; Paying for land grant, 2.073 rubles 48 kopecks; Community taxes, 2,420 rubles.

Josephstal Parish

Josephstal has 162 houses with 1,116 inhabitants, all of them being of the Roman Catholic faith. Those of other faith remain in the colony only a very short time. The parish belongs to the deanery of Odessa, diocese of Tiraspol. To this parish belongs the affiliate of Marienthal. The distance from the post office, Marjinskoe (Grossliebenthal) is 12 versts.

The Parish History

The first move to establish a parish at Josephstal was made by Duke Richelieu. The Catholic German immigrants who arrived in Odessa in 1803 and had their winter quarters there, had to turn to the Duke to ask him to make it possible for them to perform their religious duties, especially since the Catholic clergy in Odessa were all Italians who did not know the German language. Richelieu seems to have approached Father Gruber, then Father General of the Society of Jesus.

In March, 1804, the General sent Father Aloys Löffler and laybrother Georgius Lieb to the new settlement near Odessa there to minister to the souls of the Catholic colony.

Father Löffler, with his helper Lieb, seems to have accompanied the colonists from Odessa to their settlement. The settlers founded the colony in March 1804, and on March 25, 1804, Father Löffler baptized the first child.

The priests at first resided at Kleinliebenthal, but by 1805 they moved to Josephstal. The circumstances of the first priests in Josephstal were described in the diary of Father Joseph Korizky as follows: "Our priests in the Colony Josephstal near Odessa have neither a proper church nor a comfortable, healthy residence; they live very poorly. The salary is very small and the lack of provisions and other necessities is very evident. The colonists themselves are very poor and have poor houses. The air is harmful, especially to newcomers, as the wind blows mostly from the sea. The winter here is all the more troublesome. Since there is a tremendous scarcity of firewood, the people use the seaweed to heat and cook their food. This manner of heat, however, is not satisfactory, nor is this material easy to come by, since the seaweed is tied in bundles and sold at a fixed price. Forests do not grow here, or they are very scarce, and consequently wood is very expensive. In the summer, the mornings are very cool and prejudicial to health, so that if anyone goes out dressed lightly, he may get a high fever that sometimes ends in death. Therefore the inhabitants always use warm clothes during the morning.

"The fields are full of rats and snakes. It happened on one occasion when the priest returned to his mud house after a journey, he noted a peculiar smell. While he wondered about this smell, he started to hunt in every corner of the room, and alas, a large snake lay at his feet. As he searched the mud floor further, he saw a great number of snakes in his hut, so that he had to excavate the whole place in order to clean out the reptiles. One sees from this that the situation of the first priests in Josephstal was no more pleasant than, and just as dangerous as, that of the present missionaries in Africa."

Under these conditions, the priests lived a truly missionary life until 1808 when three priests had already died of "fever," and the fourth priest, Father Osmolowsky, was seriously ill. In the year 1808, Father Brzozowski, General of the Society of Jesus, wrote to the Minister of the Interior that of the four priests that he had sent to Josephstal, three had already succumbed to the murderous climate, and the fourth priest also was sick. On this account, he wrote, he was forced to send two priests at a time, so that if one were sick, the other could take his place. Furthermore, could they grant an increase in the salary of the priests, and supply free transportation to their destination.? If this suggestion could not be accepted, the General asked to be relieved of the duty of sending priests to Josephstal in the future.

The minister did not accept this proposal, and the priests were recalled from Josephstal in 1809. From then until the 27th of September, 1811, the parish of Josephstal was cared for from Odessa. As a result of the departure of the priests of the Society of Jesus, the Duke of Richelieu was placed in great embarrassment, since the Catholic settlers entrusted to him were as a result of this unable to fulfil their religious obligations. On this account, Richelieu wrote to Prince Galizin, in 1810, as follows: "In Odessa at present there is a flood of foreign immigrants, who, for the most part, belong to the Catholic faith; this has created a need for more Catholic priests who can speak German, French, Polish, and Italian here and in the neighboring Catholic colonies. Since the salary of the ministering priests is so small, it would be desirable to recruit for Odessa and colonies, Capuchin monks who live mostly from alms.

"Since, however, as I understand it, the clergy of the above-mentioned society in Russia speak only Latin and Polish, and do not know the German language, it might be possible to write to Bavaria and Tyrol, where this society has been suspended, and ask for eight Capuchin monks for Odessa and the surrounding Catholic colonies."

Prince Galizin was sympathetic to this idea, and himself negotiated with the Archbishop, Sestrinzewitsch, and Count Rumjanzow. Sestrinzewitsch answered Prince Galizin concerning this matter, stating that in the monasteries of the Capuchin monks in Russia, there was no one with holy orders who understood German sufficiently, and that it would be best to go directly to Germany. After this, Prince Galizin himself turned to Count Rumjanzow in the matter. He in turn brought the matter to the attention of the Tsar. Alexander I ordered that one get in touch with the Russian ambassador in Vienna, Count Stakelberg. The Count personally handed the request of the Russian government to Archbishop Hohenwart of Vienna and to the papal nuntio Severoli. The nuncio reported this case to the Prefect of Propaganda, but even there could be found no Capuchin monks for Odessa and Josephstal.

The Secretary of Propaganda answered as follows: "The Odessa mission until now has been looked after by Franciscans from Constantinople, but there is not a single Franciscan there now. Capuchin monks cannot be sent from the Roman province of the Order, because they cannot get passports."

The papal nuncio reported the result of this communication to Count Rumjanzow, and suggested to him for the above mission, eight priests of the Society of Jesus, priests for whom he himself would vouch in every respect.

This proposition of the nuncio was accepted, and in 1811, a priest of the Society of Jesus again came to Josephstal.

Succession of Parish Priests at Josephstal

Father Aloysius Löffler, S. J., Parish Priest from March 2, 1804 to February 7, 1807.

Father Aloysius Löffler, S.J., was born in Innsbruck on January 29, 1769; on the 24th of August, 1788, he entered the order of the Society of Jesus in Polotsk. He was one of ten pioneers who were sent to the Catholic colonies on the Volga in March, 1903. His first posting was to the Colony Preuss (Krasnopolje).

Father Löffler began his mission in the spirit of Saint Ignatius, whose spiritual exercises he presented to his parishioners in preparation for Easter confession. The wholesome effect of this action was surprising. They were shaken by the penetrating words of the priest, and the Holy Spirit entered their bosoms, so that hardened sinners who for many years had not gone to confession, again returned to the Church. Father Löffler had many unpleasant experiences, especially with mixed marriages. A certain Marie Sandos wanted to marry a non-Catholic. Father Löffler gave her the necessary instruction and admonition about this subject. However, since she did not pay any attention, he denied her absolution. So she reported the priest to Archbishop Sestrinzewitsch, who ordered Father Löffler to marry her in the Catholic Church, but before he had received this notice, he had been transferred to Josephstal, near Odessa.

Father Löffler worked with the same zeal and ardour at Josephstal as he had worked at Preuss. However, here the conditions were more difficult to deal with. The new immigrants had been thrown together from every German province. They were cold in their faith, loose in their morals, lazy in their work, poor in wordly goods, and deficient in virtues. It was necessary to bring order into this chaos. Unwearied, he was energetic in trying to lead his parishioners to fulfil their duties, to comfort them in their poverty and destitution, and to lead them onto the road of virtue.

In 1806, he built a small church and also a school, and took endless trouble trying to break the old careless ways of the colonists, in attempting to lead them to become upright people and worthy citizens. But soon his strength failed. He became seriously ill with malaria, and in 1807 had to leave the scene of his fruitful labors. He returned to White Russia. In 1814 he was made spiritual leader in the College of Uschwald, and also preacher in the College Church, in which posting, so it seems, he remained until the society was expelled from Russia. He was an Elector in 1829 in the choice of General Roothan in Rome. He died at an old age on the 30th of April, 1842, in Graz—R.I.P.

Assistant to Father Löffler in Josephstal was Father Dominikus Vinturi, S.J., 1805, perhaps only as a guest, Father Jakobus Gothot, S.J., baptized from July 1, 1806, to October 18, 1806, in which year he died in Josephstal.

One ought to pray publicly for the first and subsequent priests on Sundays and holy days.

Father Thaddaus Hattowsky, S.J., Parish Priest from February 21, to December 1, 1807.

Father Thaddaus Hattowsky, S.J., was born on the 22nd of January, 1765. He entered the Society of Jesus on February 1, 1780, in Polotsk.

He was one of the first novices in the newly opened novitiate, which had been closed since the suppression of the Society of Jesus. When he asked permission from his father to join the Society of Jesus, the latter wrote as follows: "The position of the Jesuits in White Russia is very uncertain. It could easily happen that under anti-Catholic rulers, permission could be rescinded so that the Jesuits sooner or later might be chased out, or through forcible persecution be oppressed. What would you do then, imprudent boy?"

However, the youth answered boldly and fearlessly "Dear Father; From the yoke placed on the neck of the Jesuits I will not withdraw mine. Banished, I will follow the exiled wherever they may go; life and death will be our common lot." Surprised by the answer of this precocious youth, the father gave his permission for his son to enter the order. He completed his studies with good results, became a priest, and earned great praise as a preacher.

In 1803 he came to the Catholic colonies on the Volga, where he took charge of the parish of Kasitskaja. Here he worked very ardently in the vineyard of the Lord. It is said that while there, he cured many sick in a miraculous manner. One usually saw him only in church and at the sick bed. Once it happened that a woman was sick with dropsy. Her condition was hopeless, so much so that she had received final sacraments. Then Father Hattowsky gave her "Ignatius water" to drink, and as soon as she had swallowed the water she became instantly well. The miracle healing was confirmed by more than twenty people.

In 1807, Father Hattowsky was sent to Josephstal as parish priest. Here there was much sickness at the time among the colonists. His indefatigable desire to save souls drove him to take care of the sick people himself, to comfort and worthily prepare them for the all-decisive hour to death. Through caring for the sick, he himself became infected, contracting a fatal disease.

He was given the Last Sacraments, and died quietly, resigned to God's will in Heaven, on December 1, 1807, in the colony of Josephstal near Odessa. He was steady in his duty, without complaint, quiet at work and in hardship, and true and faithful to his calling. He was a model of a true Jesuit.

Father Stephan Osmolowsky, S.J., was the assistant to Father Hattowsky from October 27, 1807, and after Father Hattowsky's death, he carried on the work until the 15th of July, 1808.

Father Aloysius Averdank, S.J.
Parish Priest from June to September 11, 1808

Father Aoysius Averdank was born on the 27th of April, 1750, and entered the order of the Society of Jesus on the 21st of October, 1769. He was the successor of the saintly Father Moritz in Marienthal on the Karaman, where he had three fruitful years of work. In June, 1808, he was transferred to Josephstal where he soon became deathly ill and died on September 11, 1808.

The superior, Father Landes, S.J., wrote of his character: "Father Averdank, whom I visited after my return to Saratov, gave the children religious instruction every day throughout Lent, at ten o'clock in the morning. It was a pleasure to listen to him,—it was impossible to present it in a more interesting way than he did. He was truly a master at this art. I was very impressed with the answers that a ten-year-old child gave to all questions that the Father asked. On Palm Sunday, Father Averdank began the holy exercises and on the first three days of the Holy Week, gave daily, three sermons and one meditation. The crowd of the faithful was quite large. They gave the greatest eulogy to the preacher through their tears and their conversions. The last three days of the Holy Week the Blessed Sacrament was set out for adoration. God blessed this good priest in that He favored him with the art of healing. More than twenty people attributed their recovery to him and among these there were some who had been very ill. Father Averdank is cheerful and content, partakes of all food brought to him, and thus creates a good impression. He often gave out alms. Every day he ate with an old Pole, with whom he could speak only by sign language. He understood music, led the singing, and for his singers he had acquired thirty pieces of music. He associated with the colonists in kindness and humility but he understood that in order to preserve his dignity, he had to be consistent and strict without hurting anyone. Even though he was very experienced, he did not fail, in all possible circumstances, to consult old or young."*

*See "Klemens"—1903.

From the 11th of September, 1808, to the 10th of July, 1810, the parish was under the care of Father Maximilian Durot, a priest from Odessa.

Father Michael Rupert Ruille
Parish Priest from August 7 to September 17, 1810

Father Michael Rupert Ruille was a Benedictine priest from the Monastery Leon, in Bavaria, which was dissolved during the rule of King Max, the destroyer of monasteries. Father Ruille was ordained as priest at Salzburg on April 10, 1792, and in 1810 came to Josephstal where he worked for only a short time. He became ill with a very violent fever and died ten days later. He was buried by visiting French cleric, who came from the Diocese Vienne, invited by the colonial Inspector Rosenkampf for this purpose. From the 17th of September, 1810, to the 27th of September, 1811, the parish was supervised from Odessa.

Father Theodor Von Monfort, S.J.
Parish Priest from September 27, 1811 to September, 1813

Father Monfort was again a Jesuit. He himself was very active in saving souls and started to build a prayer house in Franzfeld.

Father Anton Jann, S.J.
Parish Priest from the 5th of October, 1813 to June 4, 1820

Father Anton Jann was a worthy and faithful priest. He immediately started religious teaching, visited the school and preached the word of God with fervor. He finished building the Prayer House at Franzfeld, a Chapel in Marienthal and a fine church in Kleinliebenthal. In 1814 he built the first rectory in Josephstal. He also acted as judge and jury in disputes among his parishioners. When the accused, before regional or local administrations, appealed to Father Jann, the administrators would rely on his judgment. He admonished them constantly, earnestly to try to get along with each other and his inspired words impressed the irreconcilable who heard it. Father Jann was the last Jesuit in Josephstal. From June 18, 1820 to May 28, 1822, various priests were active in pastoral duties, namely Peter Stettmann, O. Karmel, Andreas Diskat and Hieronymus Hazler.

Joseph Leopold Eybel
Parish Priest from May 28, 1822 to September 12, 1830

Father Eybel came from Vilna, where he was the German

preacher. He was a big, strong man and a good speaker. He began his pastorate with great enthusiasm. He was very concerned that all his parishioners came to mass on Sundays and Holy Days. He, therefore, ruled that on these days, when the weather was favorable all affiliated parishes should come to church in a procession and there reverently attend the divine service and listen to the sermon. But, in the year 1830, the peace between the priest and the parishioners was disturbed. The priest was denounced, for keeping people in his house who were not well-behaved. The inspector, Father Musnizsky, investigated the matter and Father Eybel was temporarily removed from Josephstal. His position was taken by Father Hyazint Zagorsky from the 12th of September, 1830, to the 10th of June, 1831. Afterwards, Father Eybel returned as priest until October 1, 1833.

Bishop Kaspar Borowsky, M.S. Th.
Parish Priest from October 29, 1833 to April 2, 1835
Father Kaspar Borowsky was born on January 2, 1802 in Polenowtschine in the district of Vitebsk. He was a very conscientious priest, indefatigably active in the pulpit and confessional. The year of the great hunger, 1833, gave him a particular occasion to depict God's judgment of a sinful humanity and to urge the sinners to live a better life. In 1835, Father Borowsky left Josephstal and returned to Poland where he was active in pastoral work until he was appointed Bishop of Zhitomir. As bishop he was untiringly active establishing Christian order and discipline. Besides this, he concerned himself with the school and above all to elevate the Diocesan Seminary in order to train an intellectually educated and devout clergy. His toil soon was crowned with success. The priests of his diocese were soon the best educated and purest in the whole area. His service in public education was also recognized by the Russian Government and the Holy Father Pope Pius IX praised him repeatedly for his apostolic ardour. But his fruitful work was soon curtailed. Because he did not accede to the anti-Catholic demands of the Russian government, he was exiled to the city of Pensa in 1870. His exile lasted for twelve years. In 1882 he was recalled from exile and on March 15, 1883, made Bishop of Plozsk. But, his spirit was broken, his health failed gradually and he died, a righteous man, on January 15, 1885.

Father Michael Stankewitsch
Pastor from June 3, 1835 to 1854
For his personal history see the story of Kleinliebenthal.

Father Christopher Pietkewitsch
Pastor from January 31, 1854 to November 1, 1861

Father Pietkewitsch was born in 1822 and was ordained into the priesthood in 1847. He was a big strong man and had no small talent as an orator. He was a person of many contradictions. Sometimes he acted prudently, tactfully and well; at other times, he did just the opposite. Through this and through many offences in his life, he undermined his position and was forced to ask for a transfer. still, he left some durable memorials behind in Josephstal, for he built the present church and rectory. He was in many parishes in the Tiraspol Diocese, behaving in his eccentric manner everywhere so that in the 1870's he was retired from the Tiraspol Diocese by Bishop Zottmann. He lived for a while in Yuriev (Dorpat), where he died a few years ago.

Father Zeno Kalinowsky
Pastor from November 8, 1861 to June 21, 1862

For his personal story see Kleinliebenthal.

Father Alexander Schadursky
Priest from June 30, 1862 to January 12, 1865

Father Schadursky was born in 1804 and ordained priest in 1828. He was parish priest for a long time in Rohleder on the Karaman. He did not speak German well and, therefore, could not do much. He loved money (golden coins) and had much of it. This was the cause of his early death. He was robbed in Belzy and nearly choked, whereupon in a few hours he died.

Father Donatus Medrowsky
Pastor from January 17, 1865 to June 30, 1866

Father Medrowsky was born in 1803 and was ordained a priest in 1827. He was a Jesuit pupil and very talented. He loved poetry especially, and practiced it in several languages and form. Frequently one finds in the vital statistics, beside the baptismal record, a poem written in his own hand. He was friendly to his friends but very often hostile, and even irreconcilable, towards his enemies.

From 1866 to 1871 the parish was supervised by Father Sebald, Father Rimowitsch and Father R. Reichert.

Father Joseph Wanner
Pastor from October 14, 1871 to July 2, 1895

Father Wanner was born in the Colony Landau in Beresan in 1845. After he attended the parish school with considerable success, and received private instruction from the famous old teacher, Kaspar Jäger, he was well prepared to enter the Seminary of Saratov in 1858. He finished his studies with a good record and was ordained priest on April 15, 1867, by Bishop Lipsky. His first parish was Kasitzkaja, where he worked for several years in the vineyard of the Lord. Especially well remembered in the parish Kasitzkaja, are his moving sermons for repentance. In October, 1871, he was sent to Josephstal as pastor, where he administered faithfully the duties of a true shepherd of souls, for almost twenty-four years. Father Wanner was of medium size, healthy constitution, strong build and had a loud, firm voice. He also had the ability to speak, and a wonderful imagination which helped to make him a famous preacher. Father Wanner was capable and well informed on most scientific subjects. As a priest he strove zealously to enlighten his parishioners on their duties, to impress upon them the virtues of home and community, and to bring up their children in the fear of the Lord. His inspired exhortations in school, and in Christian teaching, and in the pulpit, are still well remembered by young and old alike. His genereosity was without limit. Constantly, he was prepared with word and deed to help the needy. When he left Josephstal he hardly had enough money to pay the fare. In the last year, he had a painful experience with several of his parishioners. He was denounced for improper remarks about a person of high rank, and as a result was transferred to Preis (Preusz) where he died an edifying death on January 8, 1898.

Jacob Selinger
Pastor from October 16, 1895 to the Present
Father Jacob Selinger was born on October 30, 1853, in the Colony Rastadt, Cherson district. In 1868 he entered the Catholic Seminary in Saratov, where he successfully completed his course and on October 31, 1876, was ordained a priest by the late Bishop Franz Zottmann. On the 17 February 1877 he received his first appointment to the Colony of Karlsruhe, where he worked very diligently and left indelible memories behind. He built there the first Gothic church in the Diocese of Tiraspol. From 1886 until 1892 he was Dean and pastor in Eichwald, where he was appointed honorary canon. In 1892 he was relieved, upon his request, of the responsibility of Dean and in 1895 was made pastor of Josephstal.

Parish Endowment
The endowment of the parish amounts to one hundred twenty dessatine of land, which was set aside by the Government for the parish on August 30, 1816. The land is presently rented out at

approximately ten to twelve rubles per dessatin. The salary amounts to three hundred rubles. The parish charges were: marriage ceremony—three rubles, baptism—1 ruble, burial—1 rubel, high mass—1 ruble, 50 kopecks, low mass—1 ruble.

The Parish Church

The first church was built in Josephstal in 1806 by Father Löffler and was dedicated in the same year by him. The church was built of fieldstone and had three altars. The main altar was dedicated to St. Joseph, the side altars to Saints Ignatius Loyola and Francis Xavier. On February 3, 1832, Inspector Musnitzsky came from Odessa and wanted to lock the Church, since it was reported to him by the Welfare Committee that this building was not safe. But, the congregation asked for a postponement of this order, promising to make the necessary repairs to the Church immediately. The Church was lengthened by several faden and a new steeple was put on it.

The New Church

The present parish Church was built in the years 1861-1862 by Father Pietkewitsch and cost roughly thirty-two thousand rubles. The Church style is Roman. It stands with the altar on the east, facing west. The Church is eighteen faden long, eight faden wide and five faden high. The steeple is seventeen faden high. The Church had a large entrance with a hall and a small door leading into the right sacristy room. On either side, there are seven windows, and two in the presbytery. The Church is surrounded by a massive stone wall. Beside the Church there are two avenues of beautiful large shade-giving trees. The interior of the Church is beautifully furnished. On the right side of the main aisle are the pictures of the Stations of the Cross, painted by Father Wanner. In the middle of the Church, toward the right side of the pulpit, hangs the very beautiful picture of Saint Anthony of Padua. Beside this is the plain confessional.

In the corner is one of the side altars, dedicated to the Sacred Heart of Jesus, whose glorious picture hangs over the altar. Above the picture of the Heart of Jesus there is a fresco of Saint Sebastian. Beside this altar is decorated with a marble tabernacle with crucifix, twelve large and four small candlesticks, and on either side, a kneeling figure of an adoring angel. Above the altar shines the beautiful picture of the Church patron, Saint Joseph with the child Jesus, surrounded by a group of angels. The presbytery has two arches and six murals. The first one on the left (epistle side) portrays the Lord with the twelve Apostles, with Christ giving

Saint Peter charge of His sheep. The second picture beside the main altar shows Saint Clemens Romanus, the third, Saint Pius V on the right, beside which hangs the picture showing the conversion of Saint Paul. The first picture covering the altar portrays the symbol of the Holy Ghost in the shape of a dove, surrounded by a troop of holy angels; the second the Last Supper after Leonardo di Vinci. Returning to the nave of the Church, on the right, one stands before the second side altar, the altar dedicated to the Blessed Virgin Mary. Above the throne is a picture of many angels. Above this picture is a mural of Saint Wendelin with the shepherd's staff, herding a flock. Two faden eastward, is the pulpit with the pictures of the four evangelists and on the balustrade four church fathers. The Church was consecrated on September 2, 1862 by Bishop Vincent Lipsky.

The School System

The first school, as well as the first Church, apparently was built by Father Löffler at the same time but there are no records available about the building itself. The second school was built by the community in 1838, and was built on the same spot where the present school-house now stands. The material for the school was obtained from the congregation and similarly the cost of the building was assessed to the heads of families. Each property-owner paid eight rubles 50 kopecks. The cottagers, sixteen in number, were assessed only two rubles 83 kopecks per family. This school-house had two large rooms: in one the school-master lived and the other was the classroom. The walls were made of fieldstone, the roof was covered with reeds.

The present new school-house was built in 1892, and contains three large rooms and living quarters for three teachers. This school-house cost two thousand rubles without the equipment. Presently, there are three teachers in Josephstal: a German teacher, who is also sacristan, receives five hundred rubles; a Russian teacher, who receives three hundred fifty rubles; a second Russian teacher receives three hundred thirty rubles. Lodging and heating for the teachers is provided by the community.

Clerical Persons from Josephstal

Father Johannes Ungemach

The first cleric from Josephstal was Father Johannes Ungemach. He was born on September 25, 1860. His parents were Joseph Ungemach and Maria Anna, whose maiden name was

Schwengler. After attending the parish school in his community and adequate private instruction, in the fall of 1875 he went to the boys' seminary in Saratov from which he graduated with distinction in June, 1879, as the best scholar. Called to the religious vocation, he devoted himself to theological studies and was ordained a priest on November 23, 1883. After he had temporarily administered the parishes of Krassna, district Bessarabia and Kasitzkaja, district Samara, he was appointed administrator at Sulz where he worked six and a half years. In the fall of 1890 he was transferred to Mannheim, and on the 25th of October, 1892, appointed pastor. In the year 1894-1895, while parish priest at Mannheim, he acted as religious instructor at the gymnasium of Odessa, while the parish was administered by a clerical Vicar. After eleven years of hard work in Mannheim, due to over-exertion, he became repeatedly ill, and because of this, was relieved of the heavy duties of the parish and appointed as religion teachers at the gymnasium in Tiflis. The climate there, however, weakened his constitution more, so that he had to give up the position after half a year. In February, 1902, he was made pastor at Berdyansk, on the Sea of Azov, where at present his ailing condition has much improved. We wish him a long life of service.

Father Johannes Vetsch
Priest in Sulz (Beresan)

Father Johannes Vetsch was born on the 25th of January, 1861 in the Josephstal colony on the Baraboi, the son of Phillipp Vetsch and Maria Anna, whose maiden name was Schneible. From the age of six until fourteen, he attended school in the colony, where even as a boy he showed love and diligence for learning and as a small altar boy, wished some day to be a priest. In 1875 the first part of his wish was fulfilled, in that his parents sent him to the seminary at Saratov in order to contiue his studies. On June 11, 1884, he was ordained priest by the late Bishop Franz Zottmann, and after his first mass at Solothurn was posted as priest administrator to Neukolonie on the Volga where he worked as pastor until 1887. In 1887, he was sent as administrator to Rothhammel (Pamatnaja) in the Kamenka deanery where, with considerable effort and sacrifice he built a fine new church. In 1894, he was moved into a similar situation at Neu Mannheim till 1899, where he built a new rectory and decorated the Church, and where his work prospered. In November, 1899, he was sent as curate to Kandel in the Kutschurgan, where he worked diligently as a pastor. Since July

185

1904 he worked as pastor in Sulz, a parish from which many small settlements have to be served.

Father Valentin Greiner
Pastor of Landau in the Beresan

Father Valentin Greiner was born in 1861 in the Josephstal Colony on the Baraboi, not far from Odessa. He was the son of a resident of Josephstal, Joseph Greiner and Mariana, whose maiden name was Selensky. After he had graduated from the parish school, he went to the Catholic Seminary in Saratov in 1875. After graduating from there he was ordained a priest by the diocesan bishop Anton Zerr on the 9th of December 1884. His first parish was far away in the Kirghiz steppe where Marienburg is located, just above the Karaman, where he worked hard for five years and built a beautiful prayer house. From Marienburg he was sent to Obermonjou on the Volga, where he also worked hard and diligently as pastor and built a pretty stone Church. After nine years and six months in Obermonjou, he was transferred at his own request to Landau as pastor, where he served for six years. In Landau he founded a poorhouse and decorated the parish Church.

Father Greiner is a trustworthy, unceasing worker in the vineyard of the Lord, namely all fields of pastoral duty. In the pulpit, in Christian teaching, at confession and in the school, he showed up regularly and very punctually to the minute. In his undertakings he is calculating and deliberate. In his demands, he is moderate and unassuming, a steady friend of peace and harmony. On the outside he appears harsh, often repelling, but inwardly he is upright and kind. His soul is free from every pretense of hypocrisy. He abhors ambiguity and hypocrisy and would not hesitate to put in their place, those displaying such characteristics.

Father Aloysius Ochs
Parish Administrator in Marienfeld

Father A. Ochs was born in 1872 (?) in Marienthal, the affiliate of the parish of Josephstal. He completed his religious studies in the Seminary at Saratov and was ordained on June 26, 1894.

Diary of the Colony Josephstal on Baraboi

1805—Many people died of fever and diarrhoea.
1820—Another epidemic raged in which large numbers of people were dying.

1830—Typhus raged, as a result of which many people have died.

1831—Many people sick with cholera, only one died. In this year there was also a big flood.

1833—Was a crop failure.

1835—In the spring there was again a big flood. In the years 1824 and 1825 locusts destroyed the hay and the wheat fields.

1838—January 2, there was a terrible earthquake so that the doors flew open, the pictures fell off the wall, the cattle tore lose from their mangers and everyone shook with fear and fright. This earthquake made a big crack in the Church so it quickly deteriorated.

1840—The wealth of Josephstal in 1840 was as follows:

Winter wheat seeded	36 Tschetwert
Rye	2 Tschetwert
Summer wheat	349 Tschetwert
Oats	187 Tschetwert
Barley	171 Tschetwert
Corn	2 Tschetwert
Potatoes	216 Tschetwert
Flax	19 Tschetwert
Horses in the village	370
Cattle	715
Pigs	30
Community bulls	4
Stallions	2

Garden Products

Community Garden	1
Private Gardens	68
In the community garden one finds fruit trees	60
Young trees, non-bearing	2,725
In the private gardens of the settlers, fruit trees	9,290
Young non-bearing trees	5,280

The fruit trees were:

apple trees	1,471
pear trees	743
plum trees	6,237
cherry trees	5,428
peach trees	44
apricot trees	632
nut trees	15

Forest

Community forest totals two dessatine with 290 forest trees and 190 mulberry trees. Around the homes of the settlers there are 1,272 forest trees.

Vineyards

The community had 72 dessiatines in the vineyards laid out in two separate areas. The number of plants were 154,200. The wine amounted to 2,974 pails. Two hundred fifty-five pails were sold at 40 kopeck per pail.

Bees

There were forty-five beehives in the colony. They produced seven pud of honey (1 pud equals 40 lbs.).

Population Statistics of 1840

Tailors.	3
Shoemakers	4
Cabinet-maker	1
Stone-masons	4
Population, both sexes	527
School children.	123
Boys	65
Girls	58
New-born.	22
Deaths.	10
Marriages	5
Homestead owners.	68
	with 415 souls
Cottagers (without property).	39
	with 110 souls
Houses in the Colony	82

Fifty houses were built of fieldstone, of lumber 32. Community income 663 rubles, 45 kopecks, Community expenses, 424 rubles, 22 kopecks. In the storage bin there should have been 478 tschetwert of wheat but there were only 13 tschetwert. The community had to pay: Tax money—982 rubles, 57 kopecks, Crown loan money—485 rubles, 71 kopecks. For regional and local administrators and secretary—239 rubles, 47 kopecks. For the upkeep of regional and local offices and the mailman—45 rubles, 80 kopecks. For the support of the priest 49 rubles, 3 kopecks. For the support of the school teacher and the school—160 rubles. Wages of the herdsmen—445 rubles, 70 kopecks.

1840—Cowherder Reis shot himself, leaving his wife and children.

1841—January 18, a terrible murder.

The priest's cook, named Ivan Sergiev, a hunchbacked Russian, killed Antona Radoll the wife of the cowherder. The murder occurred as follows: Sergiev went with Antona Radoll into the forest towards Peterstal to fish in the Baraboi with a net. In front of the fishing wharf, Sergiev threw the net over the woman's head and tried to pull her into the water. As the woman struggled, he hit her on the head with the net post so that she sank unconscious into the water. After this, the scoundrel held her head under water until she was completely dead. Then, he hurried to the parsonage, broke into the wardrobe, took 30 rubles and took to flight. On the following day, the murderer was captured and placed under guard. During the investigation, the murderer said that his wife, who works in Majaki in a wool factory, induced him to commit this murder. He was also to kill the priest to rob him, burn the parsonage and then to come to her with the money. The lawbreaker was tried in the criminal court in Odessa, where he was soon condemned to lashes and exiled to Siberia. The lashes were administered in the middle of the street in Josephstal, opposite the present new community office. At the lashing there was a monstrous crowd, as everyone came from the surrounding colonies.

The delinquent appeared, led by two lashmasters. He was laid on a broad bench with his back bared and the lashmasters stood on either side with the lashes raised, awaiting the command of the executioner. On the first whiplash, the delinquent gave a horrible scream, so that all who watched trembled. Many people in compassion burst into tears. On the second blow from the second lashmaster, the cry was much weaker and gradually decreased with future blows until by the last blow (he received 25), he moaned weakly and then became unconscious. After the lashing he was branded on the forehead, wrapped in a white cloth and laid in a wagon. Whether he died of his wounds or recovered, and was sent to Siberia, is not known.

1844—Hail damaged the entire grain crop. Ignaz Stein drowned in the well of K. Walther.

1845—The snow in the spring melted, accompanied by heavy rains. The small river Baraboi filled with an unheard-of mass of water, overflowed its banks and without warning, during the night, filled the streets. The water filled all basements and wells and entered the houses so that the people awoke and fled from their beds through the water to safety. The street was two arschine deep under water: Many cattle drowned and many calves, pigs and other small animals were swept away by the water.

1847—The grasshoppers did a great deal of damage in that they completely ate the green corn in the fields.

1853—The rectory in Josephstal burned down.

1855—Fifty-four people from Josephstal had to go to Perekop and work in salt flats for the crown.

1856—May 1, Joseph Schwengler permitted dancing in his house and was fined 7 rubles 50 kopecks by the Church. In the same year there ws a considerable loss of cattle through stock plague.

1895—Josephstal was renamed Sergiewka.

1899—In Josephstal there was a complete crop failure.

1905—There was a very poor harvest. On the night of the 21st of September there was a severe flood causing damage of over 15,000 rubles.

J. Jentsch got under the wheel of his own mill and was squashed to death. Some said he had intentionally committed suicide and for this reason he is said to haunt the place, wearing a slouched hat on his head. He was also tavern-keeper and kept false accounts. Also, his daughter Elizabeth is said to haunt the place with hair undone.

In the years 1840 to 1850, there were many pious Christian families in Josephstal. There was Georg Black with his very pious wife, Clara. During Lent they would go every week to chapel a Franzfeld and pray the rosary. There were, further, the following families of good deportment and Christian attitude:

Phillip Wilhelm—was also the best singer—and his wife, Clara; Mathias Ungemach and his wife, Theresa; Peter Schmidhausler and his wife Catherine, and Bernhard Schuh and his wife Maria-Catherine. Generally, one must say that at that time, the people were more pious than they are now. The youth frequently went to confession and communion on Holy Days, and were, therefore, not as frivolous and immoral as the youth of today.

A SHORT CHRONICLE OF

Marienthal

on the Baraboi
from 1804 to 1904

The Marienthal colony, named "Georgiewka" by the Russians, is located in the Cherson Province, of the Odessa region, in the Marinsker municipality on the small Baraboi river. It is located 25 versts from the seaport of Odessa and 9 versts from the municipal office. The Baraboi swings easterly just at the Marienthal colony for a distance of 1 verst, then turns south again. In this way it forms a somewhat oblique angle in which the colony is located. The beginning of main street runs along the left bank of the Baraboi, from the west to the east, as far as the church. Here it crosses the small river and runs from the north to the south, along the river bank. As a result of this, when water is at a high level in the Baraboi, the colony is completely divided into an upper and a lower colony. From the church eastward, there is a small lane, called the upper colony "extension," which is lined with lovely large trees. There is also a small lane in the south end which the lower colonists have named the "extension." The small houses which are built along the right side of the river bank are called chutor. The colony is completely green, and from the hill it makes a very favourable impression on the observer. The colony contains approximately 1120 souls, male and female. The number of houses is 146. The

191

occupation of the inhabitants is grain farming, vineyards, cattle raising and vegetable gardening. The important buildings in the colony are a church, 2 schools, and a community government office.

The place upon which the Marienthal colony is located, belonged to a Russian nobleman, who himself owned an estate with four small houses and six clay huts. The settling of Marienthal started in 1804 and was completed in 1809. The settlers came mostly from Alsace, the Grand Duchy of Baden, the Kingdom of Würtemberg, and some from Switzerland. The first group of eleven families came to this spot in March, 1804. Under the supervision of the colonial inspector 45 families came in the following years, until 1809 when the 60 lots were filled.

The colony was laid out by the Duke of Richelieu, and given the name of "Marienthal" by him.

List of Names of the First Settlers and
Homesteaders of the Colony "Marienthal"

House
Number:
1. Magdalena Trittenbach—later the estate went to the son-in-law, Johann Silenki.
2. Andreas Schläger—later the estate went to the step-son Joseph Braun.
3. Sebastian Jerger—the estate went to Ignaz Bienfait.
4. Joseph Unterreiner
5. Wendelin Sitter
6. Georg Laturnus
7. Anton Spitt—returned to Germany.
8. Joseph Höhn—the estate to Michael Zimmermann.
9. Jakob Bohl
10. Michael Barbie—the estate went to the son-in-law, Johann Stötzel.
11. Michael Löewenstein—the estate went to the son-in-law, Wilhelm Seitz.
12. Jakob Bös—the estate went to Joseph Ottwark.
13. Johann Kraus—the estate went to the step-brother Jakob Bast.
14. Franz Barthelmann—the estate went to Jakob Hafner.
15. Ludwig Greber—the estate went to Peter Malsam from Kleinliebenthal.
16. George Heinz—the estate went to Joseph Morse from Selz.
17. Georg Grübel
18. Joseph Wild

19. Joseph Hobehr—the estate went to the son-in-law, Martin Hellstern.
20. Jakob Schlick
21. Bartholomäus Büchel
22. Theobald Zimmerman
23. Michael Dilschneider—the estate went to Anton Ochs from Kleinliebenthal.
24. Nikolaus Lorentz—the estate went to Lorenz Bock.
25. Heinrich Schnellbach
26. Anton Gisi—the estate went to the step-son, Konrad Kopp.
27. Johann Herbach
28. Ignaz Wirth
29. Leopold Hehr
30. Philipp Ebb
31. Michael Simon—the estate went to Mathias Keszler.
32. Sebastian Klein—the estate went to Jakob Zeiler from Franz-feld.
33. Magdalena Stötzel—widow.
34. Anton Schütt
35. Michael Wirth
36. Andreas Steker—the estate went to Felix Löwenstein.
37. Michael Schäfer
38. Jakob Schnelbach
39. Joseph Kost—the estate went to Johann Zeiler from Franzfeld.
40. Joseph Gisi—the estate went to Jakob Zimmermann.
41. Jakob Müller
42. Leonard Gissel—the estate went to the step-son, Peter Schuler.
43. Benedikt Weimar
44. Daniel Hauck
45. Joseph Schnellbach
46. Johann Dielmann
47. August Klotz
48. Elizabeth Neisz widow, the estate went to the son-in-law, Andreas Ball.
49. Joseph Lagelier
50. Peter Schlechter
51. Andreas Simon—the estate went to the son-in-law, Jakob Heinz.
52. Jakob Millius
53. Jakob Eresmann
54. Nikolaus Weimer
55. George Mattern—the estate went to Rudolf Köhler from Franzfeld.
56. Anton Bauer

57. Georg Heinz
58. Johann Mansfeld
59. Joseph Ring—the estate went to Joseph Mauri.
60. Joseph Keller

In addition to the 60 homestead settlers in Marienthal there were also the following families settled: Joseph Knoll, Joseph Höhn, Joseph Fasel, Lorenz Fasel, George Dielmann, Joseph Knoll (he subsequently moved over to Karlsruhe in Beresan), Lorenz Stecker, Anton Klemens (went to Poland), Joseph Niedling, Martin Lang, Peter Fasel, Jakob Springer, Johann Andreas, Anton Kopp, Michael Thomas, Joseph Wingerter, Joseph Büchel, Franz Stetzel, Mathias Kaiser (disappeared), Sebastian Wolf, Peter Dobrowolsky (moved to Kleinliebenthal).

The Marienthal Community Land

The land of the community of Marienthal contains 2886½ dessatine of which 97¾ dessatine are pasture near Franzfeld on the Dniester. The land is bounded as follows: in the south by Neuburg, in the west by Franzfeld, in the north by Majaki, in the east by Petersthal, Josephstal and Grossliebenthal. The land is mostly level; only the Baraboi and a few ponds break the level surface and form an area of rolling country. The soil for the most part is good, rich, black earth, measuring from 2 to 3 feet thick with a subsoil of clay and in some areas also red clay and marl. With good weather the soil is very productive.

The Present Wealth and Condition
of the Colony of Marienthal

The community land at present is divided approximately as follows: for the buildings 34½ dessatine; for vegetable gardening 25¼ dessatine; gardens, 2 dessatine; for vineyards 57 dessatine; for forest 3 dessatine; ponds 7½ dessatine; clay mound, 1½ dessatine; roads 40 dessatine; hay meadows 62¾ dessatine; pasture land 302 dessatine; under cultivation 2269 dessatine. Over 600 dessatine is rented mostly from landowners of Grossliebenthal. The charges for renting are, for heavy land 15 rubles, for light land 9 rubles per dessatine per year.

In 1905 the planting in Marienthal was as follows: summer wheat, 229 dessatine; winter wheat, 1095 dessatine; rye, 34 dessatine; barley, 636 dessatine; oats, 695 dessatine; corn, 220 dessatine; potatoes, 42 dessatine. The harvest return for this year was well below half of normal.

The herdsmen were paid as follows: horse herder, 1 ruble 45 kopecks; the cow herder, 50 kopecks; the calf herder, 90 kopecks per head. Tradesmen in Marienthal were as follows: blacksmiths, 4; carpenters, 3; shoemakers, 4; cart-wrights, 3; tailor, 1; retail shops, 3; and one tavern.

The livestock—work horses, 381; young horses, 220; cows, 763; pigs, 270.

Marienthal planted many vegetables which were sold at a profit in Odessa.

Marienthal paid the following taxes: crown taxes, 291 rubles, 74 kopecks; payment for land bought, 1880 rubles, 73 kopecks; land taxes, 1176 rubles, 66 kopecks; community taxes, 2083 rubles, 58 kopecks.

The Daughter Parish of Marienthal

Since the beginning of the settlement of Marienthal and for the last one hundred years, it was affiliated with the parish of Josephstal. The inhabitants are all of Roman-Catholic faith. People of other faiths live only temporarily in the village. The community pays 140 rubles parish dues.

The Parish Church of Marienthal

The first church in Marienthal was built in 1819 by Father Jann, S.J., but because of crop failure the building could not be completed until 1821. The new church was built in 1890 by the late Father Wanner. The architectural design of the church is Roman. The church stands with the main altar on the north; it is 25 faden long, 10 faden wide and 8 faden high. The height of the steeple is 20 faden. The steeple is built into the church, and has a simple but pleasant exterior. The church has four entrances: the large door at the front under the steeple, with a gate, and one on either side of this, and one to the right sacristy room. There are windows with colored glass, six on either side, and two in the presbytery. At the entrance on the right there is a simple canopy, above which, hanging on the wall, are the Stations of the Cross; near the side door is the confessional. In the corner is the first side altar, blessed in the name of the bleeding Saviour, whose glorious picture hangs above the altar. Above the picture, there is an eye, symbol of the omniscience of God, and six bust-size pictures of the apostles. Beside this altar is the plain baptismal font. If one goes up two steps into the presbytery, one is in front of the lovely marble main altar. On the altar there is a beautiful tabernacle, decorated with two adoring angels and 12 candlesticks. Above the altar is a lovely oil painting of the Virgin Mary with the Child Jesus, surrounded by a group of angels. Saint Dominik kneels before the Queen of the Holy Rosary.

The second side altar is blessed in honor of Saint Maria Magdalena and is decorated with her lovely picture. Above the picture is the symbol of the Holy Ghost as well as six small pictures of the apostles. Near the second side door is the modest pulpit. The church owns a fine organ.

The church is built of fieldstone, and is one of the largest and finest in the Tiraspol diocese. It was worthy of soon becoming a parish church. "It was about time, for you people of Marienthal to take the necessary steps to create your own parish. Franzfeld is smaller than Marienthal, and has had its own parish for the last 50 years."

The Church Yard With the Chapel

The church yard is approximately 100 faden north-east of the church; it was set aside by the original settlers and later, because of necessity, it was constantly enlarged. As a result it is approximately 100 faden long and about the same width. In 1852 George Ochs built an attractive chapel on this consecrated land, which, however now looks quite ancient and in need of renovation. There are also a number of majestic shade trees.

The Parish School

The first school house in Marienthal was built in 1807, but by January, 1853, the school was already too small for the steadily increasing number of school children. Therefore the community, in this same year, took steps to build a new school house which is still standing. It is also built of fieldstone and is 9 faden long and 3 faden wide. For a few years the community acquired a colonist's house, which was also used as a school house. In the school yard two residences were recently built for the teachers. For the present, the space for the school yard may be considered adequate. In Marienthal at the present time there are three teachers for 114 school children. A German teacher, who is also sexton, receives 500 rubles. Two Russian teachers; one receives 350 rubles and the other 325 rubles.

There is a tremendous difference between the present and 50 years ago. In 1854 Stanislaus Schmidt from Baden was the school teacher. At that time he received 80 rubles salary and 20 kopecks per child as well as 2 dessatine of land. In this respect Marienthal has made great improvements.

Past Events and Conditions in the Colony Marienthal on the Baraboi

1805 and 1806—Many people died of fever and dysentery, so that in these years there were more graves dug than there were houses built.

1820—In March the land was surveyed. The surveyor Kuznezov with his crew, lived a whole month in the colony. The community had to board them free, and also pay Kuznezov 15 rubles.

1821—The mayor of Marienthal requested that the people be permitted to receive some wheat from the storehouse depot, because most of the colonists did not harvest enough winter or summer wheat for seed.

March 18, 1821—Inspector Repey requested six horses so that he could drive to Freudenthal. But the community refused because the arrangements for transportation had expired, and the road was extremely bad. The inspector reported this (disobedience), and requested horses for the second time, under penalty of a fine.

June 18, 1821—Circular Order from the head of the Welfare Committee: Since the people of Mannheim have perpetrated extortions on travellers on the highway through the village, because they have grazed their animals on the roadside while passing through, be it known that grazing on the roadside is permitted so long as grain fields and hay meadows are not damaged. The people of Mannheim will be strictly punished for their actions. When the fields are being ploughed, a boundary furrow for the road is to be ploughed. The main road is to be 60 faden wide, side roads 30 faden.

June 23, 1821—The whole community has to improve the ditches and roadbed on the highway from Odessa to Ovidiopol.

June 28, 1821—The stock in Marienthal was as follows: horses, 223; horned cattle, 630; sheep, 149; pigs, 149.

July 1, 1821—Lieutenant Von Löwen was appointed inspector of the Liebenthal communities.

Sept. 2, 1821—The mayor of Marienthal was fined 5 rubles for sending in a report without the mayor's signature.

Sept. 11, 12, 13, 1821—The Jewish tavern owner received permission from inspector Von Löwen to have music and dancing in the tavern in the afternoon between 4 and 10 o'clock on the church dedication festival.

Sept. 22, 1821—All Catholics who wish a catalogue of Catholic books shall send for it from Chief Justice Von Lau.

Sept. 22, 1821—Order to the mayor of Marienthal: "The Chief Justice Van Lau has asked this office to remind you of the frequently issued order with regard to the immoral colonists, who for the past 16 to 18 years have spent their time drinking. Once and for all this habit must be prohibited among people of German extraction. Consequently as of the 19th of this month, the mayor is to pay particular attention to those people who usually spend their money, which they have earned from selling produce in Odessa, on alcohol. Under order number 179 it will be necessary for him to report these people, particularly those who for the most part have lost their fortune through drinking, also those who have come to shameful death on account of it. Therefore this should be made known to all people.

"Another problem which must be corrected, and all made acquainted with this warning, is that the Highest Authority of the Odessa City Police is to take disciplinary action, by picking up those colonists who are found in wine cellars, and locking them in jail. The mayor will accordingly take the necessary steps to see that this information is made known to every one. If, as there is no doubt, such drunkards are found in the colonies, he is obliged to report the matter to the district mayor's office."—District Mayor Precht.

Sept. 23, 1821—The Chief Justice came to Marienthal; the mayor reported that everything was in order. But after he (the Chief Justice) inspected the place, he found many things not in order. On the 16th of September, of this year he gave the following order:

"To my greatest displeasure, on inspecting the region of the colony of Marienthal, I found that the colonists have not obeyed the frequently issued government orders. The walls of the lots have not been put into proper condition in relation to the streets; the gardens are surrounded only with manure and reeds. They have not at all been diligent in acquiring vines and fruit trees. Few seem to realize that they should acquire sheep and cattle for their own benefit. Consequently I order once again and for the last time, that without fail, by the 1st of October, of this year, all my previously issued 'Points of Instruction' are to be carried out. In case that this time there are still some householders who, through laziness or negligence, do not follow the government instructions, they shall lose their property, shall be condemned to do work for the Crown, or may even be sent over the border. Should the mayor's office be negligent, it will be called before a Court of Justice. I cannot over-emphasize to the mayor my complete dissatisfaction. I am astonished that the people, under my specific orders for acquiring fire fighting equipment, have not taken the necessary steps. I give the sternest order that such be obtained immediately. Further, I order that the church be surrounded by a wall, and that a bridge be built over the pond. In this the whole community must help.—Administrator Von Lau.

1823 and 1824—There was a complete crop failure so that the people had to ask for assistance from the government.

1827—The grasshoppers did considerable damage.

1831—Many people were sick with cholera, but with bleeding and peppermint drops, all recovered.

1833, 1841, 1844—These were all crop failure years because of the severe damage by grasshoppers. The fruitful years were 1825, 1829, 1837 and 1838.

1845—There was a great flood. The whole lower half of the colony and the row of houses along the valley in the upper colony were under water. Many cattle died and many people caught colds as a result of being chilled, and developed fatal illnesses. Consideration was given to tearing down all of the lower colony and rebuilding it on the hill, but because of the high cost of this undertaking it was left as it was. (From the minutes of the community committee.)

Date?—Cornelius Fix—disgusted with life, hanged himself on a tree on St. Andrew's day. His wife was bitten by a mad dog a short time before, became ill with rabies and died after eight days of severe suffering.

1850?—Johannes Höhr (Schachtel Hannes) killed a mad wolf, for which he received a reward of 80 rubles from the Welfare Committee.

1858—In Marienthal a man was killed in a brawl.

1895—Through the very highest edict of the land, Marienthal was renamed "Georgiewka."

1899—This year was a complete crop failure.

1904—A drunken man fell into a well and drowned.

1905—This was a very bad year, the people had hardly enough for bread and seed.

On the 21st of September, of this same year, there was a severe flood.

Devout persons in Marienthal were: Agatha Dielmann, whose maiden name was Mock. As a small child she was brought to Franzfeld in 1824 and adopted and raised by Balthasar Fix. Even as a child she loved to pray, and pleased her foster parents through

199

her modesty, obedience and piety. When she became a young lady she married a man named Joseph Dielmann from Marienthal, in 1843. The marriage was happy since her husband was also a pious upright Christian. But in 1855, through the terrible Crimean war, the husband contracted typhus through contact with the sick soldiers, and died.

The young woman knelt at the grave for a long time with her two children, crying and praying for his soul. She also prayed to Almighty God to comfort and fortify the widow and orphans in their new and difficult time. From this time on she lived a very quiet and secluded life, and paid the greatest attention to raising her children. As often as she had time, even on work days, she attended divine service, and tried through deeds of Christian charity, to set a good example for everyone. When her children were grown and married she devoted herself completely to a pious Christian life, very quietly at home, and not out in public, as many people do.

Often she would get up at night and secretly leave the house, and frequently even in stormy weather she would go to the chapel at Franzfeld in order to perform her devotions. People relate that she understood the poor souls in Purgatory and saved many of them. She was steady, direct and calm when she was with other people, spoke only about serious matters, and only when she was asked. Thus did this Godfearing woman lead a pious, holy life, and thereby demonstrated that virtue is not an empty sound, but a power from God, which strengthens the weak, and perhaps even makes them holy. The lady died of old age on the 14th of May, 1903. R.I.P.

Besides her, there were other pious Christian families: Jakob Heinz and his wife, Katherina; Michael Schäfer and his wife Elizabeth; and Johannes Stengler, who for many years was an assistant mayor. The oldest people in Marienthal at the present time are Joseph Materi, 87; Michael Zimmerman, 79; Katharina Zeiler, maiden name Zimmerman, 84 years old; and Katharine Zeiler maiden name Werlinger, 81 years old.

A SHORT CHRONICLE OF

Franzfeld

on the Dniester

1805 to 1905

Franzfeld, in Russian called Michailowka and also Karagol, lies on the east side of the Dniester estuary in the Cherson Province, Odessa region, municipality of Mariinskoye, 35 versts from the seaport of Odessa. The colony is laid out in a north-south direction, in the form of a terrace slope on the Dniester hills. The main street is 1.5 versts long and is planted on either side with a row of fine acacia trees. To the west of the main street one finds the so-called "Little Street," and to the north of this, the "Sparrow Hump." The houses have porches, and are built of fieldstone. They are generally attractive and are surrounded by a large wall, which is painted white on the street side.

The roofs of the houses and other buildings are usually made of reeds. At the present time there are 130 houses in the colony and 924 residents.

The setting of the colony is very lovely, the view of the Dniester estuary with its islands, fields and meadows makes a wonderful, lovely panoramic picture.

The most common occupations of the people are: grain farming, cattle raising and wine-growing. The main buildings are: a church, a school, a parsonage and a community government office.

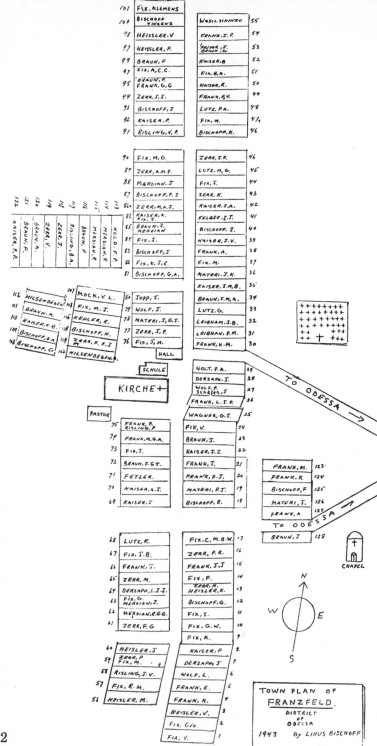

THE FRANZFELD COLONY

202

TOWN PLAN OF
FRANZFELD.
DISTRICT OF ODESSA
1943   BY LINUS BISCHOFF

The founding of the colony of Franzfeld started in 1805 and was completed in 1809. The first settlers consisted of 13 families who came in the years 1805 and 1806 from the Hungarian cities of Temesvar and Kula. All of them except three families, however, eventually settled in the adjacent Evangelical Lutheran colonies. During the period 1806 to 1809, 38 families came from Alsace and the Rhinepalatinate. Some of this last group came down on the Danube to Ismael, and by ship to Odessa. Here they were met by Franz Brittner, district mayor of the Liebenthal district, who settled them in the newly founded colony of Franzfeld. From the beginning, it was intended that Franzfeld should be settled by Lutherans, and Grossliebenthal by Catholics, however, Count Richelieu altered this plan.* The land which the new settlers occupied, previously belonged to some Russian noblemen, who had used it as pasture land, and that is why three shepherds' huts were found (there).

A long time ago, when this region was under the jurisdiction of the Greeks and Romans, this place must have been densely populated because during various excavations, one found many bones and skeletons of people throughout the whole length of the colony, as well as various eastern vessels, silver and gold objects.

List of Names of the First Settlers and Homesteaders of the Franzfeld Colony

House
Number:
1. George Heiszler
2. Konrad Götz—the estate went to Johann Heer, who married the widow.
3. Martin Heer
4. Marzel Uhl
5. Peter Heiszler
6. Christian Schmidt
7. Andreas Hätterle
8. Johann Steiert—moved to Krasna in Bessarabia in 1843.
9. Joseph Braun—shot himself on the 4th of November, 1832.
10. Nikolaus Mastio—moved to Selz in 1817.
11. Joseph Zerr
12. Johann Fix
12. Franz Heiszler
14. Peter Matery—had 7 sons and 2 daughters.

*Many Lutherans remained at first, only in the last forty years is it completely inhabited by Catholics.

15. Rudolf Merdian
16. Philipp Nold
17. Anton Zerr—had 6 sons and 4 daughters.
18. Franz Fix—the estate went to Joseph Wolf from Kleinliebenthal.
19. Michael Zerr—had 6 sons and one daughter.
20. Georg Zerr—the estate was inherited by his son, Johann Zerr.
21. Kaspar Deck
22. Georg Ulm
23. Johann Kaiser—had 5 sons and 3 daughters.
24. Joseph Braun—the estate was inherited by the son-in-law Johann Frank.
25. Joseph Braun—the estate was inherited by the son-in-law, Peter Zerr.
26. Johann Mock
27. Jakob Rheide—the estate was inherited by the step-son, Georg Riszling.
28. Jakob Bischoff
29. Jakob Braun—his widow married Anton Blattner, taking the estate with her.
30. Michael Köhler
31. Andreas Merdian
32. Philipp Job
33. Franz Leibham
34. Nikolaus Frank
35. Jakob Fix
36. Jakob Schaub
37. Joseph Riszling—his widow married Michael Stengler, taking the estate with her.
38. Maria Frank, widow. The estate was inherited by her son Jakob Frank.
39. Joseph Derzapf
40. Jakob Merdian
41. Johann Wagner
42. Konrad Busch—the estate went to the son-in-law, Michael Fix.
43. Karl Frank

Beyond the 43 homesteaders in 1816, there were approximately 15 families without land, of which over half were Lutheran. They eventually all settled in the Lutheran colonies or in the city of Odessa.

The Community Land of Franzfeld

The land of the community amounted to 2213½ dessatine of which 114 dessatine was pasture land adjacent to the Dniester.

The boundary on the south was formed by the community of Neuburg, on the west by the Dniester, on the north by the land of the city of Majaki, on the east by the communities of Petersthal and Marienthal. The landscape in the north is quite level while in the south it is more hilly. On the slopes of the Dniester hills, the soil is composed of thin layers of black earth mixed with clay, gravel and sand; in the flat country the black earth is 2 feet thick and forms a very rich soil for most cereals.

The Present Wealth and Conditions of the Franzfeld Colony

The community land is divided approximately as follows: buildings, 28 dessatine; yards and cattle range, 387 dessatine; stock lanes, 7 dessatine; vineyards, 38 dessatine; forests, 4 dessatine; meadows, 114 dessatine; vegetable gardens, 10 dessatine; stone quarry, 12 dessatine; clay pit, 1 dessatine; small hill, 12 dessatine; roads, 93 dessatine; cultivation, 1613 dessatine and 1191 faden; hay meadow, 9 dessatine. Besides this, the Franzfeld community rented 500 dessatine mostly from the Majaki Russians, at 14 rubles per dessatine per year.

The salaries of the officials and civil servants are as follows: Mayor, 15 rubles; secretary, 450 rubles, bailiff, 100 rubles. The horse herder received 1 ruble and 50 kopecks per head and ½ pud wheat; the cow herder, 45 kopecks and ½ pud wheat; the calf herder, 45 kopecks and ½ pud wheat. The herdsmen all lived in community houses. Tradesmen were: wheelwright, 3; blacksmiths, 3; joiner, 1; tailor, 1; shoemakers, 4; windmill, 1; livery stable, 1. The livestock is horses, 400; cows, 412; calves, 320; pigs, 800. Vegetable gardening was mostly for their own use, but some vegetables were sold in Majaki. Large numbers of poultry are raised in Franzfeld. The colony pays the following taxes: crown taxes, 1749 rubles, 90 kopecks; land taxes, 916 rubles, 20 kopecks; community taxes, 4665 rubles.

FRANZFELD PARISH

There are 130 houses in Franzfeld and 924 residents, male and female, and all Roman Catholics. Non-Catholics remain here only temporarily. The parish belongs to the Odessa deanery in the Diocese of Tiraspol. The Catholics of the towns of Akkermann, Majaki and those on the canals of the Dniester belong to this parish. The distance to the postoffice at Marjinskoe is 20 versts, from Majaki 5 versts.

THE PARISH HISTORY

Until the colony of Franzfeld became a separate parish, it was affiliated with the parish of Josephstal. On the 17th of January, 1852 the entire community resolved to submit the following petition to the inspector of the Roman Catholic Church of South Russia: "The community of the colony of Franzfeld, which is presently affiliated with the Parish of Josephstal, after considerable reflection and according to the unanimous opinion of the community, has decided to respectfully submit to his Reverence, the Inspector of the Roman Catholic Church of South Russia, its most ardent wish, namely the foundation of its own independent parish, and ask that this petition be considered and approved. The need for this colony, which has approximately 650 souls, to have its own parish is based on the following reasons.

1. The disadvantage for the community and for the colony of Franzfeld in particular lies in the fact that the 10 versts distance to the parish church is becoming perceptibly more difficult, particularly for those people who become suddenly ill. Some have died without receiving the last rites and without the consolation of a priest on account of this great distance.

2. It is the first duty of a Roman Catholic Christian to attend divine service on Sundays and Holy days. However the frequent obstacles, particularly the bad weather in the cold season of the year, and the high water of the Baraboi do not permit one to fulfill this duty. The circumstance needs particular consideration because, for the above reasons, the younger generation is retarded in respect to religious instruction.

It is also important to have this new parish for the benefit of the Catholics living in the surrounding Russian villages, who without any religious instruction are exposed to complete neglect and religious indifference.

For the support of the priest the community has promised the following:

1. The community promises to pay the priest 285 rubles, 71 kopecks yearly, to be paid in three installments.

2. In addition to this, each promises to pay the priest for his own church functions as follows: for a baptism, 30 kopecks; for announcement of marriage bans, 30 kopecks; for a wedding, 1 ruble; for burying an adult, 1 ruble; for burial services of a child, 50 kopecks.

Information was requested from the Franzfeld community with reference to founding a parish.

The following report was made by the Liebenthal regional office on the 17th of June, 1852, report number 2483, pertaining to further developments of this affair: "The contents of report number 28, of the Franzfeld mayor, dated the 24th of January, 1852, regarding the possibility of the Franzfeld Community founding its own parish, was reported by the Liebenthal regional office to the Welfare Committee district office on the 1st of February, 1852, number 352. Through regulation number 4849 the Welfare Committee let it be known on the 10th of June, 1852, that they had asked the Ministry of the Interior for a decision in this matter, where upon the first Department of the Imperial Government had demanded the following information:

1. Whether the other members belonging to the Josephstal Parish are in favor of this separation; and whether in case of their consent, the colony of Franzfeld would be able to maintain its own parish.

2. Whether the Franzfeld colonists are willing to renounce all further claims on Josephstal parish regarding land, church inventory, archives, and church books.

3. Whether the colonists of Franzfeld are also willing to support whatever priest is appointed, according to the 175th article of the XII volume: to give him 60 to 120 dessatine of land and also to build a house for him from their own means."

To the foregoing report the Franzfeld Community replied, that the colonies of Josephstal and Marienthal had agreed to this separation, and that they (Franzfeld community) had renounced all claim on the parsonage, the land property, and other church property of the Josephstal parish for all times. With regard to the parish land they promise to pay 500 rubles annually to the priest as rent, also they promise to build a rectory at their own expense.

The Founding of the Parish of Franzfeld was Confirmed by the Minister of the Interior

On the 3rd of May, 1853, under file No. 1052, the District Office of Liebenthal gave the following report to the Franzfeld municipal office,—"Recently the first Department of the Imperial Government advised the Welfare Committee, that His Highness, the minister, has noted from the documents presented to him, that the inhabitants of the colony of Franzfeld, which belongs to the Parish of Josephstal, wish to have their own independent parish because of the distance from the mother church; that the colonists, as confirmed by the district office, have the means to maintain a priest and to build a parsonage. The communities of the other colonies belonging to the Josephstal parish, have given their consent to the separation of the colony of Franzfeld. Consequently His Highness, the minister, has also, on his part, given permission to establish the new parish, and has on his part written to the Minister of the Interior for further orders.

In view of the correspondence between the minister of the Imperial Government, with the Minister of the Interior, the Minister of the Interior has advised as follows: that he has in this matter written to the Roman Catholic Bishop Kahn of Tiraspol, who recognizes the necessity of establishing a new parish in Franzfeld and requests that the city of Akkermann, which lies about 17 werst from Franzfeld, and 60 werst from Krasna, its present parish, be incorporated into the new Franzfeld parish.

At the same time the Minister of the Interior has decreed that in the colony of Franzfeld, a parish is to be established and that the Roman Catholics living in Akkermann are to be incorporated into the parish of Franzfeld.

The Succession of Priests

FATHER JOHANNES THEL,
Parish Priest from January 1, 1854 to September 17, 1857.

Father Thiel was born in 1807 and ordained in 1832. When he first came to Franzfeld in January, 1854, the rectory was not yet finished. On his behalf they rented a house from Rüffel. But Father Thiel did not like this house and he took lodging with Johannes Wagner near the church. Father Thiel was a strict, pious, serious priest who strove through word and deed to set a good example for his parishioners. He never went out, except to visit the sick. He performed his duties accurately according to church directions.

From the 17th of September, 1857, until the 19th of January, 1861, the parish was alternately supervised by Father Rogulsky and Prelate Rosutowitsch.

FATHER JOHANNES MICHALSKY,
Administrator from January 29, 1861 until March 10, 1862.

Father Johannes Michalsky was born in 1833 and ordained a priest in 1855, and came as a young priest to Franzfeld. His industriousness and conduct left much to be desired. He often went walking, liked to attend christenings and weddings, and often behaved improperly.

From March 10, 1862 until March 13, 1865, the parish was supervised from Josephstal.

FATHER BEDA SEBALD,
Parish Priest from 13 March, 1865 to 5 February, 1891.

Father Sebald, Capuchin monk from Türkheim near Wórisho-
fen, came to Russia in 1865 as a model priest, with professors
Michael Glossner and Willibald Zottmann. In Petersburg, Bishop
Lipsky persuaded him to take on the small but attractive parish of
Franzfeld. He agreed and came to Franzfeld.

He began his pastorate tenure with circumspection and great
spiritual zeal, gave religious courses of instruction, assiduously
preached the word of God and strove to establish order in the
colony such as existed in Germany. But the obstinacy of the
colonists disheartened him and his zeal began to cool down. Father
Sebald was subsequently assigned as pastor to Kandel where he
built a very attractive church, and was still active as spiritual
advisor until 1890. In 1890 he left Russia and returned to his
beautiful Bavaria, where he lived for a number of years in the
Capuchin monastery in Türkheim near Wörishofen. He died there
and was buried in the beautiful monastery church. In 1898 I was
there and prayed at his grave for the peace of his soul.

FATHER LUDWIG RISSLING,
Pastor from October 17, 1891 to May 9th, 1896.

Father Rissling was born in 1856 and ordained a priest on the
10th of May, 1887. He was active as pastor in various parishes. He
contracted a virulent marsh-fever (malaria), with which he is
affilicted to this day. He is an expert on the manners and customs of
our colonists and steadfastly strives to illustrate his well-liked and
superior sermons from this extensive background.

FATHER FRANZ SCHERER,
from May 9th, 1896 to February 13, 1897.

Father Franz Scherer was born in Vosnesensk in 1894. When he
had prepared himself well in the grammar-school in Odessa, he
entered the religious seminary at Saratov. After completing the
preliminary class, he withdrew and became a teacher at the
now-discontinued central school in Strassburg. In 1876 he went to
the aforementioned seminary, finished there and was ordained a
priest by Bishop Zottmann on 11 February, 1879. His first parish
was Katherinenstadt on the Volga where he worked with his whole
heart and soul, and was generally beloved. Then he came to
Rosenthal in the Crimea, where he built an attractive parsonage.
Subsequently he was at a number of different parishes, but
nowhere for long.

Faher Scherer is a good speaker but an even better beekeeper (and) as such received two diplomas in agricultural exhibits. At present, because of illness, he is living on his small estate "Argin" in the Crimea, nursing his health and tending his bees.

FATHER JOHANNES SCHAMNE,
Pastor from 13 April, 1897, until 19 August, 1901.

Father Johannes Schamne was born in Graf on the Karaman in 1841. In 1857 he entered the religious seminary at Saratov, and after finishing there was ordained by Bishop Kahn on 21 June, 1864, as the first priest from the colonists. His first assignment was as German preacher in Odessa, where initially he worked very zealously. Later on he was transferred as Pastor to Heidelberg where he was active as pastor for many years. From Heidelberg he was transferred to Franzfeld because of a conflict with the authorities. Father Schamne was an effective speaker in the pulpit and understood perfectly how to say the truth bluntly to the Franzfelders. But the Franzfelders were dissatisfied with that and said: "This man can do nothing but scold." Father Schamne died in Jekaterinoslav on 2 March, 1904. He was a capable and educated man and owned a very large library, rich in works on history.

FATHER FRANZ SCHERGER
Pastor from 7 September, 1901, to September 19, 1903.

Father Franz Scherger was born in 1867 in the colony of München, and on the 10th of December, 1895, was ordained a priest. At first he was an assistant vicar in the Wolschov parish of Severinoffka, then proctor in the seminary at Saratov. From there he was assigned to Franzfeld as pastor, where he discharged his duties for more than two years.

FATHER P. KONRAD KELLER,
Paster from 19 September, 1903, until June 11, 1904.

Father Konroad Keller was born on 1 March, 1857, in the colony of Sulz in the Beresan. After finishing at the village school, he attended, for two more years at the private schools of Karl Schneider and Franz Domansky. In the year 1875-1876 he was a teacher at Blumenfeld from where, in the autumn of 1876, he entered the Catholic seminary at Saratov. Finishing there, he was ordained a priest in Saratov by His Excellency Bishop Franz Zottmann on the 23rd of November, 1883, the feast of St. Klemens. His first appointment was in the parish of Luis on the Karaman where, however, he could not carry on for long because of illness. In 1884 he was posted to the newly-founded parish of Roshdestvenko in the Caucasus, where he was pastor for a year and a half. In 1886 he was assigned to Temir-Chan-Shura as administrator and army chaplain of the Dagestan Republic where he stayed for nine years. From Temir-Chan-Shura he was twice commanded (to go) into Turkestan as far as the Chinese border in order to bring comfort of religion to the Catholics living there. It was there, too, where he contracted an illness, uncontrollable to this day (The "Tshi fever"—rather like the African yellow fever) which even now renders him incapable of participating in the ministry. After Temir-Chan-Shura he was military chaplain for three years in Baku where, however, he kept on suffering from the virus. As a result of this he requested leave to go abroad where, in München and Wörishofen, he consulted many physicians, who provided him with very little relief. After some degree of improvement through water baths in Wörishofen, he returned to Russia, and his bishop appointed him pastor in Poniatoffka, where he was active in the ministry for almost five years. Under the instructions of Bishop Ropp he was appointed pastor in Franzfeld on 22 August, 1903. But since he kept on being sick in his new parish and was prevented thereby from fulfilling his duties, he begged his bishop in March, 1904, to release him completely from the ministry. This actually occurred in May (1904). At the present time he is living in Odessa and is occupied with the history of the German colonists in Russia.

FATHER KASPAR BUTSCH,
Substitute Pastor from 11 June, 1904 to March, 1905.
Father Kaspar Butsch was born in the colony of Katharinenthal in the Beresan and in 1904 was ordained a priest in Saratov.
Father Butsch did not like it in Franzfeld and soon had himself transferred to Nikolajev as vicar.

FATHER FERDINAND HIRSCH,
Substitute Pastor from March, 1905, till now.
Father F. Hirsch was born in 1873 and ordained a priest in 1896. For a few years he was the vicar in charge at Christina, from where he was transferred to Köhler in Kamenka deanery. In Köhler, one of the largest pastorates in the Tiraspol diocese, Father Hirsch contracted an illness, through over-exertion, which caused him to request a transfer to a smaller parish. His request was granted, and in March of 1905 he was assigned to Franzfeld where he has already recuperated and is busy working in the vineyards of the Lord.

THE PASTORAL ENDOWMENT

The Pastors salary at the founding of the parish, such as we have seen above, was 285.71 rubles and 500 rubles more instead of parish land, making 785.71 rubles in all. Today the pastor's remuneration is only 600 rubles, a potato plot and 2 dessatine of land which, however, the community gives to only those pastors whom it especially likes. In addition to heating, the pastor receives twelve carriage fares a year to Odessa. The authorized rates of surplice-fee is: 3 rubles for a marriage ceremony, 1 ruble for publication of banns, 1 ruble for a baptism, 1 ruble for burial of an adult, 50 kopecks for the burial of a child.

THE PARISH CHURCH

The first house of prayer in Franzfeld was built in 1812, stood for three years without a roof and was conpleted in 1815, then in the fall of the same year was consecrated for religious service by Father Kafasso, S.J. Superior of the Odessa Catholic missions, in the presence of Father Jann, S.J., the local pastor. The Prayer House was built of quarry-stone at the expense of the Catholic community. It had a large chapel and a room for the school-hall and cost 1300 rubles exclusive of inventory. When the chapel became too crowded later on, the separating partition was taken out, and a new schoolhouse was built (1838).

THE INVENTORY OF THE FIRST PRAYER-HOUSE

A bell weighing 4 pud cost	305	rubles
1 red damask flag—donated by Joseph Braun (Jr.) and Adam Rissling.	127	”
1 incense holder—donated by Anton Blattner	15	”
1 lamp—donated by Franz-Joseph Fix	7.30	”
1 pair of candle-sticks—donated by Joseph Braun (Sr.)	10	”
2 small candle-sticks—donated by Johannes Brust	5	”
1 bell frame with mountings	133	”
1 framed crucifix picture, pictures of St. Roch and St. Sebastian, a wooden crucifix and other pictures —gift from Father Anton Jann, S.J..		
1 image of the Blessed Virgin in glass—donated by Phillip Nold	12	”
1 image of the Blessed Virgin and St. John of Nepomuk —donated by Jacob Greiner.	4	”
St. Mary and St. Joseph—donated by Georg Heissler St. Peter and St. Magdalena—donated by Peter Matery	4	”
St. Francies Xavier—donated by Johann Kaiser	4	”
2 knee-rests—donated by Father Jann, S.J.	15	”
2 knee-rests—donated by the community	15	”
A curtain at the altar	7	”.
A tabernacle for the altar	20	”

THE LAST PARISH CHURCH

By 1849 the old prayer-house was already too small for the Catholic community of Franzfeld, so the community decided in that year to build a new church. By then the community had amassed a fairly large sum of ready money for this purpose to which came a loan of 1,000 rubles from the sheepland capital and 400 rubles from the vineyard capital, without interest.

On 6 March, 1849, the building contract with the Kishinev architect Terentii Denisov was signed. On Apil 19, 1849, Father Michael Stankievitch laid the corner-stone for the new church and the construction of the place of worship began, and fortunately was completed, in 1851, to widespread satisfaction.

The new church was solemnly blessed by prelate George Rasutovitch on 10 May, 1851, in the presence of several clergymen and a large crowd of the faithful.

The community of Franzfeld had officially invited all local government officers of the Liebenthal and Kutschurgan districts to this ceremony.

Ten years later, on 1 October, 1861, the church was consecrated with great solemnity by Bishop V. Lipsky.

The church stands in the middle of the village on the slope of the Dniester hill, with the main altar toward the west. It is 16 faden (96 feet) long, 6 faden (36 feet) wide, 3 faden (18 feet) high, built with quarry-stone, and has a roof of sheet-iron which has been painted green. The floor is overlaid with boards and painted orange. The church has three doors and sixteen windows. The tower built onto the church on its east side, is 8 faden (48 feet) in circumference and 16 faden (96 feet) high. The roof is, likewise, of sheet-iron and painted green. In the tower are two bells, one weighing 6 pud 27 pounds (267 pounds) and the other 4 pud 38 pounds (198 pounds).

In the church are three altars. The main altar is of marble, dedicated to the blessed Archangel Michael, patron saint of the church, whose beautifully painted picture shines in a gold frame over the altar. Six handsome candle-sticks, a gift of Bishop Zerr, and four silver candle-sticks next to two exquisite figures of angels in posture of supplication, embellish the altar. At both sides of the altar are wall paintings. On the epistle side (is) St. Joseph with the Christ-child (and) on the gospel side St. Anna with the Blessed Virgin, as child. The right-hand altar is dedicated to the most Blessed Virgin. The altar picture is a beautiful copy of the Madonna by Murillo; the second accessory altar is dedicated to St. Clemens Romanus, whose picture, artistically painted, is located over the altar. In addition, the church has beautiful station-pictures and several more beautiful paintings.

In 1851 the Franzfeld community purchased the old organ from the Odessa Catholic church and had it set up by the organ builder Stättlander. This organ was in use until 1904.

PARSONAGE

On the 9th of April, 1853, the Franzfeld community resolved to build a new rectory. They had 257.30 rubles of their own and they received 300 rubles on loan from vineyard-income capital. On 23 January, 1854, the building of the rectory began and it was completed in the same year. Father Thiel, the first pastor of Franzfeld, came there the 1st of January, 1854, and lived at Johannes Wagner's across from the church until the completion of the rectory.

The rectory had four rooms, was solidly built of fieldstone and had a thatched roof. In 1902 Father Scherger had two more rooms built on, and the roof covered with sheet-metal. Apart from the addition, the rectory cost 934.28 rubles. It had a patch of garden with large and pretty shade trees.

THE SCHOOL

The first schoolroom, as already stated above, was built in 1812 under the same roof with the chapel. When, in 1838, the chapel was enlarged by doing away with the partition in common with the schoolroom, a new schoolhouse with two rooms and a kitchen was built right behind the chapel. But this schoolhouse was poorly built and too low, so the community was obliged, in 1878, to build a new schoolhouse, the present one. This schoolhouse has two large bright schoolrooms which conform quite closely to modern requirements of school hygiene, and are well equipped with school furniture. In 1895 two apartments for teachers were built on the south side under the same roof with the schoolroom, so that the roof is triangular-shaped. For the 90 school children two teachers are appointed at present. The German teacher, who at the same time is sexton, receives a salary of 500 rubles. The Russian teacher has a salary of 350 rubles.

THE CHAPEL

"Blessed Virgin Heaven's gate
Comforter of the oppress'd
Let us not forsake this place
Unconsoled or unrewarded.
Mother bless thy children all
Bless them with Thine hand

See that we poor sinners all
Meet the peaceful land!"

High on the ridge of the Dniester hill stands the pretty little chapel with its slender spire, surrounded by a row of acacia trees. It looks amiably upon the village and the flat surrounding valley of the ancient Tyras spreading out in magnificent green. Concerning the genesis of the first chapel which stood near the present one, history relates the following: In 1819 Martin Busch, 19, son of schoolmaster Konrad Busch, was so (badly) crushed in the stone quarry by a boulder (which came) tumbling down that the poor fellow could no longer move a limb and was carried home unconscious. At this Konrad Busch made the vow: "If my son pulls through this with his life, then I will erect a chapel in honor of the help of the Madonna." His son recovered, grew well, but remained crippled and lived nine years more. Konrad adhered to his promise and in 1819 built a chapel on the Dniester hill. This chapel stood until 1872 (?) and was visited by many devout people of the region. In 1872 the old chapel was near the point of collapse and the present chapel was built nearby, which, likewise is visited by many pilgrims (and) Russians too. In the chapel is to be found, it is alleged, a miraculous statute of the Blessed Virgin, about whose origin I have not been able to learn anything. Many miracles are said to have occurred in the chapel, but nothing is reported about them in the church chronicle.

PERSONS of ECCLESIASTIC STANDING from the FRANZFELD PARISH

His Excellency Bishop Anton Johannes Zerr

Anton of Padua Johannes Zerr was born on 10 March 1849 in Franzfeld, where his great-grandfather had founded a new home with his four sons, after coming from Neeweiler in Alsace. He received his first instruction in the local parish school and from the local priest who took a warm interest in his acolyte. After he had reached the age of twelve, prelate Rosutovitch arranged for his admission into the Junior Seminary at Saratov, after disposing of obstacles which two persons unfriendly to his father had set up for him. On 2 November 1861 his father brought him to Odessa, from where he set out on the long road to Saratov, after first receiving the blessing of Bishop Lipsky. At the leave-taking his father addressed the following beautiful words to him:

My dear boy, farewell!
Now you go out into the world,

Take leave of your parental home,
Where parental love sustained you
Since your earliest childhood days
And shared all your joys
And healed all your sorrows;
My dear boy, farewell!

It can't be otherwise!
Childhood is done with,
Life's gravity is nearing,
Now it's: learn, do, strive,
For only the best with zest
On with loyalty, always on,
Life's no child's play;
It can't be otherwise!

God save you, my boy!
Our truest wishes do we give
As company for you, step by step,
That they from every harm to come
Shall spare your life and soul,
That bright of eye you glimpse this life,
With heart to good devoted!
God save you, my boy!

Good bye, my boy!
Time brings and takes so much
As week by week the time goes by,
When you return you then will know
The great joy of reunion
And always may that be your lot,
As long as home's right here on earth
Good bye, my boy!

His further education and preparation for the holy orders he received in the religious seminary of the Tiraspol diocese, finished there in 1870 (when) just 21 years old. In the last period of his study his health was greatly weakened, so that the school's physician sent him to his birthplace, Franzfeld, for a few months. It was the first visit he had made to his father's house; alas, his dearly-loved father was no longer among the living, he had departed this life in 1864; but that he lives on in the heart of his son is testified to by the beautiful memorial on his grave.

After he returned to Saratov, the business management of the seminary was assigned to him. Some months later he took over the French classes. On March 11, 1872, he was ordained a priest, whereupon he gave up his position in Saratov and went as substitute pastor to Krasnopoli on the Volga. After not quite five years of service, he was promoted as pastor and dean to Katherinenstadt where he officiated also as teacher of religion at the Central School. After scarcely two years his bishop called him from there to Saratov, to the seminary, as professor of dogma and metaphysics, as well as lecturer of Latin and literature. Soon afterwards he became canonical dean of the diocesan chapter and vicar general.

In the consistory of March 3rd, Leo-XIII preconized him (i.e., nominated him ecclesiastically) Bishop of Diocletianopol and transferred him to the suffragancy of Tiraspol. On May 22, he was consecrated in St. Catherine's church in Petersburg. From now on he was active mostly in the pontifical Curia and repeatedly administered the diocese in the absence of the diocesan bishop. On the 18 December 1890 the diocese of Tiraspol was transferred to him by Leo XIII with the seat in Saratov. He had taken the oath on May 1st of the same year in St.Catherine's church in Petersburg and on the 7th of May had an audience with His Majesty, Emperor Alexander III, after which he made his solemn entry into his cathedral church. In 1893 he went to Rome where, for seven weeks, he lingered at the tombs of the princely Apostles. Repeatedly he was received in audience by the Holy Father, and he spent a great deal of time at the cardinal-state-secretary's where he brought back the esteem of the diocesan clergy, which had been blackened by a clergyman in the most unscrupulous way.

Two heavy attacks of influenza left their mark on his body, completely undermining his health. Gallstones and distension of the liver increased gradually to such a great extent that no more hope for a fundamental cure could be entertained, under the burden of official business. A thorough taking of the waters of Karlsbad brought some alleviation, to be sure, (but) unfortunately for only a short time. He therefore decided to follow the advice of physicians in Paris and Berlin and tendered his resignation which, upon repeated requests, was finally granted to him in 1902.

The mild climate of Theodosia in the Crimea, where he settled after his resignation, seems to have done him a great deal of good.

Upon his departure from Saratov, he expressed his opinion to his retinue: "I am going, so it appears, toward the end of the road of my life with rapid steps. The road was fairly long, for I am already standing on the shadowy side of my life-span. For almost fifty-four years my head has worked and my heart beaten."

He is Knight, 1st Class, of the Order of St. Stanislaus, St. Anna 3rd and 1st Class and St. Vladimir 2nd class.

Father Georg Leibham, Pastor in Paninskoye

Father Georg Leibham was born in 1843 in the colony of Franzfeld on the Dniester, son of Jacob Leibham and his wife Katherine (nee Bischof). When, in 1856, the religious Seminary was set up in Saratov, Bishop Kahn invited the colonists' boys to pursue their studies there and to prepare themselves for the ecclesiastical profession. In Franzfeld ten candidates reported for the seminary. But as the time for departure from home approached, all of them became dejected, with the exception of one and that was the 13-year-old Georg Leibham who stood firmly and spiritedly by his resolve. In a great hurry, outfitting was looked after, consisting of the following articles: *1 fur coat with lining, 1 coat, 1 pair of new boots, 2 pairs of new pants, 3 new shirts, 2 vests, 1 new winter cap and 2 mufflers. Thus outfitted, he traveled to Saratov in December, 1856, with three companions, Georg Dobrowolsky, Joseph Black and Philipp Seifert. After completion of his course of instruction he was ordained a priest on 11 June, 1867, by Bishop Vinzenz Lipsky. He received his first appointment in the same year, being posted to Landau in the Beresan, where he worked zealously for two years. In 1869 he was assigned to Paninskoye where he has built a fine church and is still active there today. Father Georg Leibham was for many years teacher of religion in the non-classical secondary school at Volsk on the Volga, for which the authorities awarded him a gold breast-cross and two medals.

Father Jacob Zerr, Pastor in Kostheim.

Father Jacob Zerr was born on 1 December, 1844, in the colony of Franzfeld and was baptized in Josephstal on the 2nd of December of the same year by Father Michael Stankevitch.

His parents, Anton Zerr and Christina (nee Kaiser) have both died by now. After finishing at the village school under the teacher Johann Kiefel, he went to Saratov on 2 November, 1861, with a few more companions under the direction of Joseph Kaiser of Franzfeld, in order to enter the religious seminary there. The trip by wagon, linked with many difficulties and hardships, took a whole month. Arriving in Saratov they paused in front of the dwelling of His Excellence, Bishop Kahn. When he had conferred his blessing

---

*I give the exact account of the outfitting for the reason that the Welfare Committee had dictated (it) thus.

on them, he said: "Well, children, you must be getting hungry; in the seminary a good supper is waiting for you."

They were all glad of this news for apart from the fatigue of the trip, the youthful students felt within, an over-powering hunger. But how astonished they were when, for a "good supper," they were presented in the seminary with a tureen full of dumpling soup with dumplings the size of a ladle. Their appetite was not a little diminished by this sight, but the violent hunger demanded food, so willy-nilly, they had to fall to. The first impression for the palate of the spoiled mothers' darlings, was consequently hardly charming; but they soon forgot that, and in their happy youth gave themselves over to the hope that things would get better. After completing his seminary studies, Jacob Zerr was ordained a priest by the blessed Bishop Lipsky in Saratov on June 22nd, 1869. When, on 29 June, 1869, he was assigned his parish in Graf on the Karaman, he spent a while longer, until the 3rd of September, at Father Alexander Tortshinsky's in Tonkoshurovka so as to observe for himself to some extent the work of a parish and to get himself accustomed to it in practice. On the 8th of September he received his assignment to Kostheim as substitute pastor and on October 3rd he was already at his destination. He had to make the trip in his turn by mail-coach, since at that time there was no railroad in existence. In 1879 he was appointed pastor of Kostheim. For distinction and zeal as pastor he received a gold breast-cross in 1885 and at the same time was nominated dean of Berdyansk deanery; but in 1891 was released from the last office for reasons of health.

From 1874 to 1885 he administered a parish which consisted of 13 villages and comprised the tremendous count of 6,000 people over a distance of 115 versts. In 1885 five Polish villages separated and founded the parish of Konstantinovka. Subsequently three German villages founded a vicarage. Four German villages and one colony of Czechoslovakians and the county town of Melitopol still remained to the parish of Kostheim. During the administration of this large parish Father Zerr lost his health. Although he had spared no pains to win back such a valuable asset, his efforts had been in vain. Father Zerr still has many a recollection of his boyhood in Franzfeld. He still vividly remembers his Aunt Fränz (Franziska Zerr) at whom a wolf is said to have once sprung through the rose garden as she was walking up the hill to the chapel. Equally well (does he recall) her husband, old Hans Michel (Michael Zerr) who was once digging up healthy tendrils in his hop garden, then suddenly threw the shovel over his shoulder, ran to the village and shouted for all he was worth: "You people, the French are coming!" Both these old people had become childish.

Once in the morning his old neighbor said: "But say, Jacob, there's going to be an awful rain today." "Yes, but what makes you think so, Grandfather?" asked little Jacob. "Oh, don't you see the dreadfully dark cloud over there?" "But Grandpa," answered Jacob, "that's just the shadow of this tree." "Oh, so it is," said the old man, walking away. Father Zerr also remembers the very devout Leonhard Leibham who every day went to mass at the chapel on the hill, toward which he had worn a deep foot path. When Father Zerr took leave before his departure to the seminary in Saratov, Leonhard Leibham gave another fine speech to him and his companions, which made a great impression upon all. Yes, Leonhard Leibham was a pious man! May God give us, this day too, such pious men!!!

Father Sebastian Wolf—Parish Priest in Pfeifer in 1878.

Father Sebastian Wolf was born in Franzfeld in 1848. In 1862 he entered the seminary at Saratov, where he studied hard, and completed his studies successfully. He was ordained a priest on the 27 March 1871, by Bishop Vinzenz Lipsky. Father Wolf had great talent in learning new languages, and he also understood Latin perfectly. Consequently, soon after his ordination he was posted as teacher of Latin and religion in the lower forms of the boys' seminary. He performed this assignment with distinction. He followed the method of "saying" and "repeating." The industrious students were his favourites, and he frequently invited them to have tea with him. But the lazy ones were constantly the butt of his inexhaustible wit and satirical splintered lance, which sometimes were more severe than the welts of the school-master's rod, at that time regarded with considerable respect by many of the students.

In 1877, since he wished to have a parish of his own, Bishop Zottmann sent him to the Pfeifer Colony, on the Ilawla. But it was not his lot for long to lead those entrusted to him. Through being over zealous in his priestly duties and acquiring a feverish condition, he became seriously ill and succumbed to this disease some time later. Resigned to the will of God he died in 1878; as becomes the righteous, he received the last sacrament. He was a devout, pious, educated priest who took the saying of Saint Augustine as his guide, "A preacher who preaches well and lives well, shows the way for his people, but a preacher who preaches well and lives badly shows the dear Lord why He should condemn the preacher."

Father Joseph Matery—Died in Kleinliebenthal
on 1 March, 1888.

Father Joseph Matery was born on 31 July 1852, the son of the school teacher, Michael Matery and his wife, Annamaria Zerr. In 1865 he entered the seminary at Saratov, where he devoted himself industriously to his studies, especially of theology, and successfully completed the course. On the 6 January 1875, he was ordained priest by Bishop Franz Zottmann, and soon thereafter was sent to Göttland as acting pastor. At Göttland he was very industrious about theology, and as I understand, wrote a book, but unfortunately it has not yet been printed. He was also called to be a professor in the seminary, but was prevented by someone ill disposed (towards him). From Göttland Father Matery was sent to Eichwald and became Dean of the Berdyansk Deanery in which position he remained for 10 years. From Eichwald he was sent to Berdyansk, and after being there for approximately one year, he was sent as parish priest to Krasna in Bessarabia. In Krasna he was continuously ill, and after three months he moved to Kleinliebenthal where he died of tuberculosis on the 18 March 1888, having received the Holy Sacrament for the dying.

Father Georg Riszling—Priest of Rosenthal.
It was on the 26 August 1851, in the romantic setting of the parish colony of Selz, in the province of Cherson, that a son baptised Georg, was born to Joseph Riszling and his wife, Aloisia Hungele, in the quiet school house to which the sexton-teacher was assigned. The boy grew up there and received his primary education in the parish school, under the guidance of his father. In 1865 when the Roman Catholic seminary in Saratov was asking for students, teacher Riszling sent his son, Georg, as a candidate. After passing examinations, conducted by Father Johann Schamne of Odessa, the boy was accepted as a pupil in the seminary. In the early part of September of the same year he journeyed to Saratov in company with the other accepted pupils, namely Joseph Matery, Ferdinand Stefan and Johannes Wirth, under the guardianship of Mr. Peter Geier.

At this time this was an unspeakably difficult task, as one had to, as the people said, "go over the big ocean." From Odessa they went by steamer to Rostov, and then by ship on the Don and Volga to Saratov. The stormy trip over the Black Sea and Sea of Azov caused some fear and pain among the young students, as they all became sea sick, and had to lie down. But their guardian Peter Geier, through his tender care, soon had them on their feet again.

He took great pains to amuse and supervise his charges. From Rostov to Saratov the journey had no further incidents. Georg left the junior seminary in 1871, because of poor health, returned home to Selz, where he remained for three years as an active teacher. In 1873, along with his friend Father V. Weber, he took a trip abroad. They travelled to Vienna, Innsbruck, Trieste, Milan, Padua, Verona, Florence, then to Rome, where at the grave of St. Peter, he made a firm resolution to dedicate his life to the work of the church. On his return trip he visited the magnificent world's fair in Vienna, where at that time could be seen, every type of article of wealth and treasure in the world. In January 1875, he returned to the seminary. On the 22 June 1877, he was ordained a priest by his Excellency Bishop Zottmann, in the parish church at Semenoffka, while the bishop was making his confirmation journey. It was the first time that a priest was ordained in a country church in Tiraspol diocese.

Immediately after his ordination he was sent as acting pastor to the large parish of Köhler, where he worked for three years. As a result of overwork, he developed poor health. In 1880, at his own request he was sent to Lüzern as parish priest, where he was active for two years. In 1882, he was sent as parish priest and dean to Katharinenstadt, where he was also instructor in religion in the central school there. He remained there for 22 years and worked in peace and quiet with his parishioners who formed one-fifth of the population of Katharinenstadt.

Because of his observations and way of life, Father Riszling understood people of other religions, and was respected by them. In 1904, when Bishop Ropp wanted to move him from his parish, he became ill and asked for his discharge for reasons of health. He lived for nearly a year in Odessa, where, through bathing in the sea, he regained his health to some extent. In September of the same year, he was sent to Rosenthal as parish priest.

Father Ludwig Riszling — Parish Priest of Speier.
See above, the order of succession of the parish priests of Franzfeld.

Father Johannes Fix — Parish Priest of Pfeifer.
Father Johannes Fix was born in 1864, in Franzfeld. He completed the course of instruction for the priesthood in the seminary at Saratov, and was ordained a priest on the 6 September 1887.

Father Bernhard Leibham — Parish Priest of Baden.
Father Bernhard Leibham was born on the 19 August 1876, in Franzfeld, the son of Jakob Leibham and his wife, Theresia Zerr. He did not have a happy youth, as both of his parents died when he was nine years old, and he had to work for strangers to earn his keep. The work was hard and difficult and the pay was small. As well, the poor boy was always very pale. It happened one time that he rode two horses to water. On the way back he let the horses walk, and the side horse reared and pulled the small rider from his horse. The poor boy fell between the horses. They stepped on his foot, crushing it. The pain rendered him unconscious. He was taken to the hospital at Majaki, where he had to remain in bed for six months; but it was still not completely healed.

In 1889, his uncle, Father George Leibham took him in and through a private tutor prepared him for entry into the seminary at Saratov. In 1890 he entered the above named seminary and on completing his studies he was ordained a priest on 30 December 1901, by His Excellency Bishop Zerr. His first appointment was to Baden where, to this day, he is still working in the vineyard of the Lord. He does not enjoy very good health, nevertheless he does not lose heart, knowing that He who called him to work imparts strength, comfort and power for the working day.

EVENTS AND CONDITIONS DURING THE TIME OF THE FRANZFELD COLONY ON THE DNIESTER

1805—Martin Heer and the single man Konrad Götz, who came to this country with him, were given permission to settle in Franzfeld.

1805—A dispute between Mayor Reich and George Büchler. As the cattle were coming from the field to the watering-place, Büchler's son was about to ride with two horses through the cattle to the water. Mayor Reich told him he should wait. At this Georg Büchler came to the mayor and began to curse: "You nitwit! You simpleton! Curses on your job as mayor!" The mayor wants to send him out of the farm-yard, whereupon he seizes the mayor and chokes him; the mayor's wife wants to help her husband, whereupon he (Büchler) seizes her too and throws her to the ground. The mayor and mayor's wife flee and bring action against Büchler.**

Jan. 15, 1806—Inspector Schimiot has decreed to stop the Galliklei peasants from cutting down reeds near Majaki; the Crown is to receive a fifth of the reeds.

**Behold the respect in the presence of authority!

Jan. 24, 1806—No one is to travel to town anymore on weekdays (Odessa) except in case of necessity, or he will be arrested by the military. (The reason for this strange order is not given.)

Jan. 25, 1806—The office is to draw up a list of how many children of both sexes there are in the community, which colonist is schoolmaster and how many tables and benches are needed in the school. On the 27th of every month a list is to be sent in (showing): how many children attend school, how many already read and write and how many are still at spelling, whether the schoolmasters instruct the children properly and also whether the pastors and priests keep up their supervision of it.

Apr. 3, 1806—A list is to be presented on the harvest obtained (such) as: wheat, rye, barley, etc., and also indicate how many and what sort of tradesmen are available there (but no dabblers). The workmen are to be brought under guilds. Each worker is to present a journeyman's piece of work and appear with it at the District Office. The workmen are then to elect their master of the guild and whoever is not registered in the guild is to rate as an unqualified tradesman. The guild master has to be answerable for this. At the same time, good work must be delivered according to fixed prices; the guild master will be held responsible. (From this can be seen again how much Richelieu and Kantenius tried to help the colonists to become exemplary tradespeople to the greatest degree possible.)

Sept. 1806—Whoever wants to earn money has (the) opportunity of driving provisions from Odessa to Ovidiopol and Tiraspol. Price per tschetwert from Odessa to Ovidiopol 70-80 kopecks; from Odessa to Tiraspol 130-140 kopecks.

Sept. 21, 1806—There is to be presented the list of names of every family and orphans, and an inventory (showing) how many dessatine of land each family ploughed in the fall, how much breaking and how much previously cultivated land is tilled for seeding in the spring. For this purpose a dessatin of land is specified as follows: the dessatin has 30 charschine (instead of arschine), that is: 210 shoes wide, and 80 charschine that is: 560 shoes long.

Sept. 24, 1806—On orders of His Highness Duke Richelieu a list is to be presented of those who, for lack of provisions, will not be able to support their families until May 1st of next year (1807). Supplementing the above order: In the list are to be only those who really have no bread, especially widows and orphans who were ill all summer long; but no slackers or spendthrifts should be included.

Sept. 25, 1806—Ten kopecks must be sent in by every family for the office man and beadle; likewise the list of births, deaths, marriages and transfers, and an inventory of livestock.

Jan. 25, 1807—Order. A book about sheep-breeding is being sent to the office so as to be read often by the good managers, because the administration wants the colonists to carry on sheep-raising.

Aug. 20, 1807—Order. Those who have taken grain from the merchants for food on credit are to give it back in full, with interest, and cause the community no scandal.

Dec. 27, 1807—Two herders, one for horses, the other for oxen must stand guard over the livestock the whole night through from May 1st until the end of September. A corral shall be made to which the livestock is driven early each morning. Also a calf-tender is to be hired. The herders are to be good, honest people and not lazy and unfaithful. Two pot-hooks and a vessel full of water are always to stand ready in the village center. The night watch must always be held. A clerk is to be hired, who is to receive 50 kopecks from each family. No family is permitted to pay more for the clerk. Every family has to pay 50 kopecks a year for the letter-carrier and office attendant. Runaway livestock is to be reported. Dwellings and chimneys are always to be of clean exterior; no manure pile shall be in front of the houses and no latrines in the rooms. The embankments of the ponds shall be mended and the houses, gardens and wood-lots are to be dug round-about.

Mar. 6, 1808—It is being asked whether there is a linen-weaver in Franzfeld, who is willing to take over a weaver's loom near the district office in order to carry on his handiwork along with agriculture, seeing that this handiwork is highly important and serviceable in a community.

Apr. 1, 1808—A small packet of mulberry seeds is being sent, which seeds are to be well sown at once. But one should be on his guard here, for the State Councillor Kantenius will inspect such plantations immediately.

Apr. 17, 1808—The vintners and shopkeeper tenants are to show their old contracts to the district office to have them ratified.

Apr. 21, 1808—For the second time a quantity of mulberry seeds is being sent. The seeds are to be planted as directed and watered mornings, two or three times a week.

Apr. 24, 1808—Cattle are to be branded with the colony brand.

May 1, 1808—The district official, Barthold Ulm, is relieved of his office because of having "leaked" office business within the community. An honest man is to be chosen assistant.

May 29, 1808—It is recommended that making hay shall start on the 8th of June, if the weather is good.

June 19, 1808—A shack in Franzfeld in which a Jew lived, has collapsed; 29 timbers are offered for sale.

July 3, 1808—A list is to be presented of the newly-arrived colonists and what they have provided for themselves (the Kutschurganers and Glücksthalers are here!)

Every colonist is allowed to make hay wherever there is a stand of grass, without regard to boundary lines. New arrivals are to make enough for 6 head of cattle.

July 13, 1808—No one is permitted to sell cattle to the new colonists in order to buy inferior ones. Any transaction without a ticket from the district office is forbidden.

Aug. 21, 1808—Whenever the leaders of the newly-arrived colonists arrive in Franzfeld they are to appear in the district office in order to submit accounts for the Crown monies received on the trip.

Sept. 4, 1808—Every farmer, even the poorest one, is required to seed not less than 1 tschetwert of winter crop.

Sept. 15, 1808—Every farmer must toil two days a week for the community, the trenches (where?) must be dug a fathom deep. Every farmer must dig round about his garden and vineyard and make dykes.

Sept., 1808—The wife, Juliana, of Johann Kaminek of Kleinliebenthal, has run away from him. She is being sought.

Sept., 1808—Every colonist is to bring 5 rubles or one tschetwert of wheat to the district office for the purchase of good sheep.

Nov. 1, 1808—Every colonist is to bring one tschetwert of wheat to the store-house in Grossliebenthal, or else the military will come.

Nov. 19, 1808—The newly-arrived colonists are to swear the oath of allegiance on the 22nd of November.

Nov. 20, 1808—Those colonists who have borrowed grain seed from the general Welfare Stores must hand over 2 pud per tschetwert as a rate of interest (very high interest!)

Nov. 27, 1808—An assistant mayor and two delegates and some additional men are to come to the district government office with straw-ties in order to receive 100 vine shoots for each family.

Jan. 22, 1809—N. Mastio has been punished in Grossliebenthal with two days of communal work, with his foot in a block because he called the chief magistrate and mayor a swindler and cruelly beat Anton Laufer.

Feb. 2, 1809—The billeted Lutherans and Reformed are to be transported as far as Petersthal (to Glücksthal) in adequate vehicles on Saturday morning, February 6th (1809).

Feb. 4, 1809—*Complaint.* The Franzfelders bring action against the wine and brandy merchant because he has such wretched drinks that it makes people ill.

Feb. 16, 1809—Notice is given to all billeted Catholic colonists that every family must be equipped with a plow, shovels, and other implements. Moreover, each one must have 2 tschetwert of summer wheat, potatoes, oats and maize. Oldtime farmers can loan wheat and other things to the new colonists, on credit as cash-advance against receipt; the district office will repay the debt in February (1809). The people can get plows on cash-advance credit at the chief mayor's, Brittner. Whoever does not comply gets no payment in advance.

Feb. 19, 1809—A plot, that no livestock can get at, is to be covered with rotted manure, and when the weather permits is to be turned over, two rows deep; narrow beds prepared and mulberry seeds planted.

Mar. 13, 1809—Assistant Mayor S. Braun will be removed from office because of his conduct.

Mar. 19, 1909—Franzfeld has to hold 10 conveyances in readiness for the new colonists in order to transport them to the new colony, Glinnoi, if the order comes.

Apr. 6, 1809—All new Catholic colonists are to proceed at once (i.e, the 6th of April, 1809) with their family and belongings, in the order of their assigned settlement destination, to the new village near Shostagow on the Baraboi. At the inn on Tiraspol Street they are to encamp and wait for chief mayor Brittner who will indicate to each one his spot to move to. (And so take note if you are from Mannheim or Elsass—on 6 April 1909, you have your 100th anniversary of migration to celebrate. Let's see how you prepare for such an important day as this.)

Apr. 16, 1809—Each farmer may have only one dog, only the mayoral office may keep several. If a flayer is needed, he will be sent.

Apr. 17, 1809—The vineyards are to be cultivated, the vine-shoots received are to be planted, the mulberry seeds sprinkled daily with stagnant water, the houses repaired and white washed, yards fenced in and ditches dug. Any one wanting parsley, beets and other seeds is to procure them at the office, but (should) bring a bag along.

Apr. 28, 1809—Jakob Führer is a rebel and won't plough for the school-master.

May 15, 1809—Order. Tomorrow, Sunday the 16th of May, (1809), His Highness Duke Richelieu and another Count are coming to the colony of Franzfeld. To the mayoralty is therefore issued the order "to point out clearly to the community that each and every house is to be made spotlessly clean, the yards and lanes neat and clean, that on the whole nothing but the greatest cleanliness is to be found indoors, outdoors and on the street, failing which (if His Highness enters a house and comes across uncleanliness) not alone the householder but also the mayoralty will be severely reprimanded. From daybreak onward, 13 of the best horses must stand in readiness the whole day through so that if needed they can be harnessed immediately."

July 2, 1809—The father of every Catholic family is to appear at the church service in Josephstal next Sunday, July 4th: a new order of service will be read out.

July 10, 1809—Every 20 farmers have to deliver a wagonload of hay to Grossliebenthal for the Spanish sheep.

July 10, 1809—Martin Grossman is to receive 75 rubles in Grossliebenthal for a pair of oxen and a cart and then move to Glücksthal with the departing transport.

Aug. 20, 1809—Twenty vehicles are to drive to the new colonies (Beresan?) with wood from Odessa, for which they will be paid. The wood is at Hermann's in Odessa.

No date, 1810—The following order is issued: 1. Winter grain is to be sown and ploughing done in the fall for the spring sowing. 2. In October (1810) careful inspection is to decide whether dwellings, chimneys, gardens and vineyards are in good condition. 3. Every householder is to plant at least 10 fruit trees and several hundred vines in the fall. 4. Every householder is to clean (the) weeds, and fence in the vineyards and mulberry plantations. 5. All recommended books (in the government ofice) are to be in proper order. 6. All roads, dams and wells are to be in good condition at all times. 7. At the command of His Excellency, von Kàntenius, those officials who disobey the orders will be delivered up to the office under guard.

Jan., 1810—The question is asked whether there may not be people among the new colonists who understand how to grow madder. (Once more proof (of) how well Kantenius cared for the colonists, for the cultivation of madder is a very profitable line of business.) Furthermore: Anyone wanting his vegetable seeds is to apply at the district office. On January 26th (1810) all schoolmasters are to report to staff councillor Rosenkampf in Odessa.

Stupid people are not to be so bold as to hold discussions about political affairs, especially about war, in either inns or in private houses. Any who act in opposition to this, will be delivered up to the district office under guard. (Thus, freedom of speech among our forefathers was very limited.)

On the plea of emergency some colonists baptized their children themselves. It is ordered that no baptism may be administered, likewise no celebrations held, without the knowledge of the mayor's office.

Feb., 1810—B. Lindemann and E. Merz from Elsass got 45 strokes of the cane each for having insulted the mayor.

Feb., 1810—Since many are short of seed-grain but have much livestock, they are to sell livestock and buy seed-grain. Others must quarry stone and make wickerwork for which the Crown pays them the means with which they can buy seed-grain for themselves. But the idlers who do not merit the favors of the exalted Crown will be shipped across the border. The mayoral office is to ask each man what sort of work he will do, and then when approved send the list in to the district office.

Feb. 11, 1810—The Jew, innkeeper Moses Bastarnock, was in Franzfeld.

June 27, 1810—The Franzfeld colonists, Franz B. and Joseph Sch., were plowing together, but then fell to fighting over a hatchet which Sch. had pilfered from L. It came to a house search by the police and the hatchet was found, at which Sch. cursed the mayor and council member, for which he was put in the stocks for a whole hour.

Feb. 18, 1811—Jacob L., with his wife has stolen 71 bundles of community reeds for which he gets 40 strokes and must himself deliver 50 strokes to his wife in front of the assembled community.

Jan. 16, 1812—Joseph D. has pilfered a pole from the fishermen on the Dniester, for which he got 10 strokes of the whip in front of the whole community.

Origin of Wine and Brandy Capital

June 5, 1812—The Odessa merchants of the first guild, Georg Garri and Wilhelm Koschele, are taking over the sale of wine and brandy and other drinks in the German and Bulgarian colonies of the Cherson government for the districts of Cherson, Tiraspol and part of the Ovidiopol for two years and seven months, i.e., from 1 June 1812, to 1 January 1815, and pay 22,000 rubles rent to the general fund. The contract was approved in Odessa on 16 April, 1815. (Where did this enormous sum of money, property of the colonists, go once the Welfare committee was no longer active? Who can give accurate information about this?)

May 2, 1813—Prince Kurakin is coming into the colonies to give orders on account of the plague. All graves of those who died of the plague are to be excavated a fathom (6 feet) deep.

July 27, 1813—Since the plague has broken out again, (spreading) to Odessa and three communities, the city of Odessa is quarantined. As the investigation revealed, Jews from Balta with their wretched merchandise brought the plague and spread it into Elizabethgrad, Snamenka, Krivoe Osero and in 6 more villages, where several thousand people died within two weeks. It is strictly forbidden to take Jewish pedlars and unknown persons into the village. Likewise, no one is to pick up lost articles and bring them home. If any one of the native Jews leaves the village, he must stay on the Garandin steppe for 18 days.

July 28, 1813—Since grain vendors often enter the villages and pass the entire winter there, offer various useless wares to the colonists, and harm good morals, it is forbidden to tolerate anybody in the village without permission of Inspector Rosenkampf.

Aug. 4, 1813—The custom-house in Majaki is suing the Franzfelders. (Why, is not said.) Duke Richelieu is having the case of the Ispravnik investigated.

1813—Orders are: to keep strict closing hours for public houses. The inn-keeper may not play music without permission of the district office, failing which he will be fined up to 10 rubles.

The horse dealer, Psevan Posdeshka, wants to leave the livery stable, he insults the mayor and spits into his face. For this he gets 8 blows of the cane. (The salutary Russian switch, it is clear, had not been officially introduced at this time.)

Sept. 8, 1813—Unmarried Georg P. stole potatoes and cucumbers from Jakob Rheide, for which he is being put into the stocks and is getting 5 blows of the cane.

Sept. 18, 1813—Eva Rh. and her foster-son stole melons from Rudolf Merdian, for which both were to be put into the stocks, but they appealed to Father Jann S.J. and were sent to Josephsthal.

Oct. 17, 1813—Schoolmaster Jakob Rheide is suing the community because it is not paying him his salary.

March 4, 1814—The field-watchman, Anton P., rounds up Majaki cattle and slaughters one head, for which he gets 25 blows of the cane.

March 8, 1814—Those who are delinquent are to work one day a week in the Crown garden in Grossliebenthal. Court-days are Friday and Saturday.

March 13, 1814—The elected members of the sanitation committee are to exercise strict inspection, and if somebody in a house is afflicted with a contagious disease they are to place a guard in front of the house so that every one may keep away.

March 27, 1814—The Dniester guard is to be augmented by 3 men. Franzfeld has to put 2 men on and Freudenthal 5 men, on April 6th, to relieve the previous ones without horses. A mayor must be in command.

May 15, 1814—Court-Councillor Schuschkareff will frequently visit the colonies (to see) whether instructions given are being carried out in the colonies.

June 9, 1814—The community is giving sergeant-major Timofev the field of tilled hay to mow. Of every five piles he gets four, the community one pile.

Oct. 14, 1814—The son of the Jew, Maier Kalmann, strikes Christian Heer, son of mayor Heer, for which the Jewish scamp is punished with 15 blows of the cane.

Oct. 27, 1814—It is ordered that no one may take more than 6 per cent when lending money.

Dec. 22, 1814—Jakob Rheide received permission from Inspector Rosenkampf to depart for Selz, as schoolmaster (This J. Rheide was the step-father of Georg Rissling, from whom descend the Rissling teachers and priests).

Feb. 5, 1815—Forty bundles of reeds are to be brought to Grossliebenthal to serve for making racks for the silkworms. (And so silk culture has begun.)

Feb. 23, 1815—Court-Councillor Laskarev has given orders that land, (until now enclosed by only a furrow) shall be surveyed by dessatin in all colonies. Land may be leased with consent of the community as a whole, but not to strangers.

Feb. 26, 1815—The Jewess Haicka, who slandered M. Heer and F. Leibham, will be punished with 3 hours arrest.

March 25—Report to Inspector Hippius: The pastor in Grossliebenthal has proclaimed March 25th (The Annunciation) as a holiday throughout his parish, but the Protestants went into the fields on this day and created scandal.

April 6, 1815—The Cossacks won't let the Germans fish. (In Franzfeld 40 Cossacks were stationed until 1827 or 1828?)

April 12, 1815—All houses are to be cleaned inside and outside, because War-Governor Count Langeron is going to travel through the colonies.

July 31—None shall dare to cohabit before marriage.

August 9, 1815—Those who have cultivated silk this year and want to have it twined and wound on bobbins can send this product to the (Bulgarian) colony of Parkan, where it will be worked up on Crown machines, free of charge.

Aug. 10—Through a survey by the district office it has come to notice that the woods, gardens and mulberry plantations were entirely neglected. It was strictly ordered to restore these to good condition and to enlarge them.

Sept. 21—Orders from Inspector Meier: "Since it is known to me by experience that a few of the Liebenthal colonists take a malicious pleasure in accusing their fellow-man unjustly, or encourage others in this abomination, and after the matter is looked into and found to be slanderous, withdraw their accusations wholly or in part, I herewith order that from today onward all accusations of real substance are to be made in writing to the authorities concerned so as to put a stop to any more incidents of this sort."

(Our colonists today are still the same.)

1816—Konrad Busch (he built the first chapel) was made secretary for Franzfeld and received 175 rubles per year.

March 27, 1817—The land which had been given to each family and until now used for cattle pasture, is to be planted with various types of trees. (It appears that until now only community forests were at hand.)

Aug. 23, 1817—There was inquiry whether there were any carpenters among the newly arrived Würtembergers.

June 11, 1818—The new Würtemberg colonist, Johan Reiser, who is quartered in Franzfeld along with his whole family, has the itch; he has infected the neighbouring families as well as others, and still he will not go to the hospital.

Jan. 3, 1820—It was reported that no individual had shot on New Year's Eve. Only the military who were posted at Franzfeld at that time, had toasted the wine merchant Ross, by shooting in the New Year. The wine merchant was very proud of this.

March 3, 1820—On the border of Franzfeld there were 7 small and 2 large pickets; on the border of Alexanderhilf there were two small and one large picket. The colonists had to provide drivers for the military.

March 10, 1820—At 3 o'clock in the afternoon Philipp Job's house and all of his belongings burned, as well as 2 horses, 2 cows and 2 calves.

June 11, 1820—The community garden, located ½ werst from the colony, contains 4 dessatine and is not yet planted.

Aug. 18, 1820—There are 8 stone houses, 35 mud houses and one blacksmith shop in Franzfeld.

May 19, 1820—The mayor, Johannes Wagner, and George Heiszler from Franzfeld left for Germany on the 18th of May to get their property from there. On the 21 November they both returned safely.

Jan. 1, 1821—We have 5 bibles and 4 New Testaments. It was ordered from the Welfare office that each colonist should have a bible.

Sept. 16, 1821—The Franzfelder had to provide 2½ faden of firewood to the Cossacks every month.

Sept. 19, 1821—Kaspar Materi made a contract with the Franzfeld community to be their school teacher for which he was to receive 40 pounds of wheat and 3 rubles from each family per year.

The community of Franzfeld planted the following: rye—37 tschet., winter wheat—4 tschet., summer wheat—195 tschet., buckwheat—4 tschet., millet—1 tschet., corn—7 tschet., potatoes —142 tschet., oats—221 tschet., barley—143 tschet.

The harvest from the above planting was: rye—184 tschet., winter wheat—5 tschet., summer wheat—388 tschet., buckwheat —4 tschet., oats—280 tschet., barley 390 tschet., millet—9 tschet., corn—134 Tschet., potatoes—521 tschet., hay—369 loads (a poor harvest).

There were 1,821 trees; fruit trees in the plantation, 1,077; in individual households, 3,729. Mulberry trees in the plantation, 538; in the farm homes, 13; grape vines in the plantation, 13,195; in the farm homes, 945.

Sept. 28, 1821—The wine merchant Jakob Rösz beat up a Moldavian, because he refused to pay for some diluted whiskey. The Moldavian reported Rösz and also accused him of overcharging his customers, and of being a cheating ruffian.

1824—the harvest was better:

Seeded—rye, 293 tschet; winter wheat, 122 tschet; summer wheat, 50 tschet; oats, 74 tschet; barley, 122 tschet.; millet, 3 tschet.; corn, 10 tschet.; potatoes, 33 tschet.

Harvested—rye, 709 tschet.; winter wheat, 1,056 tschet.; summer wheat, 226 tschet.; oats, 219 tscht.; barley, 699 tschet.; millet, 23 tschet.; corn, 115 tschet.; potatoes, 72 tschet.; hay, 430 loads.

1826—For the celebration of their jubilee in the year 1826, the Franzfelders spent 26 rubles, 60 kopecks.

1827—The agricultural community of Franzfeld contained: 306 people; horses, 223; cows, 337; sheep, 206; pigs, 182; ploughs, 44; harrows, 50; wagons, 48; spinning wheels, 32; mills, 3; blacksmith, 1: shoemaker, 1.

1828—The Protestants in Franzfeld are to haul two loads of sand to make an addition to the parsonage at Freudenthal.

"There are things between Heaven and Earth which are never dreamed of in your philosophy in the schools." This expression of the great Shakespeare is demonstrated by the following occurrence.

Nov. 4, 1832—A terrible incident: The mayor, Joseph Braun, shot himself at 12 o'clock midnight, in the presence of his invited guests. But for what reason did this rich, respected man do this? Most believed he had a pact with the devil. Before I describe this incident I wish to make a remark.

It is a settled matter for every believing Christian, "that the devil goes around like a roaring lion, looking to see whom he can devour."

Through the redemption of Jesus, truly the might of the prince of darkness was broken, but not completely dispersed. Saint Augustine compared the might with which the devil takes hold of people with that of a tied up watch dog, who can only bite a person, if the person goes close enough. According to Origen, every passion has its demon, to whom it has an inner mysterious relationship. When the passion becomes so strong that the weak human being without divine grace is helpless against it, then the tyrant passion breaks all bonds, disturbs the peace of the soul and lowers the willpower with respect to the divine law, in order to subject all the soul's faculties to its tyranny. In this disturbed state the soul vacillates up and down, between light and darkness, like a magnetic needle. At this point the roaring lion in search of prey attacks the tortured soul and with his deceptive enticements lures it into his net. This is particularly true when the passion of sensual desires possesses the human being and no means of satisfying them is available except with the help of the evil one. To the question whether such a thing is possible, I reply: if human beings can be possessed by the devil against their will, which Holy Scripture, the source of truth, abundantly describes, one must admit the possibility that man can make a pact with the devil of his own free will. For the former is more difficult to understand than the latter.

I shall describe this case as the story was told to me, without vouching for its truth, except for the details mentioned in official documents. Now to the story.

Joseph Braun, also called Brauneseppel, came from Germany as a young, poor boy in 1809 or 1810, to the settlement of Franzfeld, where he worked as a hired man for some colonist there. In the neighbourhood there lived Nicholas Frank, a wealthy landowner, whose daughter, Barbara, was the prettiest girl in the district. She was surrounded on all sides by single men, causing pains of petty jealousy for poor Joseph Braun. He tried in every possible way to draw her attention, but the pretty, proud Barbara would not vouchsafe him a single word. In his despair he went into a fit of depression, and he swore to have this girl at any price.

It happened that his boss sent him, along with some other drivers, to Moldavia to get some wine. It was a quiet moonlight harvest night. When the wagons were slowly going up the hill behind Majaki, beyond the Dniester, near the colony of Palanga, Braun was the last one. He was completely lost in thought about the object of his passion, and did not notice that those he was with were far ahead, and that he had remained behind. He recalled that he had heard that the devil, when called in times of distress, comes and offers his help. He did what he had heard was necessary, and suddenly the horses stood still, and started to snort and paw. Braun became greatly frightened when he saw, standing in front of him, someone in a green mantle, wearing a large floppy hat, who spoke to him as follows: "What you were presently thinking and wishing for, you shall have, yes, even more. You will become rich and respected and you will know more than other people when you make your pact with me in blood."

There followed a terrible struggle in the soul of this unlucky fellow, but he succumbed to his strong passion and the power of the devil was victorious. Therefore he agreed to the pact and gave his signature. After returning home he soon won the favour and love of Barbara Frank, with the help of his 'Mephistopheles.' The couple was married in Josephstal by Father Oswald Rausch, S.J., on the 17 September, 1811.

The life which followed this young couple was not a happy one, as Joseph Braun soon proved himself to be a rude, rough, ungodly type of man. Because of petty jealousies he treated his wife like a tyrant. It was fortunate that they remained childless. In the company of other people he was proud, temperamental and unsociable; he was also hard-hearted towards the poor. He was forever fighting with everyone, particularly in the wine cellars in Odessa, where he was considered a hero. He was lucky in all his undertakings and the word spread around the district "that he was as lucky as the Brauneseppel." When he went hunting he would find his quarry behind the colony wine garden, whereas other hunters went as far as Majaki and found no wild game.

In his last year he was mayor, and also for a time, secretary. It happened that the people who asked to pay their taxes at that time had no money. But mayor Braun said they were lying, and would remind them that in such and such a cupboard or trunk they had so and so much money. The people were astounded at this tremendous insight of the mayor and all became terrified of him. Often he returned from the city with some gentleman, and some said that he was a free mason.

Braun lived in this manner until the time that his pact with the devil was to expire, who reminded him that the 4 November 1832, was the last day. But Braun did not want to keep the agreement and threatened to do penance, but the devil laughed and told him to hold himself ready. However, Braun was serious about doing penance and a few days ahead of time (on All Saints' Day) went to Kleinliebenthal to Father Eybel, and disclosed the above. Father Eybel gave him a note, which was to help him in the critical hour, but even with the note, Braun's luck did not hold this time. As he was returning from the border of Neuburg, and was doing something beside the road, there suddenly arose a strong whirlwind, which tore off his overcoat in which he had the note. The document which fell out, blew away in the wind. Disconcerted and without hope he returned home. On the evening of this unhappy day, he arranged a banquet and invited Philipp Job and his wife Katharina, Jacob Fix and his wife Eva, and Martin Heer* as guests. After the guests had assembled, eaten and drunk and were feeling happy, they noticed that the host was not his usual self but was depressed, seclusive and sad. So the time passed until one minute before 12 o'clock midnight. There was a loud knock on the door, frightening everybody to their feet. At the word "enter," the door opened and a form entered, covered with a green mantle, wearing a large slouched hat on his head, and carrying a book under his right arm. Without a greeting, the intruder turned towards the host, beckoned with his hand and said, "Come you, it is time." Braun shook with fright and finally, stuttering, said these words, "Go, I will soon be along." At this the door was slammed shut and the form disappeared. Then all of the guests cried, "Who is that? What does he want?" Braun quieted the guests and said, "Eat and drink, he shall wait."

After a while the host said, "Excuse me for a minute, my shoe is hurting me, and I want to tend to it." He left the table and went behind the stove where there was a small couch. The roar of a shot came from behind the stove. All of the guests screamed and jumped from their seats to look behind the stove. There lay the host in his own blood, having shot himself through the head with the iron ramrod of his hunting gun. The ramrod penetrated the beams and flew approximately 300 faden, as far as Rüffel's vineyard, where the place can still be seen today and if I am not wrong, also the ramrod. The house where this great misfortune occurred is still in

*The reporter questions whether Heer was present.

236

the "small street" but no one has lived in it since then, as one would say, because of the ghosts therein. Today the house is fallen down, only the foundation and layer of stones which are overgrown with Spanish roses are still visible.

The widow, Barbara Braun, after one year, married the neighbour, Johannes Steiert and bore him a daughter, named Johanna. In 1843, they moved to Krasna in Bessarabia. Her husband died, after which she again came to Franzfeld where she was married for the third time. She died of old age in Franzfeld, and told this story before her death, to her sister-in-law, Agatha Frank, now 77 years old, who personally told it to me. The story was supplemented by Katharine Heiszler, 84 years old, and Jacob Vogt, 92 years old, both living in Kleinliebenthal.

1833—This was a bad year.

1842—The Franzfeld colonist, Jacob Wohlgemuth (Lutheran) joined the Orthodox church in Galliklei.

1852—Taja Tabaschnik, 16-year-old daughter of the Jewish wine merchant in Franzfeld, joined the Catholic faith.

1864—Bishop Vincent Lipsky lived in Franzfeld during the summer. He went walking through the colony every day, one day turning to the right, the next day to the left. He was a great friend of the children. There was always a troop of children around him to whom he gave gifts and his blessing.

1887—In the evening of the 13 September, His Excellency Bishop Antonius Zerr came to Franzfeld from Odessa. On Sunday, September 20, after pontificial mass, he confirmed 432 persons.

1895—By a decree from the central Government, Franzfeld was named 'Michalowka.'

1901—On the 9th of June something frightful happened in Franzfeld. The single young man, Joseph Z., in a fit of madness, killed his own father, Johannes Z.

1904—On the 28 February, Joseph Frank, the oldest man in Franzfeld, died. He was born on the 14 December 1817, and baptized by Father Jann, S.J. On the 28 February 1904, he was buried by Father C. Keller.

Leonhard Leibham, son of Franz Leibham, born 1803, was a very devout man living in Franzfeld.

He was married to Katharina Merdian, who was also very devout. Leonard Leibham had gone to Jerusalem twice, the last time his wife went with him. From there he brought many articles which had been blessed, and gave them to his relatives and friends. At one time the Russians told him that Kiev was a famous pilgrimage place. So one day he prepared himself and with his own wagon, drove to Kiev. After one week he returned and indicated that he was very unhappy with his last pilgrimage. He frequently goes to the chapel in Franzfeld both by day and by night; the present chapel was built, thanks to his industriousness. He was a faithful, diligent and conscientious worker for his Master, who called him to Himself and a better home in 1875.

Archeological and Antique Discoveries in Franzfeld.

1855—Jacob Schaub found a room in a small hill, where the present stone bridge towards Majaki is located. The room was made of stones which did not come from this region. The room was two faden wide and one faden high. Around the whole wall there were shelves of hard sandstone, as in a small shop. The entrance to the room could not be identified. At the same time J. Schaub found a large earthen jug which came to a point at its base; a small earthen pitcher, three copper spoons engraved with a snake's head, two brass ear rings with an inscription and 50 arrows.

1886—Joseph Köhler found the head of a mammoth in the stone quarry. He gave it as a present to professor Wedhalm in Odessa.

1898—Jacob Schaub's son found 12 small metal plates in a hill (the plates were apparently gold). On the plates the 12 months were representged by forms of animals. He also found a large earthen jug, 8 brass buttons, and a metal plate similar to a clock face. He sold all of these to the Jew Apfelwein in Odessa for 14 kopecks.

Rudolf Kaiser of Franzfeld found two very old documents. The first one had been given to Hans Peter Frank, the executioner, in Weisenburg on the 7 December, 1680; the second one was given to Johannes Frank, executioner in Mannheim and was dated the 15 June, 1745. From this, one can conclude that the office of executioner was in the Frank family for almost 100 years.

The above chronicle was written by the author with the intention of including illustrations. However the jubilee committee was not interested, therefore the illustrations had to be left undone. So ends the chronicle of the Catholics of Liebenthal.

If the Catholics of Kutschurgan, Beresan and other communities in South Russia, wish to have similar chronicles at hand for their hundred year jubilee, I beg them to give me a written or verbal request as soon as possible (not later than the 15 February, 1906).